The Age of Youth

The Age of Youth tackles the complicated relationship between youth, national security, and education from World War I to World War II, revealing how the United States created a time-specific political and social category of youth that relied on the expectation that military-age men should devote themselves to the future of their country. Analyzing policies from the Reserve Officers' Training Corps, the New Deal, wartime military training programs, and those governing the post–World War II occupation of Japan, Masako Hattori demonstrates that the priorities of national security conditioned young people's access to education in the United States in the first half of the twentieth century, in both wartime and peacetime, and explores how the evolving link between youth, education, and national security shaped and reshaped the cultural concept of "youth" in American society.

Masako Hattori is Assistant Professor in the Department of History at the National University of Singapore.

MILITARY, WAR, AND SOCIETY IN MODERN AMERICAN HISTORY

Series Editors
Beth Bailey, University of Kansas
Andrew Preston, University of Cambridge
Kara Dixon Vuic, Texas Christian University

Military, War, and Society in Modern American History is a new series that showcases original scholarship on the military, war, and society in modern U.S. history. The series builds on recent innovations in the fields of military and diplomatic history and includes historical works on a broad range of topics, including civil–military relations and the militarization of culture and society; the military's influence on policy, power, politics, and political economy; the military as a key institution in managing and shaping social change, both within the military and in broader American society; the effect the military has had on American political and economic development, whether in wartime or peacetime; and the military as a leading edge of American engagement with the wider world, including forms of soft power as well as the use of force.

The Age of Youth
American Society and the Two World Wars

Masako Hattori
National University of Singapore

Shaftesbury Road, Cambridge CB2 8EA, United Kingdom

One Liberty Plaza, 20th Floor, New York, NY 10006, USA

477 Williamstown Road, Port Melbourne, VIC 3207, Australia

314–321, 3rd Floor, Plot 3, Splendor Forum, Jasola District Centre, New Delhi – 110025, India

103 Penang Road, #05-06/07, Visioncrest Commercial, Singapore 238467

Cambridge University Press is part of Cambridge University Press & Assessment, a department of the University of Cambridge.

We share the University's mission to contribute to society through the pursuit of education, learning and research at the highest international levels of excellence.

www.cambridge.org
Information on this title: www.cambridge.org/9781009303361

DOI: 10.1017/9781009303323

© Masako Hattori 2025

This publication is in copyright. Subject to statutory exception and to the provisions of relevant collective licensing agreements, no reproduction of any part may take place without the written permission of Cambridge University Press & Assessment.

When citing this work, please include a reference to the DOI 10.1017/9781009303323

First published 2025

Cover: FDR Visits CCC Camp #350 in Virginia's Shenandoah Valley: (Photo by CORBIS/Corbis via Getty Images)Cover design by Andy Ward

A catalogue record for this publication is available from the British Library.

A Cataloging-in-Publication data record for this book is available from the Library of Congress

ISBN 978-1-009-30336-1 Hardback

Cambridge University Press & Assessment has no responsibility for the persistence or accuracy of URLs for external or third-party internet websites referred to in this publication and does not guarantee that any content on such websites is, or will remain, accurate or appropriate.

For EU product safety concerns, contact us at Calle de José Abascal, 56, 1°, 28003 Madrid, Spain, or email eugpsr@cambridge.org

Contents

List of Illustrations and Charts		*page* vi
Acknowledgments		vii
List of Acronyms and Abbreviations		x
	Introduction	1
1	Uncle Sam's Khaki University and World War I	26
2	Educational Institutions and Military Training in the 1920s and the 1930s	61
3	The Great Depression, National Security, and the Redefinition of Youth	96
4	Conscripting Youth for World War II	129
5	Reimagining Youth during Wartime	161
6	Youth in U.S.-Occupied Japan	190
	Conclusion	216
	Index	224

Illustrations and Charts

ILLUSTRATIONS

1.1 An advertisement for the SATC promoting the program as "the Opportunity of a Lifetime" — *page* 28
1.2 Scenes from SATC training as promoted by the CEST — 58
3.1 CCC enrollees performing "review" and "colors" routines — 97
3.2 CCC enrollees at work — 114
4.1 Flag raisers on Iwo Jima, 1945 — 130
4.2 The Rough Riders on San Juan Hill, 1898 — 131
6.1 The Youth Branch meeting with Kande village representatives — 203

CHARTS

2.1 A list of ROTC institutions by region as of 1935 — *page* 87
2.2 The number of students taking the basic and advanced ROTC courses at the University of Wisconsin, 1921–29 — 91

Acknowledgments

I am deeply grateful to the numerous people from across the world who helped make this book possible. At Columbia University, where I started this project, Anders Stephanson taught me to confront difficult questions and think more broadly and deeply. Whenever I needed encouragement and support, Elizabeth S. Blackmar was there for me. Ansley T. Erickson introduced me to the history of education and taught me the importance of examining how injustice and discrimination become institutionalized in society. Christopher Capozzola not only served as an external member of my dissertation committee but also generously supported me in my academic career advancement. Hidetaka Hirota has read many chapter drafts and grant applications since the day I first met him in New York and has always encouraged me to reach higher goals. Many other Columbia faculty members, including Casey N. Blake, Alan Brinkley, Barbara Fields, Eric Foner, Ira I. Katznelson, and Jeremy Kessler, also provided invaluable assistance and guidance at various stages in the development of this project.

I also thank my teachers, colleagues, and students on the other side of the Pacific for their encouragement, assistance, and inspiration. Yasuo Endo taught me the joys of studying history when I was an undergraduate student in American Studies at the University of Tokyo and has supported me at every stage of my career since then. Thank you also to other faculty members at the university, including Jun Furuya, Kenryu Hashikawa, Fumiko Nishizaki, Masako Notoji, and Yujin Yaguchi. At Kyoto University, where I spent two years as a postdoctoral fellow, Yuka Moriguchi Tsuchiya provided me with an excellent environment in which to work on a book manuscript. I was able to complete the final stages of this project thanks to the support of my colleagues at Shujitsu University and the National University of Singapore, including Sayaka Chatani, Jack Meng-Tat Chia, Ian Gordon, Aeka Inoue, Asami Kobayashi, Chien-Wen Kung, Bruce Lockhart, Joey Long, and Satoko Mita. Students at these universities helped me refine the key points of this project by actively participating in my classes and asking intriguing questions.

Countless more mentors, colleagues, and friends across the world, within and beyond academia, supported me as well in numerous ways, from providing insightful feedback on the manuscript and guiding me through the bewildering steps involved in pursuing an academic career to supplying me with humor, coffee, shelter, breathing space, and everything else I needed to finish this project. Among them are Kathleen Bachynski, Manuel A. Bautista-González, Shumpei Goke, Masahiko Haraguchi, Yuriko Hirano, Ai Hisano, Chang Hong, Saori Hori, Yusuke Isotani, Jiao Jiao, Nick Juravich, Hideaki Kami, Shosuke Kinugawa, Naoto Kojima, Paul A. Kramer, Yoshiya Makita, Seiko Mimaki, Daniel Morales, Takahito Moriyama, Yumiko Murai, Gen Nakao, Yuki Oda, Sakurako Okuno, Yukako Otori, Kristin Roebuck, Aurélie Roy, Ian Shin, Sayuri Guthrie Shimizu, Wayan Swardhani, William A. Taylor, Allison Powers Useche, Shuichi Wanibuchi, Kohki Watabe, Mishio Yamanaka, Erika Yoshida, and Thomas W. Zeiler. I also had the privilege of presenting parts of this project at various conferences, workshops, and guest lectures, where I received constructive feedback. I am grateful to the organizers, session members, and attendees of my presentation at the American Historical Association, the Boston University Graduate Student American Political History Conference, the International American Studies Association, the International Standing Conference for the History of Education, Kyoto University, the National University of Singapore, the Nordic Association for American Studies, the Organization of American Historians, Peking University, Renmin University of China, the Suntory Foundation, and the University of Tokyo.

A number of institutions and organizations provided generous financial support at various stages of this project. I thank the American Historical Association, the American Studies Association–Japanese Association for American Studies Collaborative Committee, the American Studies Foundation in Japan, Columbia University, the Doris G. Quinn Foundation, the Franklin D. Roosevelt Library, the Japan Society for the Promotion of Science (grant numbers 18H05616 and 19J01338), the Japan–U.S. Friendship Commission (the Fulbright Program), the National University of Singapore, Shujitsu University, and the Suntory Foundation for their assistance. The Boston University American Political History Institute Outstanding Graduate Student Paper Prize, which I was honored to receive in 2015, also provided financial support and encouragement during the project's early years.

Archivists and librarians at the following institutions helped me discover and access materials crucial for this study: Columbia University Libraries, the Franklin D. Roosevelt Presidential Library, the George Washington University Special Collections Research Center, the Hoover

Institution Library and Archives, the Library of Congress, the National Archives (U.S.), the National Diet Library (Japan), NUS Libraries, the New York Public Library, New York University Archives, and the Friends Historical Library and Swarthmore Peace Collection at Swarthmore College. Special thanks to Eric Vanslander at the U.S. National Archives in College Park, Maryland, who answered my inquiries numerous times by email and in person, and, along with his colleagues, made me feel welcome every time I visited the institution.

It is an honor to have this work be included in Cambridge University Press's Military, War, and Society in Modern American History series. I am grateful to Andrew Preston, the series' coeditor, for his support of this project since it was a dissertation. He and Beth Bailey, the other coeditor of the series, as well as Cecelia Cancellaro and her colleagues at the press, patiently supported and guided me throughout the long process toward publication. An early version of Chapter 6 was previously published as "The Second Phase of War: Youth in U.S.-Occupied Japan," *Diplomatic History* 46, no. 5 (2022). Portions of Chapter 4 are based on "Mobilizing American Youth for Total War: The Selective Training and Service Act of 1940," *Nanzan Review of American Studies* 39 (2017).

Finally, I thank my family for their unwavering love and support. Mom, Ken, grandma, and grandpa, this book is for you.

Acronyms and Abbreviations

ACE	American Council on Education
ALGCU	Association of Land-Grant Colleges and Universities
ASTP	Army Specialized Training Program
AVF	All-Volunteer Force
AYC	American Youth Congress
AYCM	American Youth Commission
BDG	*Boston Daily Globe*
CCC	Civilian Conservation Corps
CDT	*Chicago Daily Tribune*
CEST	Committee on Education and Special Training
CIE	Civil Information and Education Section
CME	Committee on Militarism in Education
CMTC	Citizens' Military Training Camp
CSM	*Christian Science Monitor*
FDR	Franklin D. Roosevelt
FDRL	Franklin D. Roosevelt Library
FSA	Federal Security Agency
GHQ/ SCAP	General Headquarters of the Supreme Commander for the Allied Powers
HBCU	Historically Black Colleges and Universities
JANSSC	Joint Army and Navy Selective Service Committee
LAT	*Los Angeles Times*
MTCA	Military Training Camp Association
NACP	National Archives, College Park
NATD	National Army Training Detachments
NDL	National Diet Library
NEA	National Education Association
NSGC	National Self Government Committee
NYA	National Youth Administration
NYHT	*New York Herald Tribune*
NYT	*New York Times*
OF	Official File

RG	Record Group
ROTC	Reserve Officers' Training Corps
SATC	Student Army Training Corps
UMT	Universal Military Training
VFW	Veterans of Future Wars
WP	*Washington Post*
WPA	Works Progress Administration
YMCA	Young Men's Christian Association
YOSA	Youth Organizations and Student Activities
YWCA	Young Women's Christian Association

Introduction

For many people living outside the United States today, the U.S. armed forces may be one of the first things that come to mind when they think of the country. They may use iPhones, frequent a local Starbucks, enjoy Hollywood films, and support the United States' call for freedom and democracy, but they still have somber views of the country as a global military superpower. This is particularly true in countries where U.S. military bases are located, and historians and scholars in other academic fields alike have extensively researched how the U.S. military, its bases, and U.S. military policies have affected people and societies around the globe.[1]

In contrast, it is striking how little military issues, as well as national security issues more broadly, are brought up in conventional historical narratives on *domestic* American society, particularly those describing American society in the first half of the twentieth century. These narratives typically treat the issues as if they existed almost exclusively between 1917 and 1918, and 1941 and 1945, the periods in which the United

---

[1] Literature on this topic, as well as on the U.S. empire more broadly, is voluminous and expanding. See, for example, Paul A. Kramer, *The Blood of Government: Race, Empire, the United States, and the Philippines* (Chapel Hill: University of North Carolina Press, 2006); Alfred W. McCoy and Francisco A. Scarano, eds., *Colonial Crucible: Empire in the Making of the Modern American State* (Madison: University of Wisconsin Press, 2009); Catherine Lutz, ed., *The Bases of Empire: The Global Struggle against U.S. Military Posts* (New York: New York University Press, 2009); David Vine, *Base Nation: How U.S. Military Bases Abroad Harm America and the World* (New York: Metropolitan Books, 2015); Simeon Man, *Soldiering through Empire: Race and the Making of the Decolonizing Pacific* (Oakland: University of California Press, 2018); Daniel Immerwahr, *How to Hide an Empire: A History of the Greater United States* (New York: Farrar, Straus and Giroux, 2019); Christopher Capozzola, *Bound by War: How the United States and the Philippines Built America's First Pacific Century* (New York: Basic Books, 2020). Unsurprisingly, academic scholarship on this topic by researchers living in areas with U.S. military bases or where the United States has exerted influence in other ways is extensive as well. Works written in Japanese include Yoshimi Shunya, *Shinbei to hanbei: Sengo Nihon no seijiteki muishiki* (Tokyo: Iwanami Shoten, 2007); Hayashi Hirofumi, *Beigun kichi no rekishi* (Tokyo: Yoshikawa Kōbunkan, 2012); Ikemiyagi Yoko, *Okinawa beigunkichi to nichibei anpo: Kichi koteika no kigen, 1945–1953* (Tokyo: University of Tokyo Press, 2018).

States was officially involved in major wars. The assumption here is that military issues affected American society only when the country was driven into a war by a foreign force.[2]

Indeed, the U.S. armed forces were small compared to those of other major powers before World War II and their presence in American society in peacetime back then was not large. The global visibility of U.S. military power as we know it today is essentially a product of World War II and the Cold War. Prior to that, the country maintained enough troops to sustain an empire – in the Philippines, Puerto Rico, and Hawaii, and in Cuba, where the country exerted significant political and economic influence – and to conduct military campaigns in Latin America and Asia, but it had far fewer military outposts outside its borders than the years of World War II onwards. With the U.S. mainland surrounded by two oceans that served as natural fortresses, it was common for Americans on the mainland to believe that a foreign military attack on it was unlikely and to pay relatively little attention to military matters except when a major war occurred or was imminent.[3]

Nonetheless, the significance of military matters to American society in the first half of the twentieth century stems not so much from the sheer size of the U.S. armed forces or the degree to which most Americans constantly felt threatened by the possibility of a foreign enemy attack as it does from the extent to which diverse groups of people considered, during peacetime, military measures or measures inspired by the military as appropriate or even ideal for achieving divergent social goals of their own such as "Americanizing" immigrants or "toughening" boys. In particular, during this period, when the country faced a series of national emergencies, most notably World War I, the Great Depression, and World War II, many adults saw young people, particularly young men, as critical to overcoming these emergencies, and educating and preparing young people for national security work became a hot topic in peacetime as well as wartime. Importantly, the first half of the twentieth century was a time in which schooling beyond grammar school

---

[2] Historians, on the other hand, have extensively studied how American society in the second half of the twentieth century was impacted by the Cold War. See, for example, Elaine Tyler May, *Homeward Bound: American Families in the Cold War Era* (New York: Basic Books, 1988); Stephen J. Whitfield, *The Culture of the Cold War* (Baltimore: Johns Hopkins University Press, 1991); Laura McEnaney, *Civil Defense Begins at Home: Militarization Meets Everyday Life in the Fifties* (Princeton, NJ: Princeton University Press, 2000); Peter J. Kuznick and James Gilbert, eds., *Rethinking Cold War Culture* (Washington, DC: Smithsonian Institution Press, 2001).

[3] The global U.S. military empire, however, did not develop overnight during World War II. See Brooke L. Blower, "Nation of Outposts: Forts, Factories, Bases, and the Making of American Power," *Diplomatic History* 41, no. 3 (2017): 439–59.

was increasingly regarded as critical to one's success in life. As a result, various questions about the education of young people – who should have access to post-elementary education, how schools should prepare young people for work, and how to train young people to be good citizens – became inextricably linked to ideas about young people's roles in a national security emergency. Moreover, the very concept of "youth" in American society was defined and redefined in relation to various debates over young people, their education, and national security.

The years from World War I through World War II, then, were "the age of youth" in two senses: during this time, American adults paid close attention to young people because they believed their contribution to national security was critical to their ideal visions of American society, and who comprised "youth" was constantly redefined as a result. This book examines how this link between youth, education, and national security was developed in these years and the effects it had on young people. Although it is customary to see U.S. history from the 1910s through the 1940s as a sequence of several distinct periods – starting with World War I, followed by an "interwar" period centering on the Roaring Twenties and the Great Depression, which then gave way to World War II – these decades were a time when a wide variety of ideas concerning young people and their education were prompted by national security concerns, real and perceived.

Various factors contributed to the establishment of the connection between youth, education, and national security. First, World War I dramatically altered perceptions of national security in the United States. Specifically, during the war, Americans, as well as many other people around the world, faced a global "total war" for the first time, which required the mobilization of the country's entire population and material resources. The war – particularly its massive scale; new military technologies deployed by combatants such as airplanes, machine guns, and tanks; and the new fighting strategies required as a result – led to the transformation of ideas about national security among military leaders and other concerned adults. Upon the country's entry into the war in April 1917, the United States instituted selective conscription, which marked a departure from the country's history of obtaining wartime armed troops mostly through volunteers and sparked a fierce dispute over the appropriate age for conscription. The war also necessitated the training of soldiers in a variety of technical skills, culminating in the formation of military–educational programs in civilian colleges and universities. The idea of military training and service as an educational, formative experience was thus shaped through the American experience of World War I.

Individuals concerned with military preparedness continued to believe after the war that the next war would be of a similar kind and considered how the United States should prepare its resources for it. Moreover, many Americans considered the Great Depression a national security emergency comparable to war. Massive youth unemployment caused by the Depression, the rise of student activism in the 1930s, and the emergence of Nazi Germany drove adults' attention to young people in their late teens to mid-twenties and they discussed ways to supervise youth and guide them toward paths they considered appropriate. The selective draft in World War II built on these precedents, defining the military service of youth as an educational experience. In essence, although public interest in national security fluctuated from World War I to World War II, the idea that military training and service were educational, formative experiences for young individuals persisted and developed. In other words, as a result of the experience of World War I, national security became a recurring theme for political, educational, business, and military leaders, and how to educate the nation's youth was one of their key topics of discussion.

The second major factor that contributed to the development of the link between youth, education, and national security was the spread of the idea that education beyond elementary school was a means of achieving social mobility, vocational skills, or, more generally, a higher quality of life. Traditional routes to employment, such as apprenticeships and other on-the-job training programs, were largely superseded in the first half of the twentieth century by high school credentials, and an increasing number of young people also pursued higher education. The period in which national leaders debated how to train youth for national security, therefore, coincided with a time in which access to secondary and post-secondary education was important to a growing number of young people. This resulted in a series of debates over whether national security should be prioritized over young people's access to education. For example, a heated public debate erupted when some students were suspended or expelled from high school or college in the 1930s because they refused to participate in the Reserve Officers' Training Corps (ROTC), a program established in educational institutions for the teaching of elementary military training and which was made mandatory for male students in some institutions.

Finally, the link between youth, education, and national security developed in relation to the popularization of the concept of "youth" as a distinct period of life between childhood and adulthood that had begun in the early twentieth century as a result of factors such as prolonged education and the development of academic studies of child development. The concept was then constantly redefined as a result of the debates regarding the role of young people in national security emergencies. Furthermore, as the United States emerged as the world's superpower during World War II and the geographical scope of U.S. national security expanded, this link between youth and national security was projected onto youth in other countries, such as Japan and Germany under U.S. occupation. The cultural concept of "youth" was thus redefined by shifting U.S. national security priorities.

Various military–educational programs for young men were established during this time, as the ties between youth, education, and national security strengthened. Significantly, promoters of these programs frequently touted them as "democratic" educational programs that admitted young men regardless of socioeconomic status. The Student Army Training Corps (SATC), which existed in higher education institutions during World War I to train soldiers in technical skills necessary for the military, provided the groundwork for the subsequent development of the discourse that military training and service could be a "democratic" educational experience. Supporters of the SATC specifically praised it as a "democratic" educational opportunity that allowed young men who otherwise could not afford an education to acquire it through government funding, even though the opportunity was not accessible to many young people from minority groups. ROTC in the years following the war prompted some people to strongly criticize the emerging relationship between military service, access to education, and social class, as the educational institutions that made ROTC training mandatory for male students were predominantly public institutions. They pointed out that while young men from wealthy families might avoid the training by enrolling in private institutions without it, others who lacked financial resources could not. However, opponents of ROTC were defeated by the eve of World War II, demonstrating how the idea that military training in civilian educational institutions during peacetime was "democratic" and American had become widely accepted in American society. The World War II military–educational programs, which drew on precursors such as the SATC and ROTC, also prioritized the education of young white men who could have afforded it anyway above others of the same age group.

Consequently, these programs replicated preexisting socioeconomic and racial inequalities despite the rhetoric of "democratic" educational opportunity, making them more accessible to white men from families who could have afforded the education in the first place than to others in the same age range. In essence, while adults categorized young people in their late teens through mid-twenties as a distinct age group with shared characteristics, they also stratified them through policy, prioritizing the education of young white men with potential for national security leadership over that of others in the same age range under the name of democracy. This mechanism of designating all young people as "youth" while stratifying them based on their importance to national security was incorporated into U.S. policies for Japanese youth during the postwar occupation of Japan, as this book reveals.

The developments that took place in the first half of the twentieth century regarding youth, national security, and education were largely products of the period of total warfare. In the years after World War II, adults continued to discuss youth's role in national security crises, but the Cold War ushered in a new way of mobilizing civilians militarily. That is, the era of massive military mobilization of civilians came to an end with the emergence of new technologies like nuclear weapons and long-range missiles. As a result, rather than conscripting a large number of young men and then sorting them based on national security needs, the government began overtly deferring college students and other young men deemed useful on the Cold War home front, aligning military service more tightly with socioeconomic classes.

At the same time, conceptual and institutional developments that occurred during the first half of the twentieth century served as a foundation for subsequent developments. Historians have underscored the comparatively fair representation of social class, race, and ethnicity in the U.S. armed services from World War I through 1973, when the selective draft was the primary means of obtaining military manpower in wartime, as opposed to the post-1973 All-Volunteer Force (AVF), whose members have been drawn from "less middle class, more working class and lower income, and less educated" backgrounds. In the words of one historian, the AVF has drawn "Americans clustered toward the bottom of the income scale rather than the middle."[4] However, as I will demonstrate, mechanisms for stratifying young individuals of military age had already been implemented during the first half of the twentieth century. Furthermore, the link established between education and military service during and between the two world wars proved to have long-term consequences in other ways as well. For example, by the end of World War II, ages eighteen through twenty-five had been established as the primary age for military service, and the registration age for selective service has

---

[4] Jennifer Mittelstadt, "Military Demographics," in *At War: The Military and American Culture in the Twentieth Century and Beyond*, ed. David Kieran and Edwin A. Martini (New Brunswick, NJ: Rutgers University Press, 2018), 88, 95.

Introduction 7

remained the same until now.⁵ Moreover, from 1982 to 2021, men in those ages were required to register with the Selective Service System to receive federal aid for higher education.⁶ Understanding the evolving dynamics between national security, young people, and education and thereby illuminating the interplay between war and peace in the years during and between the two world wars is the subject of this book.

National Security, Education, and the Changing Definitions of "Youth"

As mentioned earlier, education became central to the relationship between youth and national security largely because it coincided with a time when young people were in school for longer than before due to the spread of the idea that schooling – or credentials of schools – would help them land better jobs. Until the early twentieth century, schooling beyond the elementary school level was considered a luxury limited to those who could afford it. Prolonged education was in fact often considered a barrier to one's success in life. For example, a newspaper editor in Portland, Oregon, argued in 1879 that too much education would "graduate whole regiments of sickly sentimentalists: young gentlemen unused and unfit for work."⁷ Accordingly, young people in urban areas attended grammar school for five or six years, after which they acquired vocational skills as apprentices or through on-the-job training, while their peers in rural regions juggled schooling and farm work, which meant their schooling tended to span a longer time than their urban counterparts. Either way, schooling beyond grammar school was not an option for most young people. However, with industrialization in full bloom and as an increasing number of people worked for large corporations and

---

⁵ Although no one has been drafted through the Selective Service System since the inauguration of the AVF, the requirement to register with the System has remained active.
⁶ The requirement was removed by the FAFSA Simplification Act of 2021. Director of Selective Service System, U.S. Selective Service System, "Report on Review of Processes and Procedures Employed by Agencies for Appeals by Individuals Denied Federal Benefits for Failing to Register with Selective Service System, FT2022 NDAA, Section 529A," pp. 3–4, 6, www.sss.gov/wp-content/uploads/2022/08/FY2022-NDAA-SEC.-529a-7-28-2022.pdf (accessed October 1, 2022); Benjamin Collins and Cassandria Dortch, "The FAFSA Simplification Act," *Congressional Research Service Report R46909* (updated August 4, 2022), n.p. ["Summary"], https://crsreports.congress.gov/product/pdf/R/R46909 (accessed October 2, 2022).
⁷ Harvey Kantor, "Vocationalism in American Education: The Economic and Political Context, 1880–1930," in *Work, Youth, and Schooling: Historical Perspectives on Vocationalism in American Education*, ed. Harvey Kantor and David B. Tyack (Stanford, CA: Stanford University Press, 1982), 14–15. The quote is from p. 15.

factories, rather than small shops or farms, and the number and variety of white-collar jobs expanded rapidly, both employers and employees began to see schools as a site to prepare children and young people for work. As such, secondary-school credentials became a prerequisite for white-collar jobs, and not only middle-class families but also working-class families began to send their children to secondary schools hoping that it would help their children earn a middle-class living.[8]

As a result, while only 8 percent of fourteen- to seventeen-year-olds attended secondary schools in 1900, over 44 percent of them did so in 1930. Due to the high unemployment rate of young people during the Great Depression, high school attendance further soared in the 1930s. By 1940, 73 percent of Americans in this age group were students.[9] Enrollments in higher education institutions also rose from 237,592 in 1900 to 1,100,000 in 1930, further raising the lower age limit of who should be considered as adults.[10] Although many students were unable to attend school on a full-time basis or did not graduate, and the attendance rate and the quality of education students received varied by race, class, ethnicity, gender, and region, the growth of secondary school and college attendance nationwide helped spread the idea that young people occupied a distinct social sphere. Growing up in such age-bound environments, young people themselves developed unique peer cultures and identities that distinguished them from both younger children and older adults.[11]

Prolonged schooling, along with several other factors, led to the spread of the cultural conceptions of adolescence and youth as neither childhood nor adulthood in American society. As historians have demonstrated, age categories are culturally constructed concepts. While awareness of one's chronological age had existed before then, it was during the Progressive Era – normally defined as the 1890s through the U.S. entry into World War I in 1917 – that age was normalized as one of

---

[8] Ibid., 14–22.
[9] Harvey Kantor and David B. Tyack, Introduction to *Work, Youth, and Schooling*, ed. Kantor and Tyack, 7; Kriste Lindenmeyer, "New Opportunities for Children in the Great Depression in the United States," in *The Routledge History of Childhood in the Western World*, ed. Paula S. Fass (New York: Routledge, 2013), 440.
[10] Aubrey Williams, "The Government's Responsibility for Youth," *The Annals of the American Academy of Political and Social Science*, vol. 194, The Prospect for Youth (Nov. 1937), 120.
[11] Edward A. Krug, *The Shaping of the American High School, Volume 2: 1920–1941* (Madison: University of Wisconsin Press, 1972), 120–29. For peer culture (of white, middle-class youth) in this period, see Paula S. Fass, *The Damned and the Beautiful: American Youth in the 1920's* (New York: Oxford University Press, 1977).

the fundamental social and legal categories by which individuals were defined.[12]

The various ways in which adults responded to the living conditions of young people in the Progressive Era embedded these age-related categories. For example, reformers concerned about the exploitation of youth labor embarked on wide-ranging social welfare reform projects for young people, such as the implementation of mandatory schooling and child labor laws. Others, who considered that modern technologies had rendered young people "soft," led organizations aimed at making young people physically and mentally healthy, and teaching them the essence of democratic citizenship, leadership skills, and love for nature and their country. One well-known example of this kind of organization was the Young Men's Christian Association (YMCA), which was first established in London in 1844, and then founded in the United States in 1851. The establishment of other similar organizations followed, including the Young Women's Christian Association (YWCA) in 1858 (in the United States, after its foundation in the United Kingdom in 1855), the Boy Scouts of America in 1910, and the Girl Scouts in America in 1912, although organizations for girls and young women were less likely than their male counterparts to focus on activities for mental and physical toughness, reflecting the adult organizers' gender norms.[13]

The emergence of a cultural conception of young people as a distinct age group that differed from both adults and younger children was also propelled by the establishment of child development as an academic

---

[12] Corinne T. Field and Nicholas L. Syrett, "Introduction," *American Historical Review* 125, no. 2 (2020): 371–84; Corinne T. Field and Nicholas L. Syrett, eds., *Age in America: The Colonial Era to the Present* (New York: New York University Press, 2015); Howard P. Chudacoff, *How Old Are You? Age Consciousness in American Culture* (Princeton, NJ: Princeton University Press, 1989); David I. Macleod, *Building Character in the American Boy: The Boy Scouts, YMCA, and Their Forerunners, 1870–1920* (Madison: University of Wisconsin Press, 1983). Historians have disagreed on how to describe the Progressive Era and what exactly characterized the period, but they have agreed that progressives were not a cohesive group of people and that their views on reform differed greatly. When referring to individuals involved in this tide of reform, I use "progressive" instead of capitalizing the "p" in recognition of the diversity of reformist viewpoints that were prevalent at this time. On the nature of progressivism, see Daniel T. Rodgers, "In Search of Progressivism," *Reviews in American History* 10, no. 4 (1982): 113–32; Daniel T. Rodgers, "Capitalism and Politics in the Progressive Era and in Ours," *Journal of the Gilded Age and Progressive Era* 13, no. 3 (2014): 379–86; Alan Dawley, *Changing the World: American Progressives in War and Revolution* (Princeton, NJ: Princeton University Press, 2003), introduction.
[13] Steven Mintz, *Huck's Raft: A History of American Childhood* (Cambridge, MA: Belknap Press of Harvard University Press, 2004), 192–95; Jay Mechling, "Children in Scouting and Other Organizations," in *The Routledge History of Childhood in the Western World*, ed. Fass, 421–22.

subject. Academics provided "scientific" prescriptions and advice on how to deal with young people for middle-class reformers and parents. Among the most influential was psychologist G. Stanley Hall whose book on adolescence published in 1904 popularized the idea of adolescence as a distinct life stage. Likening child development from infancy to adulthood to the Darwinian notion of human evolution, Hall defined adolescence as an emotionally turbulent yet indefatigably energetic period in which youth must be protected from the adult environment and guided carefully and slowly by adults to mature adulthood.[14] The decades in which the United States faced two world wars and the Great Depression, then, coincided with the time when the cultural and social threshold of adulthood was rising due to the spread of the idea that adolescence and youth should be differentiated from adulthood and the rising popularity of schooling beyond grammar school.

While identifying young people as a distinct age group, the rise of secondary and higher education attendance also gave rise to mechanisms that channeled young people into different educational and vocational tracks. During the nineteenth century, secondary schools primarily focused on the instruction of academic subjects and served a small number of young people, the majority of whom came from wealthy families. However, with the dramatic increase in secondary school enrollment during the first three decades of the twentieth century, educational leaders came to recognize that secondary schools need to be reformed to accommodate a wider demographic of young people.

As a "democratic" alternative to establishing separate institutions for academic education and vocational training, which many feared could result in permanent class divisions, they integrated vocational education into the conventional secondary education system and developed differentiated curricula within the same high school. However, as historian Tracy L. Steffes has pointed out, this "democratic" system operated under the supposition that children possessed intrinsically different abilities and guided them onto different paths presumably designed to enhance those abilities. As a result, the perception of high schools as democratic institutions for equal opportunity obscured and helped perpetuate structural inequality and discrimination, with certain students, particularly women, Black Americans, and others from marginalized groups, encountering greater likelihoods of being directed to vocational training and guidance for low-wage jobs, in contrast to their white male counterparts, who were more likely to be guided toward an academic,

---

[14] Mintz, *Huck's Raft*, 186–88, 196–97; Mechling, "Children in Scouting and Other Organizations," 422.

college-bound path. A similar change occurred at the level of postsecondary education as well, as an increasing number of young people sought education beyond high school. Although some people saw it as a step toward the democratization of higher education, junior colleges were established in the 1920s to cater to lower-middle-class students and to teach practical skills.[15] Thus, "democratization" talk and student stratification – ostensibly based on ability but in fact on such categories as social class, race, and gender – went hand in hand at both secondary education and higher education levels.

In short, although many young people benefited from newly created opportunities in secondary and postsecondary education, these opportunities were not equally available to all young people. Undergirding this mechanism were cultural presumptions regarding the alleged inherent abilities of people of different social, racial, ethnic, or gender backgrounds. Military–educational programs such as the SATC as well as the Selective Service System during the two world wars mirrored this pattern of channeling youth from divergent backgrounds into different tracks in the name of democratic educational opportunity. For example, selective service during these wars was described by its supporters as more egalitarian and democratic than volunteerism because it subjected all military-age men, regardless of background, to the probability of military service. Similarly, they maintained that military–educational programs like the SATC offered to draftees were "democratic" opportunities that provided higher education to young men who would not otherwise have had the opportunity. However, as I will show, young draftees were stratified once inside the military, with white men with superior educational attainment before service frequently holding the most advantageous positions.

The debates over national security, youth, and education from World War I through World War II were also shaped by changing ideas about war in American society. First, World War I not only informed Americans about the emergence of a new era of warfare; it also informed them that the new type of war could be employed for purposes unrelated to war. In the years leading up to the U.S. entry into the war in 1917, progressive reformers had been engaging in wide-ranging projects to tackle such challenges as the tremendous economic gap between the rich and the poor, the cruel living and working conditions of working-class

[15] Tracy L. Steffes, *School, Society, and State: A New Education to Govern Modern America, 1890–1940* (Chicago: University of Chicago Press, 2012), ch. 5; David O. Levine, *The American College and the Culture of Aspiration, 1915–1940* (Ithaca, NY: Cornell University Press, 1986), ch. 8.

people, especially recent immigrants from Southern and Eastern Europe in urban industrial centers, and political corruption. At first, many of them were uneasy about or against the country getting involved in the war, but as news of the war's atrocities mounted and the active engagement of the United States in the war grew more likely by early 1917, many of them expressed their support.

One reason that many cited for this change of mind was the expectation the war would yield opportunities for social reform at home and abroad. For example, John Dewey, the renowned philosopher who had previously been against the war, became one of the many intellectuals supporting President Woodrow Wilson's policies for winning what was called the war to make the world safe for democracy. Condemning pacifists who remained opposed to the war even after the country entered it as unrealistic idealists, he argued shortly after the U.S. entry into the war that the war should be used constructively to realize a democratic world. According to Dewey, the pacifists who declined to face the reality of war "wasted rather than invested their potentialities when they turned so vigorously to opposing entrance into a war which was already all but universal, instead of using their energies to form, at a *plastic juncture*, the conditions and objects of our entrance [into the war]."[16] A year later, in an article entitled "The Social Possibilities of War," he argued that the war illuminated and realized "the supremacy of the public and social interest over the private and possessive interest which might otherwise have taken a long time to construct." When used constructively, according to Dewey, the war would result in "a better organized world internally and externally," with the government regulating the economy for the common good and democracy.[17]

These individuals were neither naive nor idealistic, nor were they ignorant of the atrocities of modern warfare. Despite their hesitation about U.S. military involvement in the war, however, many reformers who eventually embraced it did so with the expectation that the U.S. entrance into the war would usher in a rare moment – a "plastic

---

[16] Italics mine. John Dewey, "The Future of Pacifism," *The New Republic*, July 29, 1917, https://newrepublic.com/article/148833/future-pacifism (accessed December 15, 2023); Robert B. Westbrook, *John Dewey and American Democracy* (Ithaca, NY: Cornell University Press, 1991), 202–203.

[17] John Dewey, "The Social Possibilities of War," *Teaching American History*, https://teachingamericanhistory.org/document/the-social-possibilities-of-war-2/ (accessed December 15, 2023).

Introduction 13

juncture" – in which society could be molded towards progressive ideals, at home and abroad, in ways inconceivable in peacetime.[18]

Not all progressives shared the view that the war could become an opportunity for social reform. Notably, the social critic Randolph S. Bourne harshly criticized his fellow progressives – especially his mentor Dewey – and their expectation that the war would yield opportunities for a better future. "If war is too strong for you to prevent," he wrote, "how is it going to be weak enough for you to control and mould to your liberal purposes?"[19] These criticisms were a minority, however, and this kind of idea – seeing war and other national security emergencies as a "plastic juncture" that can yield broad social benefits not directly related to the war – took hold across key segments of American society and remained a driving force for many political, military, and educational movements after the war. By World War II, this mindset had become so widespread that discussions on war-induced reform were in full swing way before the United States formally entered the war. For example, in October 1940, the young Arthur M. Schlesinger Jr., who would later become a leading public intellectual in American society, argued that, with all its horror, "war opens up almost revolutionary possibilities for reconstruction at home." Conscription, high taxes on the wealthy, and other governmental measures for war mobilization, he claimed, would also function as means to address social and economic inequality. Hence, just as World War I "served as a laboratory for important experiments in government control and regulation," the new war should similarly be "turned to good purposes," if it came to the United States. He argued that as war enabled a "mass psychological condition where resistance to change is at its feeblest," World War II might enable drastic governmental actions to regulate the economy, fix the wealth gap, and advance democracy in American society.[20]

Another group of people who believed that mobilizing civilians for war and other national security emergencies would have non-military effects were those on the conservative side of the political spectrum who

---

[18] David M. Kennedy, *Over Here: The First World War and American Society* (New York: Oxford University Press, 1980), 49–53.
[19] Randolph S. Bourne, "Twilight of Idols," in *War and the Intellectuals: Collected Essays, 1915–1919*, ed. Carl Resek (Indianapolis, IN: Hackett, 1999 [1964]), 57; Casey Nelson Blake, *Beloved Community: The Cultural Criticism of Randolph Bourne, Van Wyck Brooks, Waldo Frank, and Lewis Mumford* (Chapel Hill: University of North Carolina Press, 1990), 157–64; Kennedy, *Over Here*, 51.
[20] A. M. Schlesinger Jr., letter to the editor, *New York Times* (hereafter cited as *NYT*), October 14, 1940. For more on how liberals saw World War II as an opportunity to advance their agenda in domestic politics, see Alan Brinkley, *The End of Reform: New Deal Liberalism in Recession and War* (New York: Vintage Books, 1995), 175–77.

believed that the traditional U.S. military, centered on a small standing army and locally trained citizen-soldiers, was obsolete in an age of imperialism and modern military technology. These individuals became increasingly influential in the early twentieth century and especially as the possibility of the U.S. entry into World War I increased around 1915.

One of the solutions that they developed for the "modernization" of the U.S. military was the establishment of universal military training (UMT), which referred to the idea of having all young men trained by standards set by the U.S. military in basic military skills in peacetime to build a nation of citizen soldiers fully prepared to fight in a modern war. The majority of its backers were politically conservative white Anglo-Saxon male elites who were concerned not only about the position of the U.S. military in the shifting international order but also about the rapid transformations in American society brought on by industrialization and mass immigration. Consequently, they believed that UMT would not only increase military preparedness but also have social benefits, such as physically and mentally "toughening" young American men, bringing people from various socioeconomic backgrounds together, and "Americanizing" immigrants. This idea of turning immature youth into mature adults through military training and service eventually shaped policies concerning the mobilization of young people for World War I; it continued to shape debates over youth and national security in the years that followed.

In the years in which educational credentials were considered crucial for one's success in life and when youth was increasingly regarded as distinct from adulthood, therefore, various American adults contemplated how to prepare and mobilize young people for modern warfare or invoked national security threats for objectives that were not necessarily related to them. Young people, including teenagers, had served in past U.S. wars, but predominantly as volunteers. The implementation of a large-scale military draft during World War I marked a fundamental departure from the volunteer system on which the United States had traditionally relied. The question was, then, could the state *compel* young people whom society considered as not yet adults to serve the country, militarily or otherwise, in times of national emergency? If so, on what grounds? Hence, preparing youth for national security duties emerged as a significant policy domain where divergent views regarding the relationship between youth, the nation, and education converged and clashed.

These debates and their consequences, moreover, were tightly connected to the predominant sense of manly citizenship. The demand for boys and young men to receive military training surged at the turn of the twentieth century, with proponents arguing that such training would "toughen" boys and young men both physically and mentally in addition to boosting national defense and strengthening the armed forces; the idea that linked military training with manliness continued to shape arguments for military training and service throughout the first half of the twentieth century.[21] The typical image of the American soldier remained that of a young man, not a young woman, even though women of all ages served in the military throughout U.S. history. Rather, it was assumed that women would perform supportive duties on the home front. During World War I, while male high school students were encouraged to prepare themselves for future military service, female students were encouraged to support men from home, such as by joining the Junior Red Cross and participating in wide-ranging projects like food conservation, planting vegetables, and fundraising.[22] In the years after the war, when military training of young men was hotly debated in the public, calls for the military training of girls and young women remained rare.[23] In World War II, women were depicted in popular culture as "objects of obligation" for which men fought. Government officials and media outlets urged men to fight for their wives and girlfriends as well as for universal human rights.[24]

With military training and service firmly connected to masculinity, femininity was even stigmatized as symbolizing unpatriotic, cowardly citizens unwilling to serve the country. For example, a university chancellor, speaking at a 1922 meeting of college presidents and ROTC representatives to promote compulsory military training in higher education institutions, castigated the growing tide of the antiwar movement

---

[21] For the cultural history of manliness at the turn of the twentieth century and how it shaped policy, see Kristin L. Hoganson, *Fighting for American Manhood: How Gender Politics Provoked the Spanish-American and Philippine-American Wars* (New Haven, CT: Yale University Press, 1998); Gail Bederman, *Manliness & Civilization: A Cultural History of Gender and Race in the United States, 1880–1917* (Chicago: University of Chicago Press, 1995); Michael H. Hunt, *Ideology and U.S. Foreign Policy* (New Haven, CT: Yale University Press, 1987).

[22] Randall Curren and Charles Dorn, *Patriotic Education in a Global Age* (Chicago: University of Chicago Press, 2018), 62–63.

[23] For a rare example of an attempt to have high-school girls drill, see Richard Welling to William J. O'Shea, May 16, 1933, Richard Welling to Harold G. Campbell, May 16, 1933, William J. O'Shea to Richard Welling, June 2, 1933, all in "Military 1930–33" folder, Box 68, National Self Government Committee Records, New York Public Library (hereafter cited as NSGC Records). More common was the enlistment of girls as "sponsors" of boys and men in military training to give "glamour and feminine appeal" to the training. Edwin C. Johnson, "Main Issues in the Junior R. O. T. C. Controversy," *Harvard Educational Review* 9, no. 4 (1939): 478, a reprint of the article filed in "Military in General Corres. 1936–40" folder, Box 68, NSGC Records.

[24] Robert B. Westbrook, *Why We Fought: Forging American Obligations in World War II* (Washington, DC: Smithsonian Books, 2004), 69.

after the end of World War I as symbolizing how American society was "rapidly becoming feminized."[25] The establishment of masculine citizenship in American society also led to the development of rules prohibiting homosexuality in the military and disqualifying servicepeople regarded as homosexual from veteran benefits including education.[26] The development of the ties between young heterosexual men's educational opportunity with military training and service that this book explores, in turn, reveals how access to education, when linked to national security, placed other young individuals in a secondary status.

The debates over youth, education, and national security also highlighted the pervasive racism in American society. For example, Black men's access to military–educational programs was conditioned by institutionalized racism in the military and American society at large, which assumed that Black men were unqualified for officer positions or military positions requiring highly technical skills. Although secondary education and higher education grew in the first half of the twentieth century, access to these opportunities for Black youth remained severely limited. The debates over youth, national security, and education, and the supposedly "democratic" educational programs that they created, therefore, demonstrate how the discourse of military training and service as democratic educational opportunities built on and reinforced preexisting racism in American society.

Some readers may not find the increased access to education provided through military service to be a problem. After all, military–educational programs such as the SATC did allow some young men who would not otherwise have been able to attend college to obtain an education. However, justifying these initiatives merely on the basis of promoting equal educational opportunity, as their proponents did, overlooks the structural inequalities firmly rooted in American society, which shaped discourses and policies regarding youth, education, and national security. First, young men from wealthy families did not have to go through military training programs or risk their lives to acquire an education. Furthermore, while ROTC, which still exists today, is now recognized as a pathway to a military career and a way to fund a college education, it was not until after World War II that four-year scholarships and avenues to active officer positions were made available to students who participated in ROTC programs. Put simply, before that period, students who were obligated to participate in ROTC training did not receive the

---

[25] "Says Opposition to War Is Feminizing Americans," *NYT*, December 3, 1922.
[26] Margot Canaday, *The Straight State: Sexuality and Citizenship in Twentieth-Century America* (Princeton, NJ: Princeton University Press, 2009), chs. 2 and 4.

same kind of financial or professional benefits as ROTC students today. Finally, these options were not equally accessible to all young people. The labeling of these programs as democratic by their supporters reflected a larger trend in American society of categorizing and stratifying young people depending on their perceived value to the national good and doing so in the name of democracy.

Rethinking the "Interwar" Period in U.S. History

By revealing how military and national security concerns influenced the education of young people in the years during and between the two world wars, this study joins the growing scholarship that rethinks the boundaries between wartime and peacetime, as well as the place of war and the military, in conventional U.S. historical narratives. As stated earlier, war and military issues have often been portrayed as abruptly entering American society and then vanishing within a brief time, with little impact on society in peacetime. In this type of narrative, World War I reaches American society in 1917 and then fades in 1918; World War II enters the same society in 1941 and then recedes in 1945.[27]

Multiple factors have contributed to the persistence of this perception of war as brief deviations from peace, such as the popular U.S. self-perception of the United States as a peaceful nation and the growing invisibility of war to most Americans in the twentieth century (due to changes in the nature of warfare and military technology, as well as the fact that wars have been fought outside the U.S. mainland). Historian

---

[27] The "rise and fall" of the New Deal state, for instance, has long been the main chronological framework used to explain twentieth-century U.S. political history. It traces the formation of an active federal government in the 1930s, its tenure through the mid-1960s, and its eventual "fall" signified with the election in 1980 of Ronald Reagan as U.S. President. While this is certainly an essential and central aspect of twentieth-century U.S. political history, in this version of U.S. history, World War II usually serves only as a backdrop or incorporated as one of many factors that led to changes in the New Deal order. Steve Fraser and Gary Gerstle, eds., *The Rise and Fall of the New Deal Order, 1930–1980* (Princeton, NJ: Princeton University Press, 1989). The division between wartime and peacetime is also evident in the narratives about education and youth in twentieth-century United States. The literature can be largely divided into two categories: studies that deal with wartime (World Wars I and II) and those that deal with the years when the United States was not formally involved in those wars. For a historiographical review of American education in World War II, see Charles Dorn, *American Education, Democracy, and the Second World War* (New York: Palgrave Macmillan, 2007), 13–18. For a historiographical review of the relationship between federal policies (including world war and Cold War policies) and U.S. higher education, see Christopher P. Loss, *Between Citizens and the State: The Politics of American Higher Education in the 20th Century* (Princeton, NJ: Princeton University Press, 2012), introduction.

Michael S. Sherry points out that the United States is "a nation deeply wedded to and defined by war, though maddeningly reluctant to admit it."[28] Marylin B. Young also articulated a common American self-perception of the United States: that the United States is not "an aggressor, because, by definition, it does not commit aggression. The hostility of others to the United States cannot, again by definition, be a response to American actions, because the United States does not invite hostility but only reacts to it."[29] The idea that the United States only enters a war when attacked by a foreign enemy and only stays in it for a short time has frequently shaped historians' understanding of twentieth-century U.S. history. This idea has not only obscured the profound and long-lasting effects that U.S. military operations, engagement in wars, and occupations have had on other countries and societies but also diverted historians' attention away from the fundamental and enduring impact that military and national security issues have had on American society and people.

In light of this, a rising body of historical scholarship published in recent decades has challenged the conventional dichotomy between war and peace in U.S. history narratives or demonstrated the long-term changes that war and wartime mobilization made in various arenas, ranging from the jurisdiction of the federal government and American people's understanding of their relationship with the government to social policymaking and U.S. perceptions of global order.[30] From a

---

[28] Michael Sherry, "War as a Way of Life," *Modern American History* 1, no. 1 (2018): 95.

[29] Marylin B. Young, "The Age of Global Power," in *Making the Forever War: Marilyn B. Young on the Culture and Politics of American Militarism*, ed. Mark Philips Bradley and Mary L. Dudziak (Amherst: University of Massachusetts Press, 2021), 15–16. For an analysis of how the physical distance from the front lines of war – and thus from dead soldiers – led to apathy toward war in American society today, see Mary L. Dudziak, "'You Didn't See Him Lying...Beside the Gravel Road in France': Death, Distance, and American War Politics," *Diplomatic History* 42, no. 1 (2018): 1–16.

[30] Laura McEnaney, "Nightmares on Elm Street: Demobilizing in Chicago, 1945–1953," *Journal of American History* 92, no. 4 (2006): 1265–91; Laura McEnaney, *Postwar: Waging Peace in Chicago* (Philadelphia: University of Pennsylvania Press, 2018); Mary L. Dudziak, *War Time: An Idea, Its History, Its Consequences* (New York: Oxford University Press, 2012); Michael S. Sherry, *In the Shadow of War: The United States since the 1930s* (New Haven, CT: Yale University Press, 1995); Daniel Eugene Garcia, "Class and Brass: Demobilization, Working Class Politics, and American Foreign Policy between World War and Cold War," *Diplomatic History* 34, no. 4 (2010): 681–98; Christopher Capozzola, *Uncle Sam Wants You: World War I and the Making of the Modern American Citizen* (New York: Oxford University Press, 2008); James T. Sparrow, *Warfare State: World War II Americans and the Age of Big Government* (New York: Oxford University Press, 2011); Ira Katznelson, *Fear Itself: The New Deal and the Origins of Our Time* (New York: Liveright Publishing, 2013); Jennifer D. Keene, *Doughboys, the Great War, and the Remaking of America* (Baltimore: Johns Hopkins University Press, 2001); Elizabeth Borgwardt, *A New Deal for the World: America's*

different angle, other scholars have provided new perspectives on the United States in the 1920s and 1930s by challenging the conventional narrative that characterizes the country at this time as "isolationist." In other words, they have highlighted the country's significant involvement in world affairs in fields like culture, the economy, and disarmament in these decades, and advocated for a new understanding of U.S. relations with the rest of the world during this time that goes beyond the conventional explanation based on the binary between "isolationism" and "internationalism."[31] Building on these studies, I challenge the conventional view that holds that American society in the first half of the twentieth century had little to do with military and war issues outside of times in which the country was engaged in major wars and demonstrate how integral national security and military concerns were to ideas about youth and education across war and peace.

What emerges as significant in the narrative that unfolds in the chapters of this book is not so much the military itself as it is the diverse imaginations, primarily held by civilian adults across the political spectrum, regarding what the training and service in or inspired by the military could do for the education of young people and to yield other benefits such as political and social reform. Even in the 1920s, when there was little immediate military threat, ROTC was maintained in over 120 higher education institutions across the country on the assumption that it would not only benefit national defense but also make young men better citizens. The rise of Nazi Germany in the 1930s contributed to a negative image of the military training of youth, but even then,

---

Vision for Human Rights (Cambridge, MA: Belknap Press of Harvard University Press, 2005); Thomas W. Zeiler, David K. Ekbladh, and Benjamin C. Montoya, eds., *Beyond 1917: The United States and the Global Legacies of the Great War* (New York: Oxford University Press, 2017); Thomas Childers, *Soldier from the War Returning: The Greatest Generation's Troubled Homecoming from World War II* (Boston: Houghton Mifflin Harcourt, 2009). A number of works by political scientists have also been published on this subject. See, for example, Edwin Amenta and Theda Skocpol, "Redefining the New Deal: World War II and the Development of Social Provision in the United States," in *Politics of Social Policy in the United States*, ed. Margaret Weir, et al. (Princeton, NJ: Princeton University Press, 1988), 81–122; Ira Katznelson and Martin Shefter, eds., *Shaped by War and Trade: International Influences on American Political Development* (Princeton, NJ: Princeton University Press, 2002); Bartholomew Sparrow, *From the Outside In: World War II and the American State* (Princeton, NJ: Princeton University Press, 1996).

[31] Daniel T. Rodgers, *Atlantic Crossings: Social Politics in a Progressive Age* (Cambridge, MA: Belknap Press of Harvard University Press, 1998); Dawley, *Changing the World*; Emily S. Rosenberg, *Financial Missionaries to the World: The Politics and Culture of Dollar Diplomacy, 1900–1930* (Durham, NC: Duke University Press, 2003); Brooke L. Blower, "From Isolationism to Neutrality: A New Framework for Understanding American Political Culture, 1919–1941," *Diplomatic History* 38, no. 2 (2014): 345–76.

Americans had a wide range of ideas about what positive good educating youth through the military could achieve to build a better society.

In fact, the lines separating war and peace were not always evident to Americans living at the time. For example, ROTC was established in 1916 and maintained throughout the twentieth century; it still exists today. Many government agencies established for World War I functioned as the institutional basis for New Deal programs, which in turn served as the backbone for the U.S. war effort during World War II. The Selective Training and Service Act of 1940, which became the basis of the U.S. selective service policy throughout World War II, was signed into law on September 16, 1940, more than a year before the country officially entered the war. These policies, I show, led to a larger shift in the ideas about young people in the United States, and underscore how national security concerns redefined young people's place in society across wartime and peacetime.

By examining the link between national security, youth, and education, this book, then, presents a "transwar" approach to twentieth-century U.S. history. "Transwar" is an analytical approach developed in recent decades by Asian history scholars to challenge the long-standing linear trajectory assigned to twentieth-century Asia, which treats the end of World War II in 1945 as the sole significant break that transformed the region overnight from one ruled by the Japanese empire to one shaped by U.S. Cold War hegemony. They instead see the period as a complex, multi-layered one shaped by various nationalist, political, and imperialist forces, as well as multiple turning points.[32] In short, "transwar" challenges linear narratives of the twentieth century, as well as the chronological dichotomy between war and peace, while recognizing the profound political and social ramifications of imperialism and total war. As such, it enables a multi-layered analysis that transcends but

---

[32] Reto Hofmann and Max Ward, introduction to *Transwar Asia: Ideology, Practices, and Institutions, 1920–1960*, ed. Reto Hofmann and Max Ward (London: Bloomsbury Academic, 2022), 1–13. I am grateful to Elizabeth Blackmar for bringing up the idea that this work is about "transwar" in a conversation we had, and to Kristin Roebuck for introducing me to pertinent scholarship in Kristin Roebuck, review of Masako Hattori, "The Second Phase of War: Youth in U.S.-Occupied Japan" (*Diplomatic History* 46, no. 5 [2022]: 960–83), H-Diplo Article Review 1183, *H-Diplo*, https://networks.h-net.org/node/28443/discussions/12867730/h-diplo-article-review-1183-roebuck-hattori-%E2%80%9C-second-phase-war (accessed June 12, 2023). See also Andrew Gordon, "Consumption, Leisure, and the Middle Class in Transwar Japan," *Social Science Japan Journal* 10, no. 1 (2007): 1–21; Su Yun Kim, "Transwar Continuities of Colonial Intimacy: Korean–Japanese Relationships in Korean Cinema, 1940s–1960s," *Asian Studies Review* 45, no. 3 (2021): 400–19; Yasushi Yamanouchi, J. Victor Koschmann, and Ryūichi Narita, eds., *Total War and 'Modernization'* (Ithaca, NY: Cornell University Press, 1998).

incorporates war and peace and takes into account multiple factors that shaped society over time.

Of course, one cannot examine U.S. history using the same parameters or time frame. However, taking a "transwar" look at American society in the years from World War I to World War II allows us to grapple with the complex and fundamental ways in which war and military issues shaped American society across wartime and peacetime. This book, in essence, sheds light on the intricate web of social and political contexts in which these issues shaped American society as the country went through a series of national security emergencies, from World War I to the Great Depression and to World War II.

A "transwar" approach to U.S. history also enables us to see how American perspectives on the geography of U.S. national security changed over time. The individuals who established ties between youth, education, and national security from World War I through World War II did so solely in response to perceived national security threats to the U.S. mainland. In other words, considerations about potential dangers to U.S. territories overseas and people living there were not raised in their debates on youth, education, and national security. Nor was there substantial debate over what role youth should play, if ever, in maintaining the existing U.S. empire. Yet, as the United States emerged as the world's superpower after World War II and the U.S. sense of national security changed, the ideas about youth and national security that had been developed in American society in the years before then came to influence how Americans interacted with the societies and people in other parts of the world. Tracing ideas about national security across war and peace, therefore, sheds light on how they evolved over time and influenced U.S. perceptions of other societies and countries.

Finally, I reveal the central role that educational leaders played in developing the ties between youth, education, and national security. Young people's educational paths were largely determined by the system older adults created, and many educators, including college presidents, administrators, and faculty members, and the educational associations they represented, were deeply involved in policymaking that connected education and national security. Not all educators were on board and this book reveals a strong force of educators who were vehemently opposed to the educational profession's involvement in tying educational opportunities to military training and service. For example, some progressive educators who had supported the U.S. involvement in World War I, including Dewey, eventually lost faith in war's potential to change the world after realizing that the war failed to produce the social reconstruction they had anticipated both at home and abroad.[33] However, the efforts to put young Americans under governmental administration for national security emergencies, perceived or real, earned remarkable support from educators across the political spectrum. The educators' motives varied – some were driven by patriotism, others attempted to secure financial resources for their institutions, and still others collaborated with the government hoping that it would lead to better educational policies for young people – but they collectively contributed to institutionalizing the idea that military training and service was an educational experience.

The ties between military service and access to education that these educators helped develop had lasting consequences. Recent studies have revealed how the military has attracted young people into the AVF, since the termination of the draft in 1973, by combining military service with non-military benefits that included educational and career opportunities as well as healthcare and pension.[34] This book describes the origins of this relationship between education and military service. Indeed, the long-term consequences of the shift that took place in the first half of the twentieth century concerning youth, access to education, and national security are still felt across the United States today, from the way Americans conceive of adolescence and youth, the enduring ties between education and military service, to the idea that military training creates better citizens.[35]

A note on my use of the term "national security" should be added here. Because of its geographical location, the United States was, until the early twentieth century, largely free from the fear of being attacked or invaded by foreign powers. The idea of the United States as naturally protected by the two oceans prevailed, and even during World War I, Americans knew that physical attacks on the U.S. mainland were highly unlikely. Even with the rise of Nazi Germany and Imperial Japan in the

---

[33] Westbrook, *John Dewey and American Democracy*, 239, 275–79.
[34] Jennifer Mittelstadt, *The Rise of the Military Welfare State* (Cambridge, MA: Harvard University Press, 2015); Beth Bailey, *America's Army: Making of the All-Volunteer Force* (Cambridge, MA: Belknap Press of Harvard University Press, 2009).
[35] The history of the development of ties between youth, education, and national security also touches on the scholarship on the state's management of its population. See, for example, Rachel Louise Moran, *Governing Bodies: American Politics and the Shaping of the Modern Physique* (Philadelphia: University of Pennsylvania Press, 2018). Some scholars have used Michael Foucault's theories of biopolitics and governmentality to explain the state's regulation of youth in the twentieth century. See Anna Anderson, "Toward a Genealogy of the Liberal Government of Youth," *Journal of Youth Studies* 21, no. 4 (2018): 459–75; Gordon Tait, "Re-assessing Street Kids," *Youth Studies Australia* 11, no. 2 (1992): 12–17; Howard Sercombe, "Youth Theory: Marx or Foucault?" *Youth Studies Australia* 11, no. 3 (1992): 51–53.

1930s, many Americans on the U.S. mainland still considered themselves safe from enemy attacks and were thus unwilling to engage in geopolitical matters abroad. It was precisely this reluctance of the American public to have the country intervene in the shaky international order that led to the invention of the modern idea of national security by those wishing to aid the Allied powers, as historian Andrew Preston has demonstrated.[36] The "interventionists," as they are often called, in their attempts to garner support for greater involvement of the United States in the European crisis in the late 1930s, propagated the idea that international security and the security of the United States' core values were interdependent. While "security" until then had largely indicated the social and economic security of the individual, in the late 1930s, President Franklin D. Roosevelt and his interventionist allies increasingly used "national security" to indicate the interrelatedness of the domestic and international spheres.[37]

Yet, if it was only in the late 1930s that national security as a term signifying the geopolitical connectedness of American society to the broader world became widespread, the idea of envisioning the nation under threat by both domestic and international factors had already entered policymaking debates by then. Indeed, as the following chapters show, politicians and military and educational leaders alike rarely used the term "national security" to describe their social and educational concerns; however, they propelled the blending of domestic and international concerns, as exemplified by how they paired young people's educational opportunities with military service. This vision of national security that emerged during the years from World War I to World War II would set the stage for the Cold War "national security state."[38] Highlighting the ways the events in the years during and between the two world wars drove this powerful social change, this book reconceptualizes the political–cultural history of the twentieth-century United States, showing how national security concerns informed policies in the years during and between the two world wars with long-term consequences for the country and its youth.

---

[36] Andrew Preston, "Monsters Everywhere: A Genealogy of National Security," *Diplomatic History* 38, no.3 (2014): 491–92.

[37] Ibid., 492–97.

[38] On the rise of the national security state in the early Cold War years, see Michael J. Hogan, *A Cross of Iron: Harry S. Truman and the Origins of the National Security State, 1945–1954* (Cambridge, UK: Cambridge University Press, 1998); John Lewis Gaddis, *Strategies of Containment: A Critical Appraisal of American National Security Policy during the Cold War*, Revised and Expanded Edition (New York: Oxford University Press, 2005); Sherry, *In the Shadow of War*.

Chapter Outline

This book is organized chronologically. The first chapter explores the debates over the establishment of the selective service system, especially over the appropriate age for conscription, and military–educational training programs during World War I. The debates around such policies helped set the stage for a broader redefinition of youth, education, and national security in the years to come. By examining the debates over ROTC courses that were made mandatory for male students in some civilian higher education institutions, Chapter 2 sheds light on the evolution of the relationship between higher education institutions and the military during the years between the two world wars. Building on the ideas developed in the 1910s on the relationship between citizenship and masculinity, supporters of the program argued that it had great value in "toughening" young men and instilling a sense of citizenship in them, as well as strengthening the military preparedness of the country. Opponents of ROTC questioned the legitimacy of imposing military training on students in public institutions who could not afford to attend private institutions that did not have the requirement, shedding light on the relationship between social class, national security, and access to higher education.

As discussed in Chapter 3, many leaders in government and academia considered the Great Depression as a national security emergency comparable to war. Franklin D. Roosevelt famously likened the Great Depression to war in his first inaugural address in 1933, asking U.S. Congress to give him "broad executive power to wage a war against the emergency, as great as the power that would be given to me if we were in fact invaded by a foreign foe."[39] As a result of the many debates around the high rate of youth unemployment and the federal programs intended to combat it, "youth" was defined as wards of the federal government in need of adult supervision. In the late 1930s, as the nature of the national security threat shifted from the Depression to war, the New Deal initiatives for youth were transformed into military preparedness projects, illustrating the porous nature of the line between wartime and peacetime in this period. Chapter 4 explores the debates over selective service in World War II, particularly those centered on what made the conscription of minors "democratic." Chapter 5 examines how, as a result of World

---

[39] Quoted in William E. Leuchtenburg, "The New Deal and the Analogue of War," in *Change and Continuity in Twentieth-Century America*, ed. John Braeman, et al. (Columbus: Ohio State University Press, 1964), 105.

War II, the relationship between youth, their role in national security, and their education was redefined once again.

As the United States emerged from World War II as the world's predominant power, U.S. definitions of youth and their role in national security were exported to countries where the United States wielded influence. Chapter 6 explores how, during the U.S. occupation of Japan, American ideas of youth and national security shaped U.S. occupiers' attitudes toward young Japanese. The occupation period also marked the end of the period in which total war defined the relationship between youth, education, and national security, and the Cold War prompted another shift in that relationship. However, the connections established between military service and education in the years from World War I through World War II proved enduring, and they continue to shape the educational experiences of many young people in the United States today.

1 Uncle Sam's Khaki University and World War I

On October 16, 1918, approximately eighteen months after the United States entered World War I, *Outlook*, a weekly magazine published in New York City, ran an editorial correspondence about young men who had just moved to Cambridge, Massachusetts, to join the Student Army Training Corps (SATC) – a military–educational program established by the War Department in over 500 postsecondary education institutions across the United States to prepare young men for military service. The program consisted of two sections: the Collegiate Section, which trained high-school graduates and young men with comparable educational attainment in advanced technical skills needed in the military and as officer candidates, and the Vocational Section, which trained grammar-school graduates in basic technical skills that met military needs. The SATC students were to be voluntarily inducted into the military, wear a uniform, and abide by army regulations. They would receive a private's pay while being trained for military duty by federal government funds at civilian colleges for two to nine months before being assigned to a position in the military based on their abilities as determined by the military.[1]

The author of the *Outlook* piece emphasized the diverse socioeconomic backgrounds of SATC enrollees and the SATC's potential to open the door to higher education for individuals who might otherwise have found it out of reach. Among the young men that the piece featured were Tom, Harry, and Ned (all names are pseudonyms). Tom was an eighteen-year-old, preparatory-school graduate who had just entered Harvard College. He had intended to enlist in the military because he was eager to contribute to the war effort, but because the military rejected him for what he

---

[1] E. H. A., "The S. A. T. C.," editorial correspondence, *Outlook*, October 16, 1918, pp. 251–52, filed in Folder 10, Charles Riborg Mann Papers, #1048, Southern Historical Collection, The Wilson Library, University of North Carolina at Chapel Hill (online collection, hereafter cited as Mann Papers); Committee on Education and Special Training, Advisory Board (hereafter cited as CEST Advisory Board), *Committee on Education and Special Training: A Review of Its Works during 1918* (Washington, DC: War Department, [1919]), 25–26, 76, 84.

saw to be a minor reason (no specific reason was named in the article), he came to Cambridge instead. He was overjoyed when U.S. Congress passed an amendment to the Selective Service Act in August 1918, which lowered the draft age from twenty-one to eighteen, only to find out that eighteen-year-olds were designated as the last group to be called, decreasing his chances of getting drafted. But soon thereafter, he learned about the establishment of the SATC. As a regular student at Harvard, Tom was eligible for the Collegiate Section unit established at the university, enabling him to follow his desire to take an active part in the war.

Harry and Ned, the two other men featured in the article, were in a different situation. Harry did not have a high-school diploma. He had to leave high school before receiving it for reasons unstated in the article and since then had worked while taking courses at night school. His night-school certificate would not have qualified him for Harvard normally, but he did qualify for the same Collegiate Section unit at Harvard that Tom joined. Finally, Ned, the third young man mentioned in the article, had never received a high-school education. He was not qualified for the Collegiate Section unit at Harvard, but he was for the nearby Massachusetts Institute of Technology (MIT)'s Vocational Section unit.

The author of the *Outlook* piece described the SATC as "the greatest step forward in democratic education" that provided access to higher education not only for preparatory-school graduates like Tom, who would have gone to college anyway, but also for disadvantaged young men like Harry and Ned. The author suggested that Ned, who had not attended high school due to misfortune, might now be able to outperform elite men like Tom at college and in the military.[2] The SATC was framed as a democratic educational opportunity in other publications as well. For example, the *Engineering News-Record* called the program "Uncle Sam's khaki university" in which "[d]emocracy and merit will dominate," referencing the U.S. Assistant Secretary of War's description of the SATC as the "University of Uncle Sam."[3] An advertisement of the SATC that appeared in the Philadelphia *Evening Public Ledger* called it the "Opportunity of a Lifetime" in which young men could study for free and even get paid for it (Figure 1.1).[4] Some students also seem to have been excited at the establishment of SATC as a means of opening the doors of higher education to those who had previously deemed it out of reach. The student newspaper at the University of Wisconsin stated that

---

[2] E. H. A., "The S. A. T. C.," 251–52.
[3] "The University of Uncle Sam," *Engineering News-Record*, August 29, 1918, page number unidentifiable, filed in Folder 10, Mann Papers.
[4] Advertisement, *Evening Public Ledger* (Philadelphia, PA), September 26, 1918.

S.A.T.C.

STUDENTS' ARMY TRAINING CORPS

Offers Special Training for Military Service to Youths Between 18 and 20 Years Old

Here's the Opportunity of a Lifetime for You Chaps Who Just Registered to Fit Yourselves for Responsible Posts in the National Army.

Uncle Sam will give you a technical education free—and pay you while you are learning. Here's the plan:

The Government has established Students' Army Training Corps at the universities and colleges listed below. They have been selected and approved by the War Department—your local draft board will assign you to the one you select.

A student entering the S. A. T. C. is not given deferred classification or temporary exemption from service. On the contrary, he automatically becomes a member of the regular army, lives in barracks and draws a private's pay of $30 a month. The Government also pays for his "keep" and tuition.

If you are a high school graduate, or having thirteen units of college preparatory work, you will receive special technical training which will fit you to perform important medical, engineering and general military duties.

You also will receive adequate military training.

If you show that you are made of the right stuff you may win an appointment to an Officers' Training Camp. Or you may be allowed to continue in the educational institution for such special technical training as the needs of the service require.

Further information concerning the S. A. T. C. may be obtained on application, either in person or by letter, to any of the following institutions:

UNIVERSITY OF PENNSYLVANIA
PHILADELPHIA, PA.
TEMPLE UNIVERSITY
PHILADELPHIA, PA.
ST. JOSEPH'S COLLEGE
PHILADELPHIA, PA.

DREXEL INSTITUTE
PHILADELPHIA, PA.
VILLANOVA COLLEGE
VILLANOVA, PA.
PENNSYLVANIA MILITARY COLLEGE
CHESTER, PA.
FRANKLIN AND MARSHALL COLLEGE
LANCASTER, PA.

BUCKNELL UNIVERSITY
LEWISBURG, PA.
ALBRIGHT COLLEGE
MYERSTOWN, PA.
URSINUS COLLEGE
COLLEGEVILLE, PA.

Figure 1.1 An advertisement for the SATC promoting the program as "the Opportunity of a Lifetime."
Advertisement, *Evening Public Ledger* (Philadelphia, PA), September 26, 1918.
Image provided by: Penn State University Libraries; University Park, PA.
Retrieved via the Library of Congress. In the public domain.

it was the "greatest opportunity ever offered to young men in the world's history [...]. For once in the history of our country [...] a young man does not have to depend upon fortunate circumstances and environment to give him a higher education."[5]

Many higher education administrators and professors joined the chorus of acclaim for the SATC's "democratic" potential, but as the following pages reveal, many of them had other reasons to praise the program as well. For some, it was an opportunity to demonstrate to the American public the social value of higher education, which had often been seen as useless. Others saw the SATC as a financial boon that helped their schools recover financially from the substantial drop in enrolment and inflation caused by the war. Finally, many of them had long been supporters of military training of young men in peacetime and had worked to have higher education institutions contribute to the war effort once the United States entered the war. To them, the establishment of the SATC signified a moment in which their long-standing commitment to national security bore fruit.

The entry of many young men into the armed forces, therefore, sparked an array of discourses and expectations about what it could accomplish for larger aims, even within the restrictions imposed by wartime necessity. This chapter examines the debates surrounding the conscription of young men, particularly those below the age of majority, for the war, the establishment of military–educational programs such as the SATC, and the role of the educational elite in establishing such programs.

Individuals who saw the positive aspects of the SATC were not uncritical of the program. The *Outlook* article explained how, unlike college students in peacetime, SATC students could not choose their own courses since they were predetermined by the military and would not be able to attend college for four years. Similarly, the *Engineering News-Record* article gently criticized how the SATC was planned based solely on military requirements and without regard for civilian requirements for engineers.[6] Yet, it is noteworthy how they nonetheless framed the SATC as a "democratic" opportunity that enabled young men like Harry and Ned to pursue higher education. This mirrors how civilian mobilization for the war, dubbed "the war to make the world safe for democracy," was frequently couched in democratic terms in the United States. As this chapter explores, selective service, which was first established in April

---

[5] Quoted in Carl S. Gruber, *Mars and Minerva: World War I and the Uses of the Higher Learning in America* (Baton Rouge: Louisiana State University Press, 1975), 231.
[6] E. H. A., "The S. A. T. C.," 252; "The University of Uncle Sam."

1917 and would define military service in the United States during both world wars, was also framed in democratic terms.

As a wartime measure, it was evident to all that the SATC's sole purpose was to contribute to the urgent objective of winning the war and was therefore distinct from the democratization of higher education during times of peace. Indeed, the program opened the opportunity to study at such prestigious universities as Harvard or MIT to young men who would not have envisioned doing so without it, but their education came only with their voluntary induction into the military, and their studies were restricted to subjects determined by the military, such as carpentry, radio operation, and automobile repair. Moreover, their training would only last for two to nine months, depending on their age and the SATC division for which they registered. Finally, this "democratic" path to a college education through military service was closed to many others in the same age range, such as women, men deemed physically unqualified for military service, men above military age, and conscientious objectors, and because of structural racism in American society and within the military, it was less accessible to young Black men than white men.

In short, while many SATC supporters claimed that the program "democratized" higher education, implying that it increased access to higher education for those without financial means, the program was more a manifestation of how attempts to democratize education in civilian society (which frequently embraced classifying young people into different educational tracks based on such categories as race, ethnicity, gender, and social class) and the mobilization of civilians for war (which required the stratification of civilians based on their military usefulness) neatly overlapped.

Selective service and the SATC were products of the U.S. entry into World War I, but they were also based on other social and political developments concerning military service and access to education in American society that originated earlier in the twentieth century. For example, the "democratic" rhetoric used to describe the SATC also had roots in the several years preceding the U.S. entry into the war, when the country debated military preparedness. As this chapter explains, the establishment of the program was built on nationwide debates that took place prior to the U.S. entry into the war over mobilizing civilians, especially young men, for military preparedness. Among such debates were those over universal military training (UMT), which referred to the idea of a national military training program that would train all young men of the country in basic military skills in order to build a nation of citizen-soldiers universally trained in times of peace and fully prepared to fight in a war, that evolved in the early 1910s and peaked in the first few years of World War I. These debates, as well as the debates over the Selective Service Act of 1917, which established the first universal conscription law in U.S. history, revolved around the questions of what age groups should serve and how the country would prepare its largely untrained youth for modern warfare. They also became the basis of the establishment of military training programs in civilian educational institutions. The debates that developed around the UMT, the Selective Service Act, and the SATC would set the stage for an evolving discourse in the following decades regarding youth, education, and national security.

Universal Military Training and the Establishment of Selective Service for World War I

The ideas about youth, education, and military service that emerged during World War I grew out of broad redefinitions of youth and national security in American society in response to the changing nature of warfare and shifting geopolitical concerns. Prior to the war, the United States procured wartime armed forces based on volunteerism, and the wartime military included individuals of a wider range of ages. In the colonial period, colonial governments (except for that of pacifist Pennsylvania) required all free white men between the ages of approximately seventeen and sixty to be members of a local militia and be ready to take arms in times of emergency. The 1792 Militia Act provided for the organization of state militias by men between eighteen and forty-five years old, but calls into federal service were limited to specific conditions enumerated in the U.S. Constitution. By the mid nineteenth century, commitment to state militias had become less universal among white men in Northern states, as the threat of being attacked by a neighboring external force had diminished and privately organized (and officially recognized) volunteer militia companies had emerged and replaced some of the roles of state militias. Despite these changes, the image of a two-tier army consisting of a small standing army at the federal level and citizen-soldiers eager to respond to calls to take up arms in an emergency, but otherwise living as civilians, had come to be idealized as the U.S. tradition of national defense, in contrast to Europe's large standing armies and powerful central governments.[7]

---

[7] John Whiteclay Chambers II, *To Raise an Army: The Draft Comes to Modern America* (New York: Free Press, 1987), 14, 28–29, 36–39; Gene M. Lyons and John W. Masland, *Education and Military Leadership: A Study of the R.O.T.C.* (Princeton, NJ: Princeton University Press, 1959), 28; Marvin A. Kreidberg and Merton G. Henry, *History of Military Mobilization in the United States Army, 1775–1945* (Washington, DC: Department of the Army, 1955), 3–4.

Conscription was implemented during the U.S. Civil War (1861–1865), due to high fatality rates and prolonged fighting, but its impact on acquiring soldiers was limited. In 1862, the Confederates subjected white men between the ages of eighteen and thirty-five to the draft (expanding it to seventeen to fifty years old in 1864 and, out of desperation, to enslaved men towards the end of the war), while the Union did the same for men between the ages of twenty and forty-five. Both sides used the draft, though, mainly for reasons other than the draft itself: for the North, it was largely a symbolic act of demonstrating to the public the government's resolve to avoid disunion; for the Confederates, it was primarily a means of compelling volunteers to serve out the remainder of the war. The draft remained unpopular because there were ways to avoid it, such as hiring substitutes and gaining vocational exemptions, and because draftees were seen as being unpatriotic. As a result, conscripts made up a small percentage of either army.[8]

The idea of ensuring national defense with a small standing military and a large pool of wartime volunteers was challenged at the turn of the twentieth century, when military technology advanced considerably, European competition for colonies and naval power increased, and the United States acquired territory overseas. Responding to the changing international order, some Americans launched a determined campaign to reform the traditional U.S. military policy, which they perceived as being outdated. These were mostly professional elite men who were overwhelmingly white, Anglo-Saxon Protestants who resided in the major hubs of the Northeast and the Midwest. Their spokesmen included Theodore Roosevelt, the U.S. President (1901–1909); Elihu Root, the prominent lawyer and politician; and General Leonard Wood, Army Chief of Staff (1910–1914). Many of these men were pivotal figures in U.S. imperialism – Roosevelt rose to national prominence as the "Rough Rider" hero of the Spanish–American War; Root, as U.S. Secretary of War, oversaw the country's colonial possessions acquired as a result of the war; and Wood led the Rough Riders in 1898 and then served as Governor-General of Cuba and the Philippines. As such, they were committed to the expansion of U.S. power abroad.[9]

Envisioning a future of the United States as a major player in world politics, these men believed that the country lagged behind European powers in modernizing military institutions. They called for the

---

[8] Chambers, *To Raise an Army*, 41, 45–46, 50–51.
[9] Chambers, *To Raise an Army*, 74–81; John Dickinson, *The Building of an Army: A Detailed Account of Legislation, Administration and Opinion in the United States, 1915–1920* (New York: Century, 1922), 27–28.

expansion of the U.S. military through measures such as strengthening naval power, increasing the size of the regular army, creating a national reserve, and, most importantly, as this chapter discusses, institutionalizing UMT. By adopting UMT, they contended, the United States would replace state militias with a national reserve ready to be mobilized for war and strengthen the military more economically than enlarging the standing army, which they thought was undemocratic, costly, and un-American. Standing together under the banner of efficiency, professionalism, and nationalism, their movement eventually grew into a major driving force of a military preparedness movement that developed in response to the outbreak of World War I in Europe.[10]

Their plans for military reform reflected a wider Progressive-Era ethos of a stronger federal government, efficiency, and faith in professional expertise, but also bore the imprint of the social and political conservatism the proponents inherited from their privileged backgrounds. Many of these men were driven by a fear of the "degeneration" of American manhood amidst what they perceived as the social disorder generated by industrialization, the decline of frontiersmanship, and mass immigration from southern and eastern Europe into rapidly expanding urban centers.[11] In addition to the diffusion of military knowledge among young men and training them militarily, therefore, these men believed that UMT would solve domestic problems. In other words, they thought that it would alleviate the growing tensions among different classes and ethnic groups and "Americanize" immigrants. Theodore Roosevelt, for example, envisioned it to be a way for "the son of the multi-millionaire and the son of the immigrant ... sleep under the same dog-tent and eat the same grub."[12] The military tent, he mused, "will rank next to the public school among the great agents of democratization."[13]

Plans to train leadership for UMT-trained citizen-soldiers were also developed. In 1913, Leonard Wood and several college presidents held summer military training programs in Gettysburg, Pennsylvania, and Monterey, California, for college students and high-school graduates over age eighteen. Over 200 students paid their expenses to experience drilling, military tactics, rifle practices, and other basic training. The

---

[10] Chambers, *To Raise an Army*, 74–81.
[11] Ibid., 89–101. See also Anders Stephanson, *Manifest Destiny: American Expansion and the Empire of Right* (New York: Hill and Wang, 1995), ch. 3.
[12] Quoted in Michael S. Sherry, *Preparing for the Next War: American Plans for Postwar Defense, 1941–45* (New Haven, CT: Yale University Press, 1977), 28.
[13] Quoted in Chase C. Mooney and Martha E. Layman, "Some Phases of the Compulsory Military Training Movement, 1914–1920," *Mississippi Valley Historical Review* 38, no. 4 (1952): 641.

planners did not think that a short summer program alone would ready students for military service, but they believed that these programs would effectively popularize the need for peacetime preparedness and the usefulness of military training for youth leadership and discipline to the broader American public.[14]

Based on this experimental program, a military training camp program named the "Plattsburg camps" was launched in 1915 by the Military Training Camp Association (MTCA), another group of elite men propagating military preparedness established earlier that year (the "Plattsburg" in this context is typically spelled without an "h" at the end). The camps, based in Plattsburgh, New York, offered young business and professional men, as well as students, summer military training.[15] Reflecting their racism and the prevailing military norm that only white men could be officers, these camps were reserved exclusively for white men. Leonard Wood, for instance, resisted having candidates "with whom our descendants cannot intermarry without producing a breed of mongrels; they must at least be white."[16] Grenville Clark, a Wall Street lawyer in his early thirties from a prominent upper-class family, led the MTCA. The MTCA would continue to be a leading proponent for UMT after World War I and would spearhead the drive for the passage of the Selective Training and Service Act of 1940, utilizing its extensive connections with political and corporate leaders of the country.[17] Some educational leaders, such as university presidents, administrators, school principals, and superintendents, who came from the same socioeconomic background as these preparedness advocates, and who wished to instill a sense of patriotism and discipline in young people, also supported UMT and the Plattsburg camps. Plattsburg's Advisory Committee of University Presidents consisted of the presidents of Princeton, Harvard, Yale, Alabama, Michigan, Lehigh, and Virginia Military Institute.[18]

These preparedness advocates and their UMT idea helped create some of the groundwork for development in the American understanding

---

[14] Kreidberg and Henry, *History of Military Mobilization*, 213; Chambers, *To Raise an Army*, 79; Dickinson, *Building of an Army*, 6.

[15] Chambers, *To Raise an Army*, 79, 82–83; Kreidberg and Henry, *History of Military Mobilization*, 213.

[16] Quoted in David M. Kennedy, *Over Here: The First World War and American Society* (New York: Oxford University Press, 1980), 161. See also Chambers, *To Raise and Army*, 93.

[17] Chambers, *To Raise an Army*, 83. For Clark and his involvement in Washington politics, see Nancy Peterson Hill, *A Very Private Public Citizen: The Life of Grenville Clark* (Columbia: University of Missouri Press, 2014).

[18] Gruber, *Mars and Minerva*, 220.

of the relationship between education and military service in the years ahead. The Plattsburg program dealt with a small minority of young men in the country, but the proponents considered it an important step toward the realization of UMT. With many supporters in the educational leadership, they also helped set the stage for other military–educational programs like the SATC described at the opening of this chapter – and which is discussed further below – as well as the Reserve Officers' Training Corps (ROTC), which will be discussed in Chapter 2. Many UMT advocates would become central in the drive for the passage of the Selective Training and Service Act of 1940. Universal military training would never be adopted, but the idea underlined a larger evolution in the legal and political discourse around youth, education, and military service in the United States.

The preparedness movement gained momentum in American society after American passengers were killed by the German submarine attack on the British passenger liner *Lusitania* on May 7, 1915, and debates over the country's stance on World War I and whether or how to strengthen national defense intensified as diplomatic relations with Germany deteriorated and the U.S. entry into World War I became increasingly probable in early 1917. Universal military training, essentially a peacetime preparedness measure, was now discussed alongside universal service in wartime, with the two measures often muddled or confused. This enabled preparedness advocates to seize this "plastic juncture" to further their objective of strengthening the military establishment in both peacetime and wartime by requiring all young men to participate in military training.

In February 1917, for example, William Howard Taft, former U.S. president and preparedness advocate, called for universal service of at least one year to be performed by every man between nineteen and twenty-four years old to meet the present emergency and in the years after the war. He believed that military training and service was part of every man's duty, in peace as well as in war, and contended that conscription would "discipline our native young men" and "teach them respect for authority," while making new immigrants loyal to the United States. To Taft, the volunteer system on which the country had relied unfairly pushed military service on patriotic men while exempting "those who can only be dragged in by ultimate recourse to law."[19] Harvard University philosopher and UMT advocate Ralph Barton Perry likewise argued that military training was "everybody's business, not that of any one class, either a leisure class or a desperate class ready to serve for small pay."[20]

---

[19] "Conscription Urged by Taft as We Face War," *Log Angeles Times*, February 5, 1917.
[20] "Both Sides on Conscription," *Boston Daily Globe*, March 11, 1917.

Calls for military preparedness, however, were met by a powerful counterforce comprised of anti-preparedness advocates with various motivations, and fighting UMT became one of their shared causes. Opposition to UMT came from around the country. Supporters of the locally controlled militia tradition feared the escalating federal intrusion into the tradition (in fact, they had been fighting with the federal government, which wished to federalize state militias, over the control of the militias; as a compromise between the two groups, a portion of state militias had been organized as the National Guard in 1903, allowing greater federal control in exchange for greater federal funding), pacifists denounced it as militarism, and individuals on the left of the political spectrum saw it as a business elite's plan that forced workers to subordinate individual interests to national defense.[21]

Given how divisive it was and how it represented a significant departure from the nation's prior reliance on volunteers, President Woodrow Wilson and his administration took considerable time to consider and deliberate before deciding to call for selective conscription at the onset of the U.S. entry into the war. In fact, Wilson had been opposed to compulsory military training in peacetime and instead attempted to strengthen the military by increasing the size of the regular forces and creating a national volunteer force to replace the locally administered National Guard.[22] As the U.S. entry into the war became more likely in early 1917, however, he appears to have become convinced that in wartime, a selective draft was the most effective way of sufficiently and rapidly enlarging the armed forces with the least disruption to the national economy. A growing number of liberal and progressive public figures, including educator John Dewey and commentator Walter Lippmann, publicly or privately indicated support for selective wartime conscription, which also prompted Wilson to adopt the measure.[23]

Military leaders and many others around him were now persuaded that selective service was not just about choosing who should serve; rather, it was about compiling a national database of all available men for war work and categorizing them into various jobs – both on the home front and in the military – that would maximize the effectiveness of the nation's war effort. When viewed from this angle, the dependence on voluntarism would have the unfavorable consequence of permitting men to serve in positions that were not optimal for the country as a whole and could severely disrupt the war effort. By the time the country entered the war,

---

[21] Chambers, *To Raise an Army*, 70, ch. 4.   [22] Ibid., 103–107.   [23] Ibid., 125–28.

therefore, Wilson seems to have endorsed the idea that a wartime army of civilians should be raised exclusively by the draft.[24]

In his speech before U.S. Congress asking for a declaration of war against Germany on April 2, 1917, Wilson clarified his intention to augment the wartime army by selective conscription. He stated that the declaration would "involve the immediate addition to the armed forces of the United States already provided for by law in case of war at least five hundred thousand men, who should, in my opinion, be chosen upon the principle of universal liability to service."[25] Congress would then debate in the coming days what "universal liability to service" entailed as they worked out a conscription law. The debates would revolve around who should be conscripted, how the draft should look, and, more significantly, what age groups should be conscripted, all of which in turn forced legislators and the public alike to rethink the country's ideas about youth, national security, and education.

On April 7, the day after Congress approved the resolution declaring war on Germany, Secretary of War Newton D. Baker submitted to Congress the bill to establish the draft. In addition to expanding the regular army and the National Guard, he asked for a selective draft that would immediately conscript 500,000 men between the ages of nineteen and twenty-five, with the possibility of inducting another 500,000, to realize an initial goal of 1.2 to 1.7 million ground troops. He requested that certain individuals, such as government officials, men engaged in industries essential for wartime production, men with dependents, and those deemed "unfit" for service be exempted.[26]

Upon introducing the bill to the Senate, Senator George E. Chamberlain, chairman of the Senate Committee on Military Affairs, echoed Baker's insistence on the need for a draft, explaining that the volunteer system would not suffice. He believed that military service was "the highest duty of the citizen" that should in no sense be regarded as a voluntary offering. The volunteer system, to Chamberlain, was "undemocratic, unreliable, extravagant, inefficient, and above all, unsafe."[27] Baker added that other countries had proven the system inappropriate, as it had resulted in "the earliest sacrifice of the bravest,

---

[24] Ibid., 134–36, 268; Kreidberg and Henry, *History of Military Mobilization*, 242–43.
[25] "Address by the President of the United States" (S. Doc. No. 5), April 2, 1917, 65th Cong., 1st sess., *Congressional Record* 55, pt. 1: 103.
[26] Chambers, *To Raise an Army*, 153–54; "Details of the Army Bill," *New York Times* (hereafter cited as *NYT*), April 6, 1917.
[27] Dickinson, *Building of an Army*, 59–61 (the quotes are from p. 59 and p. 61).

most zealous, and active men." In other words, he argued, it unfairly led to the "early sacrifice of the best men of the country."[28]

Voices that completely rejected the Selective Service Act remained in the minority, as the country had already entered the war and it was evident that an urgent increase in the armed forces was required. Nevertheless, some individuals criticized the Act as un-American and proposed that the volunteer system be tried first. A representative of the American Federation of Labor declared before the House Committee on Military Affairs that the "American labor movement has always been against compulsion, and especially against militarism in all of its forms," and urged the committee to try the voluntary system before adopting conscription.[29] Conscription "is a form of coercion which is absolutely averse and absolutely contradictory to everything that America has ever stood for," the social reformer Jane Addams of Hull House argued. If the country were to fight Prussianism, "do not let us begin by taking the most offensive system of Prussianism and adopting it in this country."[30] Despite these criticisms, the debate around selective service centered less on whether to adopt the measure than how to do it, raising questions regarding what age range should be liable.

It is noteworthy that when he introduced the bill to Congress, Baker asked for the conscription of nineteen- and twenty-year-olds, which were below the age of legal adulthood in most states of the country. The administration preferred young men for a few reasons. First, their absence was considered less likely to disturb the essential industries on the home front.[31] Second, young men were considered tougher and more easily manageable than older men. In the words of Provost Marshal General Enoch H. Crowder, who oversaw the preparation of the Selective Service System and who would administer it throughout the war, men of eighteen to twenty years old were "the soundest and most pliable military material."[32] Finally, conscripting younger men was considered less costly as fewer would be married men requiring dependency allotments.[33]

The idea of nineteen-year-old soldiers was not new, as teens had served as volunteers in the country's past wars. However, considerable opposition was expressed by legislators to conscripting men under the age of twenty-one, as they believed that allowing minors who were

---

[28] U.S. Congress, House, Committee on Military Affairs, *Selective-Service Act: Hearings before the Committee on the Bill Authorizing the President to Increase Temporarily the Military Establishment of the United States*, 65th Cong., 1st sess. (Washington, DC: GPO, 1918), 14, 17.
[29] Ibid., 235. [30] Ibid., 238, 239. [31] Ibid., 5, 8.
[32] Quoted in Chambers, *To Raise an Army*, 197. [33] Ibid., 155.

capable of military duty to voluntarily enlist and subjecting all men in the age group to selective conscription were entirely different. They frequently argued that men below age twenty-one were physically and mentally too young for military life, connecting legal adulthood with the maturity required for military service. One of them, for example, stated "I do not believe the country is willing to accept the proposition of making it a war, as they say, by the *children* of America."[34] Another argued that the bill put the burden of military service only on a small proportion of men out of the total U.S. population, and a large portion of them would be "boys," who were "not old enough to make a contract! These boys are not even citizens."[35]

Many of these people insisted on conscripting older men instead of men below the age of twenty-one, including a senator who argued that he saw no valid reason why physically fit men up to forty-five years old should not be considered for the draft, on the grounds that they "have had 26 years more of the benefits of government than has the boy of 19." According to him, many of these older men were eager to serve, and many were veterans of the Spanish–American War or militiamen armed with rich military experiences. Until it became necessary, boys should be allowed to "finish their education, their apprenticeship in trade, [and] their preparation for life," he insisted.[36]

In connecting the legal majority with the maturity required for military duty, these legislators emphasized that minors did not enjoy the rights that adults enjoyed, notably voting rights. Specifically, some believed that it was unfair to force men who did not have the right to vote to serve, while others indicated that the lack of righting votes meant that these minors were not mentally mature enough to fight. The House Committee on Military Affairs, for example, decided that it would "never vote for a bill that would authorize the Government of the United States to conscript a boy 19 or 20 years of age and who did not have the right to vote," and proposed instead that the age range be twenty-one to forty so that "the burden shall be spread on all the *mature* men of the country."[37] A representative argued that he "could not vote to conscript the *boys* who

---

[34] Emphasis added. House Committee on Military Affairs, *Selective-Service Act*, 149 (see also p. 292).

[35] Senator Kenneth McKellar (TN), speaking on S. 1871, April 24, 1917, 65th Cong., 1st sess., *Congressional Record* 55, pt. 1: 1014.

[36] Senator Charles E. Townsend (MI), speaking on S. 1871, April 24, 1917, 65th Cong., 1st sess., *Congressional Record* 55, pt. 1: 1009.

[37] Emphasis added. Representatives S. Hubert Dent, Jr. (AL) and Frank Wheeler Mondell (WY), speaking on H.R. 3545, April 23, 1917, 65th Cong., 1st sess., *Congressional Record* 55, pt. 1: 960; "Raise Age Limit for the New Army," *NYT*, April 14, 1917.

are not old enough to vote and force them to do the fighting for the *men* of this Nation."³⁸ The contrast between "men" and "boys" here is significant as is how the distinction between the two overlaps with the legal distinction between minors and majors. The link between majority, maturity, and military service would be shaken in the 1930s and the 1940s, as later chapters of this book will demonstrate.

In response, proponents of the conscription of minors argued that taking young men was a "universal practice" adopted by European countries, but they also shared their opponent's perception of nineteen-year-olds as immature "boys," arguing that the advantage of military service was turning "boys" into "men."³⁹ By so doing, they connected military service to education. In response to a congressman's question as to whether boys still in school could be exempted or whether the maximum draft age could be raised to thirty, Baker responded to both in the negative, arguing that taking men between the ages of twenty-five and thirty would have a negative impact on the country's economy, that allowing students to remain in school would favor boys whose parents could afford to keep them in school, and that "the greatest education a man can get, valuable as formal education is, is to serve his country in an army in a time of stress." According to him, the Civil War had shown that men whose college career had been interrupted by the war acquired "a training and an equipment in the service which made them the men of mark in the generation that they came into as men."⁴⁰ As we have seen, this idea – that military training and service was an educational, formative experience that would transform boys and young men into adult men – was also expressed by preparedness and UMT advocates prior to the U.S. entry into World War I; it would be repeated in the following decades by supporters of both peacetime military training and wartime conscription of young men.

Despite the Wilson administration's and military authorities' vigorous push to enlist men under the age of twenty-one, Congress ultimately agreed that conscription should be limited to "men" and not "boys." On April 28, 1917, when both chambers of Congress voted for the bill, they rejected the conscription of nineteen- and twenty-year-olds. The

---

³⁸ Emphasis added. Representative Percy E. Quin (MS), speaking on H.R. 3545, April 23, 1917, 65th Cong., 1st sess., *Congressional Record* 55, pt. 1: 981. See also Representative Samuel J. Nicholls (SC), speaking on H.R. 3545, April 23, 1917, 65th Cong., 1st sess., *Congressional Record* 55, pt. 1: 973; Representative William J. Fields (KY), speaking on H.R. 3545, April 28, 1917, 65th Cong., 1st sess., *Congressional Record* 55, pt. 2: 1519.
³⁹ Senator Henry Cabot Lodge (MA), speaking on S. 1871, April 23, 1917, 65th Cong., 1st sess., *Congressional Record* 55, pt. 1: 943.
⁴⁰ House Committee on Military Affairs, *Selective-Service Act*, 129–30.

Senate decided that the draft age should be twenty-one to twenty-seven. The House voted that it should be twenty-one to forty. On May 10, a compromise was agreed on, fixing the range at twenty-one to thirty, both inclusive.[41] The Selective Service Act of 1917 thus established the principle that only men who were legally adults (i.e., age twenty-one and older) should be conscripted.[42] This principle, however, would be soon challenged, as the war demanded the deployment of additional troops.

Drafting Minors

The Selective Service System soon established a system to classify registrants into five groups, Classes I through V. All registrants by default belonged to Class I, which consisted of men to be inducted first. Class I, in Crowder's words, was composed of "those whose withdrawal from domestic and industrial connections would create the least disturbing effect upon the current of our national life."[43] Class I men were most likely to be single men and married men without dependents, as well as unskilled laborers. Men who were granted deferments and exemptions for reasons such as having dependents, engaging in a job crucial for the home front, or being physically "unfit" for military service, were reclassified into Classes II to V. The military's aim was to obtain military manpower only from Class I men.[44]

Class I alone was supposed to supply enough draftees up until January 1919, but the war did not proceed as predicted. In the spring of 1918, Russia withdrew from the fighting. As a result, Germany relocated its eastern-front troops to France. Out of desperation, the Allies urged President Wilson to send additional troops, which he proceeded to do

---

[41] "The Conscription Bill," editorial, *Washington Post*, May 8, 1917; Chambers, *To Raise an Army*, 166–67; "Selective Draft Is Finally Agreed On," *San Francisco Chronicle*, May 11, 1917.

[42] Even after the Selective Service System was implemented, a volunteer route remained for a time. It was discontinued in December 1917, in the Army, and in August 1918, in the Navy and Marine Corps. *An Act: To Authorize the President to Increase Temporarily the Military Establishment of the United States*, Public Law 65-12, *U.S. Statues at Large* 40 (1917–1919): 81; U.S. Congress, Senate, Committee on Military Affairs, *Amending the Draft Law: Hearings before the Committee*, vol. 1, 65th Cong., 2nd sess. (Washington, DC: GPO, 1918), 29; E. H. Crowder, *Second Report of the Provost Marshal General to the Secretary of War on the Operations of the Selective Service System to December 20, 1918* (Washington, DC: GPO, 1919), 6, 224.

[43] Crowder, *Second Report of the Provost Marshal General*, 12.

[44] Ibid., 169–74; "Appendix: Section 268 – The Questionnaire," *Congressional Record* 56, pt. 9: 9399; "Only First Class to Be Called Out for Duty in Army," *Atlanta Constitution*, January 4, 1918.

by sending additional troops immediately and authorizing the General Staff's request to triple the size of the American Expeditionary Force in Europe by the spring of 1919 and further enlarge it later that year.[45] However, doing so meant that Class I would be exhausted by September 1918. Rather than inducting men from the deferred classes, the Office of the Provost Marshall General, which oversaw the draft, decided that the age groups subject to selective service should be enlarged so that an additional supply of draftees could be taken from newly registered Class I men. The Office undertook a series of simulations, calculating the number of men that would be available for service if the draft age was expanded to the range of nineteen to forty, nineteen to forty-five, or eighteen to forty-five. It concluded that only the last option could provide the required number of draftees without drawing from deferred classes.[46]

At the instance of the Secretary of War, a bill was introduced to Congress on August 5, 1918, expanding the registration to those eighteen- through forty-five years old.[47] Legislators worried that drafting older men, who were more likely to be in managing positions in various business and industrial sectors and more likely to be fathers, would spark opposition from industrial and labor leaders as well as the general public, but, as discussed below, they were also concerned about or opposed to conscripting "boys" who had not reached the age of majority.

The relationship between legal majority, mental and physical maturity (or the lack thereof), and military service loomed larger than in 1917 as the likelihood of conscripting young men under age twenty-one increased. A legislator stated that boys under age twenty-one "are children; the law declares they are children and they are immature."[48] Another argued that an eighteen-year-old boy was "only a child yet, clinging to the knees of that mother [...]; a tender bud blooming into manhood." He argued that the boy should be offered "his opportunity in the battle of life by enabling him to have an education and to develop the character that at that age alone can be perfected," instead of giving him to "the battle of bullets and the grave while cowardly men stand back and receive the benefits of this death."[49] Another legislator likewise argued

---

[45] Chambers, *To Raise an Army*, 196; Crowder, *Second Report of the Provost Marshal General*, 25.
[46] Crowder, *Second Report of the Provost Marshal General*, 25, 312.
[47] S. 4856 and Provost Marshal General to the Chief of Staff, War Department, both reprinted in 65th Cong., 2nd sess., *Congressional Record* 56, pt. 9: 9200–9201.
[48] Representative Frank Clark (FL), speaking on H.R. 12731, August 22, 1918, 65th Cong., 2nd sess., *Congressional Record* 56, pt. 9: 9379.
[49] Representative John Austin Moon (TN), speaking on H.R. 12731, August 23, 1918, 65th Cong., 2nd sess., *Congressional Record* 56, pt. 9: 9425.

that boys below age twenty-one had "not reached that state of mental maturity which renders them capable of casting an intelligent vote." Taking them and sending them overseas would "seriously interfere with their school life, which is so vitally important to them as well as to the future of our country."[50] Many of the legislators against the lowering of the draft age insisted on taking older men in the deferred classes first.[51]

It is noteworthy how these legislators argued that military service would cut off education, as most men in the United States between eighteen and twenty years old then were out of school. Attending high school, let alone college, was not yet a practice shared by the majority of people in the country. Out of the roughly three million men between the ages of eighteen through twenty, only approximately 165,000 were attending a higher education institution and 100,000 were in high school.[52] The bill's supporters thus pointed out, quite correctly, that, contrary to the argument of their opponents that the bill would deprive youth of educational opportunities, few men aged eighteen through twenty were enrolled in educational institutions.[53] A representative argued that many men at that age were "anxious and willing to take a part in this great world war." He criticized his opponents, claiming that eighteen-year-olds were mature enough to fight: "You are thinking too much of the boy who is mollycoddled at home. You are not thinking of

---

[50] Representative John Wesley Langley (KY), speaking on H.R. 12731, August 23, 1918, 65th Cong., 2nd sess., *Congressional Record* 56, pt. 9: 9432. See also Senator William Fosgate Kirby (AR), speaking on S. 4856, August 22, 1918, 65th Cong., 2nd sess., *Congressional Record* 56, pt. 9: 9349; Representatives William Gordon (OH) and William J. Fields (KY), speaking on H.R. 12731, August 22, 1918, 65th Cong., 2nd sess., *Congressional Record* 56, pt. 9: 9375; Senator James Kimble Vardaman (MS), speaking on S. 4856, August 24, 1918, 65th Cong., 2nd sess., *Congressional Record* 56, pt. 9: 9476–77; Senator William Borah (ID), speaking on S. 4856, August 24, 1918, 65th Cong., 2nd sess., *Congressional Record* 56, pt. 9: 9464.

[51] Representative William R. Wood (IN), speaking on H.R. 12731, August 22, 1918, 65th Cong., 2nd sess., *Congressional Record* 56, pt. 9: 9384. Some legislators representing agricultural regions of the country argued that this was a class and regional issue as well, insisting that "slackers" were "hiding behind" war industries as white-collar workers while farmers were being conscripted. Representative Rufus Hardy (TX), speaking on H.R. 12731, August 23, 1918, 65th Cong., 2nd sess., *Congressional Record* 56, pt. 9: 9434.

[52] Senate Committee on Military Affairs, *Amending the Draft Law*, vol. 2, 93, 97; U.S. Congress, House, Committee on Military Affairs, *Selective-Service Act: Hearings before the Committee on H.R. 12731, Amending the Act Entitled "An Act to Authorize the President to Increase Temporarily the Military Establishment of the United States," Approved May 18, 1917*, 65th Cong., 2nd sess. (Washington, DC: GPO, 1918), 36.

[53] Representative John Humphrey Small (NC), speaking on H.R. 12731, August 23, 1918, 65th Cong., 2nd sess., *Congressional Record* 56, pt. 9: 9441.

the real red-blooded American youth of 18 who has been out for years making a living for himself and his family."[54]

Interestingly, however, both chambers of Congress added their own educational provisions to the War Department bill. The House Committee on Military Affairs added a measure allowing the Secretary of War to assign soldiers to educational institutions for technical training, which the War Department had recommended at the last minute.[55] On the other hand, the Senate Committee on Military Affairs suggested that those who volunteered or were drafted under the age of twenty-one and served in the military be eligible for a government-funded education at approved educational institutions *after* the war.[56]

The House agreed to its Military Affairs Committee's proposal without much debate, as the representatives were informed by military representatives that plans to use educational institutions for technical training by the military were already underway (which were to materialize as programs such as the SATC). They also agreed that modern warfare required skilled men and that such plans would prevent the country from facing a future shortage of college-trained specialists.[57] On the other hand, the Senate committee's amendment drew numerous reservations from senators before finally being agreed on it, most of which were related to the uncertainty involved in estimating the cost. Indeed, as some of them said, no one could forecast how long the war would last, how many men in the proposed age would return, and how many would want to take advantage of this benefit. Furthermore, one senator stated that such a program amounted to "unreasonable paternalism," while others expressed reservations due to the lack of precedent for federal involvement in educational matters.[58] The supporters of the provision, on the other hand, argued that it would show gratitude to those who offered to make the ultimate sacrifice for their country and that it would help young veterans compete with men who were able to receive a

---

[54] Representative Thomas Spencer Crago (PA), speaking on H.R. 12731, August 23, 1918, 65th Cong., 2nd sess., *Congressional Record* 56, pt. 9: 9431–32.

[55] Representative S. Hubert Dent Jr. (AL), speaking on H.R. 12731, August 22, 1918, 65th Cong., 2nd sess., *Congressional Record* 56, pt. 9: 9365.

[56] The length of education was to be equivalent to the period in which the individual served in the military, but not exceeding two years. "Changes of Draft Age," *Congressional Record* 56, pt. 9: 9230.

[57] Representative S. Hubert Dent Jr. (AL), speaking on H.R. 12731, August 22, 1918, 65th Cong., 2nd sess., *Congressional Record* 56, pt. 9: 9365; Representative C. Pope Caldwell (NY), speaking on H.R. 12731, August 23, 1918, 65th Cong., 2nd sess., *Congressional Record* 56, pt. 9: 9422.

[58] Senators William Alden Smith (MI), Kenneth D. McKellar (TN), and John Wingate Weeks (MA), speaking on S.4856, August 26, 1918, 65th Cong., 2nd sess., *Congressional Record* 56, pt. 10: 9515–16, 9519.

traditional education. Moreover, they predicted that the cost would be acceptable since most young veterans would not take advantage of this provision anyway and instead work after demobilization.[59]

These educational provisions, in a conscription bill, hinted at the growing involvement of the higher education sector in the military training and service of young men as detailed later in this chapter. They also show how military service and education were gradually being linked in the thoughts of many of the country's lawmakers. After a congressional conference committee discussed the disagreements between the two chambers of Congress over the amendments to the bill, the Senate provision, which would have provided veterans with an opportunity for postwar education, was withdrawn due to the inherent uncertainty. It was agreed that it would be "best to adopt that provision [of the House] for taking care of the young men now, rather than in the future." The final bill that was eventually passed by both chambers of Congress in late August, therefore, lowered the draft age to eighteen while also adopting the House provision which allowed soldiers to be assigned to technical training during the war.[60] It contained a section stipulating that the Secretary of War was authorized to "assign to educational institutions, for special and technical training, soldiers who enter the military service under the provisions of this Act in such numbers and under such regulations as he may prescribe" and to contract with educational institutions for the subsistence, quarters, and military and academic instruction.[61] This and a War Department order issued simultaneously with the passage of the amendment authorized the SATC mentioned at the beginning of this chapter.

Although men as young as eighteen years old could now be drafted, many Americans remained uneasy about doing so. Upon signing the bill into law at the end of that month, President Wilson tried to allay their discomfort by emphasizing that young men had served voluntarily since the country's earliest days and had convinced the military authorities that

---

[59] Senators William Borah (ID), George E. Chamberlain (OR), and James A. Reed (MO), speaking on S. 4856, August 26, 1918, 65th Cong., 2nd sess., *Congressional Record* 56, pt. 10: 9515, 9519–20; roll vote on S. 4856 Committee amendment, August 26, 1918, 65th Cong., 2nd sess., *Congressional Record* 56, pt. 10: 9521.

[60] U.S. Congress, House Committee of Conference, *Conference Report (to Accompany H.R. 12731)*, 65th Cong., 2nd sess., report no. 763 (Washington, DC: GPO, 1918), 6; Senator George E. Chamberlain (OR), speaking on "Universal Military Training and Education," August 30, 1918, 65th Cong., 2nd sess., *Congressional Record* 56, pt. 10: 9680.

[61] *An Act Amending the Act Entitled "An Act to Authorize the President to Increase Temporarily the Military Establishment of the United States, Approved May 18, 1917,"* Public Law 65-210, *U.S. Statues at Large* 40 (1917–1919): 957.

they held the highest combatant qualities. He added that their "youthful enthusiasm, their virile eagerness, [and] their gallant spirit of daring make them the admiration of all who see them in action."[62] Furthermore, in the following month, September 1918, he designated ages nineteen to twenty, as well as thirty-two to thirty-six, as the groups subject to the earliest call among the new registrants to delay the draft of the youngest and oldest men in the draft age.[63] When the armistice was signed on November 11, 1918, local draft boards had just completed the classification of registrants between ages nineteen and thirty-six and were embarking on the task of classifying eighteen-year-olds and men above age thirty-six. The new draft age allowed the Army to register a total of over twenty-four million men by then and to secure necessary fighting forces only from men classified in Class I.[64]

The Creation of the Student Army Training Corps

By the time President Wilson signed the amendment to the Selective Service Act in August 1918 expanding the age groups for the draft and establishing the educational provisions, a network of support had already been built among prominent educational figures interested in the relationship they saw between education and military service. For example, many college and university administrators, as well as some faculty members, were avid supporters of UMT, as previously mentioned. These educators, like many other civilian advocates of UMT, tended to emphasize its educational value, claiming that it would teach young men discipline, order, and toughen them mentally and physically. And like other UMT advocates, they claimed that UMT promoted democracy since it would bring together young men from across socioeconomic backgrounds.[65] Many higher education leaders also saw their institutions as having a role to play in training young men militarily. In 1915, Harvard offered a course in military science and established a regiment to prepare students for reserve officer positions, while Princeton offered a military history and policy course.[66] To a *New York Times* questionnaire in January 1915 asking presidents of major higher education institutions in the country about their opinions regarding

---

[62] "The President's Proclamation of August 31, 1918," reprinted in Crowder, *Second Report of the Provost Marshal General*, 311. See also pp. 25–26.
[63] Crowder, *Second Report of the Provost Marshal General*, 179.   [64] Ibid., 2–3.
[65] Gruber, *Mars and Minerva*, 221.   [66] Ibid., 222.

military training of students, two-thirds of the twenty-seven presidents that replied favored the measure.[67]

After the United States entered World War I, educational leaders ardently backed the country's war effort. One of them described their enthusiasm as "almost pathetic."[68] It was not driven solely by the pressing need to win the war. Rather, the U.S. entry into the war provided another incentive for them to support the military training of students and strengthen the connection between the federal government and educational institutions – an increasing number of college-age men now enlisted or were drafted into the military rather than attending college. The sharp drop in student enrollment caused widespread disruption in colleges. It had a particularly significant impact on private universities, which relied financially on student tuition. Public universities were not as financially dependent on it, but they also faced financial difficulties because of wartime inflation.[69] Fearing repercussions, financially and otherwise, colleges and universities across the country actively promoted their institutions to the public in ways they had never done previously, claiming that pursuing higher education was advancing the war effort. Emory College in Georgia, for example, urged high-school seniors to "ENLIST IN COLLEGE IN ORDER TO RENDER YOUR COUNTRY A LARGER SERVICE."[70]

Higher education representatives also appealed to the federal government for financial help by emphasizing the value of higher education in producing engineers, doctors, scientists, and other specialists essential to winning the war. Additionally, they argued that if the colleges were left depleted, a long-term lack of trained men in various sectors of American society would continue after the war.[71] In response to the educators' request for help, in the summer of 1917, Secretary of War Baker created an educational advisory committee to serve the Advisory Commission of the Council of National Defense, which then launched discussions on the role of schools in the country's war effort. The work of this committee would lead to further cooperation between educational institutions and the government, which in turn would prompt the establishment of the military–educational programs explored below.[72]

---

[67] Ibid.; "College Heads for War Drills," *NYT*, January 24, 1915.
[68] Senate Committee on Military Affairs, *Amending the Draft Law*, vol. 2, 101.
[69] Gruber, *Mars and Minerva*, 227.
[70] Emphasis in original. Quoted in David O. Levine, *The American College and the Culture of Aspiration, 1915–1940* (Ithaca, NY: Cornell University Press, 1986), 25.
[71] Ibid., 26.
[72] Ibid., 27; Senate Committee on Military Affairs, *Amending the Draft Law*, vol. 2, 91.

Furthermore, in January 1918, some of the major educational associations in the country created the Emergency Council on Education to strengthen and consolidate the war effort of postsecondary education institutions. This was soon renamed the American Council on Education (ACE). Its members included the Association of American Universities, the Association of State Universities, the National Education Association, the American Association of University Professors, and other groups that represented educational institutions, especially higher education institutions, around the country.[73] In the following decades, the ACE would grow into a leading mediator between the federal government and the education sector.

In the months leading up to the passage in August 1918 of the amendment expanding the draft age and establishing the educational provision, educational leaders worked with the military to create military–educational programs in civilian educational institutions. Doing so met the military's needs as well. Soon after the United States entered the war, military officials realized that the country was running low on draftees with technical expertise essential to the military, ranging from carpentry, blacksmithing, and construction, to electrical work, radio operation, and automobile driving and repairing.[74] Trade tests that the Army's Committee on Classification of Personnel conducted indicated that only 6 percent of draftees could be classed as "experts," 28 percent as "journeymen," and 40 percent as "apprentices," while the rest could only be rated as having very limited trade experience.[75] The convergence of the military's and educational institutions' interests – the military needed to train draftees in technical skills, and many educational institutions were facing financial difficulties and wished to demonstrate their contribution to the war effort – led to the establishment of the Committee on Education and Special Training (CEST) in the War Department in February 1918, with the mission of coordinating the relationship between educational institutions and the military and developing training

---

[73] "The Emergency Council on Education: Report of Committee on Organization," n.d., n.p., Records of the American Council on Education, Box 26, "Establishment of Emergency Council on Education, 1918" folder, Hoover Institution Library & Archives, Stanford, CA (hereafter cited as Hoover Institution Archives); Gruber, *Mars and Minerva*, 98.

[74] C. R. Dooley, *Final Report of the National Army Training Detachments Later Known as Vocational Section, S. A. T. C.* (Washington, DC: War Department, Committee on Education and Special Training, 1919), 13; CEST Advisory Board, *Committee on Education and Special Training*, 11; Emmett J. Scott, *Scott's Official History of the American Negro in the World War* ([United States]: [publisher not identified], 1919), 328.

[75] Dooley, *Final Report*, 13–14.

programs that met mutual interests.[76] The committee would create and administer military–educational programs on college campuses such as the SATC.

The CEST was composed of three to five representatives from the Army (the number changed from time to time) and was advised by a civilian board of seven educators each representing engineering education, vocational education, higher education, or agricultural education.[77] It is noteworthy that some of the people who would spearhead the military training of young men or seek to strengthen the relationship between youth, education, and the federal government throughout the next few decades were members of this committee or its advisory board. For example, the chairman of the CEST's Civilian Advisory Board was Charles R. Mann, a physicist who had been an associate professor at the University of Chicago (1907–1914) and an investigator for the Joint Committee on Engineering Education of the National Engineering Societies and Carnegie Foundation for the Advancement of Teaching (1914–18). Mann would continue to serve the War Department after the war (1919–25) and direct the ACE (1922–34.)[78] Additionally, one of the members of the CEST was Grenville Clark, the prominent attorney and a leading force behind the MTCA and UMT movements, who at the time was assisting the Adjutant General's Department with the classification of inductees. He would become one of the principal drafters and promoters of the 1940 Selective Training and Service Act.[79] Harvard philosopher and UMT advocate Ralph Barton Perry, who had entered the Army after the U.S. entry into World War I, also became a CEST member in May 1918.[80]

In April 1918, the CEST established its first military–educational program, the National Army Training Detachments (NATD), which were vocational training detachments set up in educational institutions to train technical workers for the military, such as automobile drivers, blacksmiths, and carpenters. The CEST made contracts with a total of

---

[76] Ibid., 14.
[77] Three military representatives were initially intended to be included in the committee, but sources indicate that the actual number changed over the committee's existence. CEST Advisory Board, *Committee on Education and Special Training*, 11–12, 23, 35, 101.
[78] "Charles Riborg Mann (1869–1948)," Folder 1, Mann Papers; "Charles Riborg Mann," in *Who Was Who in America: A Companion Biographical Reference Work to Who's Who in America*, vol. 2 (1943–1950) (Chicago: A. N. Marquis, 1963 [1950]), 343.
[79] Dooley, *Final Report*, 14; CEST Advisory Board, *Committee on Education and Special Training*, 11; Hill, *A Very Private Public Citizen*, 69.
[80] CEST Advisory Board, *Committee on Education and Special Training*, 12; "Ralph Barton Perry," in *The Gifford Lectures*, www.giffordlectures.org/lecturers/ralph-barton-perry (accessed February 22, 2023).

157 institutions, such as colleges, universities, and trade and normal schools, for this purpose. In this program, the CEST sent 750 Army officers, 100 quartermasters, and some medical officers to the participating institutions as instructors. Students were to be voluntarily inducted into the military on special calls issued by the Provost Marshal General. Any man who had received a grammar school education or its equivalent was eligible to apply.[81] Some courses required instructors with special vocational and trade skills and experience that school faculty did not possess, so skilled industry mechanics were recruited as instructors. Local businesses, such as tire manufacturers and railroad shops, offered their facilities to the NATD when equivalent facilities were not available at the schools.[82] Daily instruction involved six hours of vocational training and three hours of military instruction. Each course, most of them two months in length, was divided into three classes of different levels, each for students rated as "experts," "journeymen," and "apprentices," respectively. Upon completion of the course, each student was assigned to military duty according to their grades, usually infantry units or the Field Artillery.[83] By the armistice, the program had trained 130,000 men.[84]

Even before the NATD was established, it was evident that the Army would soon face a shortage of a different type of man – officer candidates and individuals with higher-level technical abilities than those addressed by the NATD.[85] In March 1918, while planning the NATD program, therefore, the CEST began developing a second military–educational program. This materialized as the SATC, which was to be established in college-level institutions with a hundred or more male "able-bodied" students over age eighteen. The SATC, despite only existing for a brief period toward the end of the war, inaugurated a new relationship between higher education and the military. As discussed below, its establishment across hundreds of universities manifested the role of higher education in wartime and its impact on young people's lives.

The SATC was initially established by a War Department order in June 1918. In the plan that was announced then – about two months

[81] Senate Committee on Military Affairs, *Amending the Draft Law*, vol. 2, 92; CEST Advisory Board, *Committee on Education and Special Training*, 13, 16–19.
[82] CEST Advisory Board, *Committee on Education and Special Training*, 15; Dooley, *Final Report*, 71, 111–12.
[83] Dooley, *Final Report*, 29, 91; Scott, *Scott's Official History*, 332–33; CEST Advisory Board, *Committee on Education and Special Training*, 15–16.
[84] The NATD would become the Vocational Section of the SATC in the fall of 1918, as will be explained later in this chapter. The total number of men trained in the NATD includes those trained as SATC Vocational Section students. CEST Advisory Board, *Committee on Education and Special Training*, 18.
[85] Ibid., 22.

before the passage of the selective service amendment lowering the draft age to eighteen – college students from ages eighteen to twenty-one were to be encouraged to voluntarily enlist in the military and participate in the program. They would then be put on furlough status while receiving the training, and would not be called to active duty before age twenty-one (which was then the minimum draft age), except in urgent military necessity. Because they were not called for active service, they would not receive any pay or allowance. The aim was to prepare students for military service while also preventing "unnecessary and wasteful depletion of the colleges through indiscriminate volunteering."[86] The Army was authorized to enlist 150,000 college-age men in SATC units. The enrollees were to engage in military instruction for ten hours a week while conducting regular academic work, which would be further supplemented by a six-week summer training camp.[87]

However, the draft law amendment of August 1918 that lowered the draft age to eighteen meant that a drastic change for the SATC plan was required, as the passage of the Act meant the induction of practically every college student over the age of eighteen and who was deemed physically fit, rather than just those who were older than twenty-one. Consequently, the CEST revised its plan for the SATC accordingly. It decided to have eligible students be voluntarily inducted into the military and give them full military status while readying them for service. In other words, while SATC enrollees in the June 1918 plan were considered students, those in this new plan were, by definition, soldiers receiving training in educational institutions. In this new plan, SATC students would be Army privates on active duty. Like ordinary draftees, they would wear uniforms, live in barracks, receive a monthly allowance of thirty dollars, and be subject to military discipline and regulations. They would engage in military drilling eleven hours a week and follow special curricula prescribed according to their age, the program they entered, and military needs. The subjects taught were to be military related, such as military law, hygiene and sanitation, and map-making. Academic subjects such as languages, history, and economics were to be modified to meet military ends.[88] This new program was named the

---

[86] Senate Committee on Military Affairs, *Amending the Draft Law*, vol. 2, 92; CEST Advisory Board, *Committee on Education and Special Training*, 22–23, 57 (the quote is from p. 57.)

[87] John Garry Clifford, *The Citizen Soldiers: The Plattsburg Training Camp Movement, 1913–1920* (Lexington: University of Kentucky Press, 2015), 256–57; Senate Committee on Military Affairs, *Amending the Draft Law*, vol. 2, 92–93; CEST Advisory Board, *Committee on Education and Special Training*, 62.

[88] CEST Advisory Board, *Committee on Education and Special Training*, 24–26; Gruber, *Mars and Minerva*, 217–18.

Collegiate Section (or Section A) of the SATC, whose educational qualification was a four-year secondary school education or its equivalent. To allow men who did not meet the academic qualification to serve in the SATC, the NATD units were incorporated into the SATC as the Vocational Section (or Section B), into which individuals with a grammar school education might be voluntarily inducted.[89]

The application process differed between the two sections of the SATC, but the general idea was to enlist as many qualified men as needed. Section A applicants needed to be accepted into the educational institution of their choosing to become SATC members, whereas Section B applicants were required to apply at a local draft board. Section A institutions were to admit students based on preexisting admission standards until October 1, 1918, when a new college admission system adapted to military demands would take over. In the new system, applicants would be selected based on their experience and educational background, a personal interview, and the standard army intelligence test.[90] Even before October 1, however, many institutions lowered the standards to admit a greater number of students. This included some of the most selective universities in the country, such as Harvard, whose president announced in early September that upon the opening of the term on September 23, the university would "receive not only the regular candidates for a degree who have passed the entrance examinations for the college, but also as student members of the SATC applicants over eighteen years of age who have graduated from any good high school or had an education equivalent thereto."[91] This adjustment in admission standards enabled young men like Harry (one of the three men introduced at the beginning of this chapter) to attend Harvard.

Upon completing the SATC program, students were either to be transferred to a central officers' training camp, sent to a noncommissioned officers' training school, assigned to further work in the school or vocational training in the military, or sent to a cantonment for duty as a private, depending on their abilities as rated by the military.[92] The length of time a student remained in the Collegiate Section depended on his age. Corresponding to the order and timing in which men were called under the Selective Service Act, twenty-year-olds were to remain in college for three months, nineteen-year-olds for six months, and

---

[89] CEST Advisory Board, *Committee on Education and Special Training*, 25–26, 66–68, 139; Dooley, *Final Report*, 5.
[90] CEST Advisory Board, *Committee on Education and Special Training*, 30, 67–68, 75.
[91] Quoted in Gruber, *Mars and Minerva*, 228.
[92] CEST Advisory Board, *Committee on Education and Special Training*, 76.

eighteen-year-olds for nine months. This arrangement was made so that students would not remain in SATC after most men of the same age had been called into military service. In other words, it was to guarantee that the SATC would not create a "privileged class enjoying partial immunity from [the] draft." The Vocational Section was a two-month program.[93]

The new SATC was officially authorized by the August 1918 amendment to the Selective Service Act and a War Department order that was issued simultaneously with the passage of the amendment.[94] On October 1, 1918, 140,000 men nationwide were sworn in as SATC privates. The hosting institutions received tuition fees, as well as 1 dollar per diem per student for subsistence and housing, from the federal government.[95] Colleges and universities welcomed the SATC enthusiastically. The ACE conducted a massive campaign in the summer of 1918 to promote the SATC as part of their broader campaign to publicize the contributions of higher education institutions to the war effort. In a letter to college presidents instructing them on how to publicize the SATC, ACE's campaign director proclaimed with excitement that "Now is the great day for American education!"[96] In addition to relieving higher education institutions of financial concerns, the SATC offered an opportunity for the higher education representatives to demonstrate their patriotism and convince the broader public that higher education was socially useful and meaningful.[97]

Faculty members of wide-ranging expertise became involved in the SATC. For example, humanities and social sciences scholars taught the War Issues Course, an important component of the SATC curriculum that was designed to teach students the historical and economic causes of the war and enhance student morale.[98] A system to rate and sort the students was devised by Edward L. Thorndike of Columbia University, an authority in the field of educational psychology, although armistice came before this system was implemented.[99]

Some faculty members and college administrators eventually became dissatisfied with the curricular and institutional adjustments imposed by the SATC. For example, final program reports collected from SATC's

---

[93] Ibid., 25, 76, 84 (the quote is from p. 25). The SATC had Navy and Marines divisions, although they were smaller than their Army counterpart. Ibid., 105–10.
[94] Ibid., 26, 65.   [95] Ibid., 78–79; Levine, *American College*, 28.
[96] Robt. L. Kelly, letter draft (no addressees), August 2, 1918, and Robt. L. Kelly to the State Directors and College Presidents, August 29, 1918, American Council on Education Records, Box 26, "Commission on Students War Service 1918" folder, Hoover Institution Archives.
[97] Gruber, *Mars and Minerva*, 230.   [98] Ibid., 238–39.
[99] CEST Advisory Board, *Committee on Education and Special Training*, 31.

Vocational Section institutions show that some academic officials questioned the effectiveness of imposing military discipline on students. A University of Oklahoma representative stated that the "general effect of military training and discipline on the quality of work was detrimental" and believed that "the men would have done more work and better work if they had not been under military discipline."[100] A response from Lafayette College also questioned the merit of military discipline, stating that the "men who developed the greatest interest in their work did not do so because of the military training or discipline, but because of ambition to advance or because of a desire to be of additional value to the service."[101]

Others, however, credited military training and discipline for producing effective soldier-mechanics and instilling in students the vision of "a finer type of citizenship."[102] Overall, representatives of the participating institutions reflected favorably on the program, noting that it provided them with a unique opportunity to interact with young men who would not have otherwise attended college, that it prepared young men for citizenship responsibilities and better living, and that it persuaded them of the value of vocational training at the college level.[103] As historian Carol S. Gruber has observed, objections from educators to the "militarization" of colleges were largely absent. According to Gruber, they complained about the "malfunctioning of the program, not about its purpose."[104] In the ensuing decades, they would continue to embrace higher education's new role in national security.[105]

With the armistice in November 1918, the SATC was terminated, and its 165,000 members were promptly demobilized.[106] Although the program existed for only a few months, a total of 525 institutions, spread throughout the mainland United States, as well as one each in Hawaii and Puerto Rico, had participated.[107] C. R. Mann, the chairman of the advisory civilian board of the CEST, later recalled that the SATC had been "a genuine national university – the University of Uncle Sam, in which every boy had an opportunity with every other boy to render his utmost service to the nation."[108]

---

[100] Quoted in Dooley, *Final Report*, 117. [101] Quoted in ibid., 119.
[102] Quoted in ibid., 126. [103] Ibid., 126–31. [104] Gruber, *Mars and Minerva*, 251.
[105] In various other ways, college educators contributed to the war effort. For example, psychologists viewed selective service as an opportunity to test the newly-developed method of measuring individual intelligence, the IQ test. Christopher P. Loss, *Between Citizens and the State: The Politics of American Higher Education in the 20th Century* (Princeton, NJ: Princeton University Press, 2012), ch. 2.
[106] CEST Advisory Board, *Committee on Education and Special Training*, 33.
[107] Ibid., 26, 87–93. [108] Quoted in Clifford, *The Citizen Soldiers*, 258.

Mann's remarks about the SATC were consistent with the main idea underlying selective service: selective service and the SATC both assigned individuals to positions that would maximize their contribution to the country's war effort and couched it in democratic terms. To that end, the SATC gave a wider spectrum of people a taste of higher education, and there were certainly meritocratic features: men without a high-school education were offered the chance to demonstrate their ability to undertake officer training, and if successful, to be transferred from the Vocational Section to the Collegiate Section. Conversely, students in the Collegiate Section could be transferred to the Vocational Section if their abilities were determined to be more appropriate for the latter.[109] Likewise, a study of men who finished NATD training at selected institutions indicates that 20.6 percent of them had not completed elementary school and only 20.4 percent were high-school graduates. The NATD, therefore, provided two months of campus life to young men who might not have otherwise stepped into a college.[110]

However, as a wartime measure, the extent to which the military–educational programs "democratized" higher education was strictly limited. Clearly, the military's role was not to empower young people from disadvantaged backgrounds. Upon establishing the NATD, for example, the CEST made clear that its primary purpose was to train soldiers. In the instructions sent out to commanding officers at the participating schools, it stated that the Army was "not a collection of men in trade occupations, but is an organization in which the men are first and last, soldiers, many of whom possess special vocational ability as a part of their equipment."[111] As such, the courses were to be tailored not to the average student but to the best, so that those considered bright could learn to perform increasingly difficult tasks, while the less promising worked on lower-level tasks that presumably suited them. The CEST encouraged instructors to carefully monitor students to make sure they were placed in courses suited to their "native ability and previous experience."[112] The military's goal in these programs was, unsurprisingly, strictly military: to determine each student's military potential, cultivate it, and assign them to tasks that appeared to be most beneficial for the military.

Therefore, although military representatives also referred to the idea that these military–educational programs "democratized" higher education by making it accessible to young people who were previously unable

---

[109] CEST Advisory Board, *Committee on Education and Special Training*, 26.
[110] Dooley, *Final Report*, 96–97.   [111] Quoted in ibid., 29.
[112] Ibid., 30–31, 36–37. The quote is from p. 31.

to afford it, the idea arose primarily as a result of the convergence of various civilians' interests. For example, legislators and the Wilson administration sought to assuage public opposition to the conscription of minors by rewarding soldiers with education, higher education leaders wished to persuade the public of the social value of higher education, and progressive reformers hoped that the horrific war would at least serve as a "plastic juncture" for expanding access to higher education. These diverse interests merged with the imperative military need to train soldiers in practical skills, thereby establishing the military–educational programs as a democratic education opportunity.

It is also important to highlight that the claim that the SATC was a "democratic" educational opportunity was built on prevailing social and racial inequalities in American society. According to Army test results, the educational level of U.S. soldiers in World War I varied by race and ethnicity. While native white soldiers had received a median number of 6.9 years of education before entering the military, immigrants had received 4.7 years and Southern Black soldiers had received 2.6 years.[113] This reflected the significant disparity in American society in the quality and length of education that children of different racial and ethnic backgrounds could get, as well as the systemic biases in educational testing that favored native white children.[114] Because admittance to the SATC was based on prior academic achievement, it benefitted individuals who were least affected by existing educational inequities.

The effects of the SATC on Black Americans exemplify how the "opportunity of a lifetime" was not accessible to many young soldiers from minority groups. As explained below, racial segregation and discrimination in the military, which assigned Black men to segregated units and assumed that officers were white men even in those units, as well as preexisting discrimination in education and American society broadly, disqualified many Black men from the SATC.

As historians have shown, systematic discrimination and segregation in the South, where the majority of Black Americans lived, relegated the quality of Black children's grammar school education and their accessibility to education to a level significantly lower than that of white children, and when combined with economic discrimination, high school and higher education were beyond reach to many of them.[115]

---

[113] Kennedy, *Over Here*, 188.
[114] Carlos Kevin Blanton, "From Intellectual Deficiency to Cultural Deficiency: Mexican Americans, Testing, and Public School Policy in the American Southwest, 1920–1940," *Pacific Historical Review* 72, no. 1 (2003): 41–44.
[115] James D. Anderson, *The Education of Blacks in the South, 1860–1935* (Chapel Hill: University of North Carolina Press, 1988). See especially ch. 6.

Significantly, according to Emmett J. Scott, an African American journalist who was appointed as a Special Assistant to the Secretary of War to address racial issues during the war, Black soldiers were not considered eligible when the military initially decided to establish a technical training program; only with Scott's insistence did the War Department include them in the plan.[116] Even then, the SATC remained essentially a racially segregated program, with fifteen Collegiate Section units and ten Vocational Section units established in historically Black institutions (these institutions were mostly located in the Jim Crow South, but they also included a few outside the South, such as Wilberforce University in Ohio and Lincoln University in Pennsylvania.)[117] Outside the South, where school segregation was not legally instituted, Black students were nonetheless denied admission to SATC units in some colleges, to which the National Association for the Advancement of Colored People raised their concern. In response, the War Department announced that "No color line will be drawn in inducting men into the S. A. T. C. Colored men eligible for induction will be inducted at institutions which they attend and will not be required to transfer to other institutions," clarifying that it did not intend to introduce the color line to schools that did not have one. At the same time, however, it announced that it did not intend to break down the color line at institutions where it had already been drawn.[118]

Sources indicate that the quality of education offered to these units contradicts the CEST's claim that it trained men of draft age "irrespective of nationality, race, intelligence and education" (Figure 1.2).[119] The stance of the military on racial issues in the SATC reflects its focus on the goal of winning the war, the systemic racism ingrained in the institution, and its overall policy of not intervening with racial issues in American society. Additionally, the fundamental purpose of war mobilization measures such as selective service and the SATC, once again, was to assign individuals to duties that would help the country's war effort, not to address inequality. Therefore, the military's assessment of which positions Black soldiers should be assigned to was shaped by these factors, naturalizing the low quality of training delivered to Black soldiers in the SATC. The "democratization" of higher education through

---

[116] Scott, *Scott's Official History*, 329.
[117] CEST Advisory Board, *Committee on Education and Special Training*, 87–93.
[118] Scott, *Scott's Official History*, 338–40. The War Department's announcement is quoted in p. 338.
[119] Dooley, *Final Report*, 32.

The job of the Committee of Education and Special Training of the War Department was to train men of draft age for the United States National Army along specialized technical lines, irrespective of nationality, race, intelligence and education

Figure 1.2 Scenes from SATC training as promoted by the CEST. Note the contrast between facilities for white students (top) and facilities for Black students (bottom).
C. R. Dooley, *Final Report of the National Army Training Detachments Later Known as Vocational Section, S. A. T. C.* (Washington, DC: War Department, Committee on Education and Special Training, 1919), 32. In the public domain.

military training programs such as the SATC operated within the framework of preexisting racism.

The mobilization of young Americans for World War I established the basis on which Americans in the following decades discussed the relationship between youth, education, and national security. The 1917 Selective Service Act established the principle that only men who had reached the age of majority would be drafted and that their liability stemmed from the legal rights they possessed, most notably the right to vote. The need to draft men under the age of twenty-one, therefore, sparked a heated debate in 1918 over what justified compulsory military service of minors. The 1918 amendment to the Selective Service Act established a precedent of drafting eighteen-year-olds and its passage reflected legislators' recognition of some of the ideas that had been forming for some time, since the rise of the preparedness and UMT movements, and would be pronounced in the following decades to support military training and service of young men – that young men made better soldiers in modern warfare and that military training and service would turn "boys" into "men."

Nonetheless, even though the realities of war necessitated the passage of the amendment lowering the draft age to eighteen, Americans in 1918 were still concerned about drafting minors. The link between legal majority, mental and physical maturity, and military duty remained strong, and minors were still regarded as "boys" in need of adult guidance and education. The educational provisions that the House and the Senate each agreed on illustrate the strength of this bond. The House's proposal – to have soldiers receive training in civilian educational institutions – did not specify age eligibility, but the programs they authorized, such as the SATC, by default, trained young men in their late teens to early twenties. The Senate's provision – to reward soldiers under the age of twenty-one with postwar educational benefits – specifically limited the qualification to soldiers who entered the service as minors. As the subsequent chapters of this book will show, the link between legal majority and military duty (or between legal minority and education) would be shaken in the decades that followed.

Second, the institutional relationship that the war established between higher education and military training would be further strengthened in the following decades through the development of programs such as ROTC and wartime measures in World War II. As the subsequent chapters will reveal, the debates over these programs would revolve around the unsettling connection between military training and access to education. Furthermore, the Senate's educational proposal of 1918, which would have provided young veterans with educational opportunities, died at that time, but the idea of the federal government rewarding veterans with education would be materialized in World War II as the G.I. Bill of Rights of 1944, which allowed veterans of that war to pursue an education with federal support after demobilization and which led to the considerable expansion of higher education institutions in the second half of the twentieth century.

Finally, the war left a lasting impact on the ideas about the nature of higher education and its place in American society. For example, many instructors of the War Issues Course considered the course a positive experience, as it cut across departmental lines and promoted interdisciplinary cooperation among professors who had previously been isolated in their respective academic departments. They also found in the course a way to make the undergraduate curriculum more relevant to contemporary issues. The adoption of the Contemporary Civilization course, modeled after the War Issues Course, by Columbia University in the fall of 1919 symbolized how the SATC and higher education's cooperation with the military influenced postwar curricular reform in higher education institutions.[120] The SATC also helped form a public consensus that higher education was socially valuable, especially in technical and practical training, and helped boost enrollment in the years after the war. "In the public eye World War I transformed the college student from a frivolous young fellow into a prospective leader of society," observes educational historian David O. Levine.[121] Most importantly, educational leaders now had the ACE, a new home to discuss political actions and a wealth of experiences from which to build future partnerships with the federal government. After the war, they would gradually come to believe that their cooperation with the military during World War I had not been ideal, as it gave the military too much power over them, but they would still use the bittersweet memory of the war to improve their relationship with the military. As Chapters 3–5 demonstrate, the ACE would spearhead higher education's involvement in federal policymaking concerning American youth in the Great Depression and World War II, with many of its central members holding important governmental and educational positions that connected the political and educational worlds.

---

[120] Gruber, *Mars and Minerva*, 243–44.
[121] Levine, *American College*, 24. See also pp. 39–41.

2 Educational Institutions and Military Training in the 1920s and the 1930s

In the fall of 1939, twelve-year-old Paul Brinkman of Augusta, Georgia, crossed state lines to enroll in North Augusta High School in South Carolina. He had been expelled from Richmond Academy, Augusta's public high school, for refusing to take the mandatory Reserve Officers' Training Corps (ROTC) course on religious grounds. ROTC, established by the National Defense Act of 1916, offered elementary military training to male students in secondary and higher education institutions with the aim of providing basic military knowledge and training to the students and spotting potential reserve officers. In 1935, 139 secondary schools across the country (such as civilian high schools and secondary-level military schools) had ROTC units, with 83 making enrollment mandatory for male students. In the same year, 117 higher education institutions had ROTC units, with 82 requiring male students to participate for the first two years.[1] Brinkman's father, an evangelical minister, requested intervention from the state Board of Education and the governor, but both declined.[2]

Brinkman's supporters questioned the legitimacy of requiring students in civilian educational institutions, particularly public schools, to

---

[1] U.S. Congress, Senate, Subcommittee of the Committee on Military Affairs, *Compulsory Military Training: Hearings before the Subcommittee on S. 3309*, 74th Cong., 2nd sess. (Washington, DC: GPO, 1936), 217–19; "Higher Educational Institutions Having Courses in Military Training," a list provided by the War Department printed in the *Congressional Record* at the request of Senator Lynn Joseph Frazier (ND), speaking on H.R. 11035, March 18, 1936, 74th Cong., 2nd sess., *Congressional Record* 80, pt. 4: 3930–31.
[2] "For Conscience's Sake," editorial, *Atlanta Constitution*, November 8, 1939; "Misunderstanding, Somewhere," *Atlanta Constitution*, September 28, 1939. See also "Appeal on R. O. T. C. to Be Heard Today," *Atlanta Constitution*, October 4, 1939; "Georgia Objector Enrolls His Son in Carolina School," *Atlanta Constitution*, November 8, 1939; "Conscientious Objectors and Compulsory Drill," *News Bulletin of the Committee on Militarism in Education* (December 1939), 3, filed in "Military in General Corres. 1936–40" folder, Box 68, National Self Government Committee Records, New York Public Library, New York, NY (hereafter cited as NSGC Records). This last source gives the boy's last name as "Brickman." This chapter uses "Brinkman," following the *Atlanta Constitution*.

undergo military training. In the United States, the term "academy" often refers to institutions that prepare students for military careers, and the Richmond school board justified its decision to expel Brinkman by claiming that it had been a military school for a long time.[3] Nonetheless, the *Atlanta Constitution*, a local newspaper, condemned the deprival of Brinkman's right to attend a local public school. If the Academy wished to maintain itself as a military prep school, the editors argued, it should do so by refraining from accepting state school funds. They continued: "Educational institutions supported by state funds, collected from all taxpayers, are supposed to be open to any boy or girl who can meet the scholastic requirements. To make acceptance of military training in such schools conditional for admittance is to adopt the methods of Stalin, of Hitler and of Mussolini."[4]

Brinkman's was not an isolated case. Rather, in the years between the two world wars, multiple students in higher education institutions and secondary schools were expelled or suspended for refusing to participate in mandatory ROTC training. The commitment of public schools and universities to mandatory military training conditioned access to post-elementary education for young people who could not afford to attend a private institution that did not have the requirement, and sparked a heated debate over whether students could be compelled to take military training and whether national security should be prioritized over students' access to education in peacetime. This chapter explores these debates and sheds light on the tensions that existed and grew between access to education and national security in these years, as well as the consolidation of the relationship between educational institutions and the military through ROTC.

---

[3] There is considerable ambiguity regarding the definition of "military school" here. A War Department study of ROTC conducted in 1945 counts Richmond Academy as one of 94 civilian schools with a junior ROTC unit, not one of 40 military schools with one. On the other hand, Richmond Academy's former website explains that the school "became a military school after the Civil War." The school's current website has no information on the school's history of military training. Millard W. Hansen, "A History of the Reserve Officers' Training Corps and the 55C (National Defense Act) Schools, 1939–1944," April 1, 1945, n.p. (p. 6 of "Chapter VI – The Junior Division ROTC"), "History of the ROTC" folder, Army Service Forces, Director of Military Training, Army Specialized Military Training, 1942–46, Historical File, Records of Headquarters Army Service Forces, Record Group (hereafter cited as RG) 160, U.S. National Archives at College Park, College Park, MD (hereafter cited as NACP); "Homepage," *Academy of Richmond County* (the former website of the school archived online), https://web.archive.org/web/20071011024142/http://arc.rcboe.org/home.aspx (accessed June 14, 2023); *Academy of Richmond County*, www.rcboe.org/arc (accessed July 31, 2023).
[4] "For Conscience's Sake."

The supporters of military training in educational institutions drew on many of the ideas underlying the universal military training (UMT) and Plattsburg movements that gained momentum in the several years before the U.S. entry into World War I; that is, they sought to strengthen not only military defense but achieve domestic goals such as "toughening" young men and preserving the social order by training students militarily. Some readers may wonder if financial support for students through ROTC scholarships was among the key reasons why some people supported ROTC in this period, but this was not the case. ROTC in higher education institutions consisted of two courses: a two-year basic course, which was required in some schools for first- and second-year students, and a two-year advanced course for third- and fourth-year students who were chosen to continue by the institution's president and instructor of military training. Only advanced-course students were qualified for financial aid, which meant that ROTC was not a means for young people who could not otherwise afford a college education to obtain one. Furthermore, the two-year basic course did not qualify its graduates for service in the U.S. armed forces. In short, the purpose of ROTC in these years was not solely military. Rather, it reflected a combination of national defense interests and goals that were not strictly military. The ultimate defeat of opponents of ROTC by the end of the 1930s suggests that American society had come to accept the teaching of military subjects in civilian educational institutions.

Despite the lasting impact of the preparedness movement and broader ideas about national security that emerged during World War I on young men's access to education, military matters are rarely featured in narratives of American society in the 1920s and 1930s. According to the standard narrative, after the armistice in November 1918, American society returned to "normalcy," promptly demobilizing the wartime troops. The narratives about the "interwar" years are typically centered on the "New Era" of the 1920s – a decade marked by the rise of consumerism and urbanization, along with nativism and prohibition – as well as the Great Depression and the New Deal reforms of the 1930s. Historians have challenged the portrayal of American society in this period as inward-looking or isolationist by revealing wide-ranging interactions of American people with the wider world – economically, culturally, and militarily.[5] Yet, the assumption that real military presence *inside*

---

[5] Daniel T. Rodgers, *Atlantic Crossings: Social Politics in a Progressive Age* (Cambridge, MA: Harvard University Press, 1998); Alan Dawley, *Changing the World: American Progressives*

American society did not resurface until the Japanese attack on Pearl Harbor in December 1941 remains.

Indeed, the U.S. armed forces faced significant budget cuts during this time, as did the general public's lack of interest in military matters, which was exacerbated by the long-held belief that a large standing army was incompatible with American society. Having rejected its commitment to the League of Nations, U.S. Congress cut down the military budget significantly, if not to the prewar level. By 1924, the national defense budget had declined from 11 billion dollars in 1919 to 500 million dollars.[6] The Great Depression further reduced military strength "below the point of safety" in the words of Douglas MacArthur, then Army Chief of Staff.[7] George C. Marshall, Army Chief of Staff during World War II, later recalled that the years between the two world wars had been the Army's "Dark Ages," in which the institution was "gradually being starved into a condition almost comparable to its pre-Spanish–American War condition."[8]

However, although the presence of the military in American civilian life diminished after the end of World War I, the armistice did not bring a complete return to the military of the nineteenth century. Among the lasting repercussions that the war left on Americans concerned with national security was the idea that the nature of war had fundamentally changed. In Secretary of War John W. Week's words, the war shattered the illusion that national defense could be "secured by the maintenance of a small Navy and diminutive Army, a delusion that was frightfully costly in men and money and brought us to the realization that national defense in the larger sense depends upon the whole people and that modern wars are waged by nations in their entirety."[9] The war thus

---

in *War and Revolution* (Princeton, NJ: Princeton University Press, 2003); Brooke L. Blower, "From Isolationism to Neutrality: A New Framework for Understanding American Political Culture, 1919–1941," *Diplomatic History* 38, no. 2 (2014): 345–76; Emily S. Rosenberg, *Financial Missionaries to the World: The Politics and Culture of Dollar Diplomacy, 1900–1930* (Durham, NC: Duke University Press, 2003).

[6] In 2023 U.S. dollars, this represents a decline from approximately 192 billion to 8.7 billion dollars. The conversion was performed by "Purchasing Power Today of a US Dollar Transaction in the Past," *MeasuringWorth 2023*, www.measuringworth.com/ppowerus/ (accessed March 3, 2023).

[7] Quoted in Michael Matheny, "When the Smoke Clears: The Interwar Years as an Unlikely Success Story," in *Drawdown: The American Way of Postwar*, ed. Jason W. Warren (New York: New York University Press, 2016), 157.

[8] Michael Sherry, *Preparing for the Next War: American Plans for Postwar Defense, 1941–45* (New Haven, CT: Yale University Press, 1977), 3; Mark Skinner Watson, *Chief of Staff: Prewar Plans and Preparations* (Washington, DC: GPO, 1950), 3–5, 26.

[9] [Conference on Training for Citizenship and National Defense (hereafter cited as Conference on Training),] *Special Report of the Secretary of War to the President on the*

convinced military policymakers and other concerned adults in the United States that modern warfare required technically skilled personnel knowledgeable in subjects such as engineering, chemistry, and mathematics at all levels of the mobilization machinery, on the home front and the battlefields. In addition, they came to believe, the country required a literate, physically strong, highly motivated citizen army fully trained in peacetime and prepared to take arms in case of an emergency.[10] These people included UMT supporters, who saw the institutionalization of ROTC as a step toward the realization of UMT.

On the other hand, the experience of a brutal modern war inspired robust anti-war and pacifist movements in the United States and elsewhere in the world.[11] From their perspective, military preparedness signified to the rest of the world that the United States was preparing to fight another war. These two significantly different groups – one advocating for military preparedness and the other calling for disarmament – clashed over the issue of military training in educational institutions, especially the question of whether it should be compulsory for male students in public institutions.

As previous studies of ROTC have shown, many educational leaders, including college presidents, school board members, and educators holding federal government positions, aggressively sought to fortify their relationship with the military.[12] Along with UMT advocates and patriotic groups, these educators believed that every male citizen, especially students in publicly funded institutions, should be prepared to serve their country and that military training was beneficial for their health and discipline. They fiercely defended military training in educational institutions against oppositional groups such as those of students, pacifists,

---

Conference on Training for Citizenship and National Defense, 1922 (Washington, DC: GPO, 1923), 6, filed in "Report of the Conference" folder, Records of the Conference on Training the Youth of the Country for Citizenship and National Defense, October 1922–June 1923, Operations and Training Division (G-3), Records of the War Department General and Special Staffs, RG 165, NACP.

[10] Committee on Education and Special Training, Advisory Board (hereafter cited as CEST Advisory Board), *Committee on Education and Special Training: A Review of Its Works during 1918* (Washington, DC: War Department, [1919]), 49–52.

[11] Lawrence S. Wittner, *Rebels against War: The American Peace Movement, 1933–1983* (Philadelphia: Temple University Press, 1984), ch. 1; Robert Cohen, *When the Old Left Was Young: Student Radicals and America's First Mass Student Movement, 1929–1941* (New York: Oxford University Press, 1993).

[12] Michael S. Neiberg, *Making Citizen-Soldiers: ROTC and the Ideology of American Military Service* (Cambridge, MA: Harvard University Press, 2000); Candice Bredbenner, "Searching for the Civic Soul of the University: Higher Education, Citizenship, and the Debate over Military Training in the Interwar Period," in *The Meaning of Citizenship*, ed. Richard Marback and Marc W. Kruman (Detroit, MI: Wayne State University Press, 2015), 225–48.

and college faculty that saw it as militaristic, pedagogically unsound, and un-American, and even criticized the military for not doing enough for the maintenance of ROTC. The examination of educators' commitment to mandatory ROTC training highlights how these educators contributed to the prioritization of national security needs over students' access to education in peacetime and how World War I triggered a broader reevaluation of the role that educational institutions should play in national security.

Although military training was conducted in both secondary schools and higher education institutions, their relationships with the federal government differed. Studies of military training during these years have largely focused on compulsory ROTC at the college level, but examining the interplay between debates over military training in secondary schools and higher education institutions illuminates how the line between secondary school students and college students was drawn in relation to military obligations. In other words, increasing national attention was paid to military training in colleges and universities, which solidified higher education's relationship with the military and established the idea that secondary school students were too young to fight.

The percentage of young men who went through military training in these years is not large. At the secondary education level, in 1920, there were 126 ROTC units in the country (90 in public high schools and 36 in military academies), with the total enrollment numbering 57,707 (44,852 in public high schools and the rest in military academies.) This was a small fraction of the approximately 1,100 public high schools eligible for an ROTC unit (with a total enrollment of boys at approximately 350,000). When it came to the total number of boys of high-school age in the country, the impact of ROTC was even less significant. Out of the approximately 4,000,000 boys in this age bracket, 9 percent were eligible for membership but only a little over 1 percent were enrolled.[13] At the college level, approximately 20 percent (57,749) of male freshmen took ROTC courses in 1938, at a time when roughly 15 percent of Americans of ages eighteen to twenty (half of whom were women) attended college.[14] Moreover, higher education and secondary

---

[13] Pearson Menoher, memorandum, June 14, 1920, and C. R. Mann, memorandum, December 4, 1920, p. 1, both in "Junior R. O. T. C. Conference FY 1921" folder, Operations and Training Division (G-3), General Correspondence of the Advisory Board, 1919–1925, Records of the War Department General and Special Staffs, RG 165, NACP.

[14] Hansen, "A History of the Reserve Officers' Training Corps," n.p. (p. 7 of "Chapter III – Training Program: Administration"); John R. Thelin, *A History of American Higher Education* (Baltimore: Johns Hopkins University Press, 2004), 205.

education were not equally accessible to young men across class, race, and ethnicity. All the above indicates that only a small minority of young people were directly affected by ROTC training.

Yet, an increasing number of young people pursued secondary and higher education after World War I, and the institutionalization of ROTC in civilian educational institutions, as well as the denial of students who wished to avoid military training, had an important symbolic meaning for American society – that civilian educational institutions now trained young men militarily not only in wartime but in peacetime. National security thus affected young people's access to education in peacetime and consolidated a long-term relationship between education and the military.

Debates over Military Training of Boys in the United States before ROTC

The idea of training youth militarily in educational institutions had existed since the early nineteenth century, when the public school system evolved in the United States, and calls for military training in public schools below the college level waxed and waned with real and perceived crises in the domestic or international order. During the U.S. Civil War, for example, the city council of Bangor, Maine, instituted a "Volunteer Drill Company" in the city's public high school, in which male students engaged in military drilling for two hours a week.[15] Another wave came in the 1890s, when large-scale immigration from southern and eastern Europe, labor conflict, rising prominence of women in public life, and growing imperial ambitions of the United States prompted some Anglo-Saxon elites to advocate for military training as a method of "Americanizing" immigrants, stabilizing social order, "toughening" boys and young men, and fulfilling the country's new role as an empire.[16] In January 1895, for example, a bill that provided for all boys of age eleven and older in public schools in New York State to be organized into a military organization called the "American Guard" was presented to the state legislature. Its chief promoter was a New York "post" of the patriotic Grand Army of the Republic, which had also championed the move to have the stars and stripes raised at every public school in the

---

[15] Randall Curren and Charles Dorn, *Patriotic Education in a Global Age* (Chicago: University of Chicago Press, 2018), 59.
[16] David I. Macleod, "Socializing American Youth to Be Citizen-Soldiers," in *Anticipating Total War: The German and American Experiences, 1871–1914*, ed. Roger Chickering and Stig Förster (Washington, DC: German Historical Institute; New York: Cambridge University Press, 1999), 137–66.

country to foster patriotism among pupils, which included many recent immigrants.[17] Supporters of military training around the country maintained that it would make boys physically and mentally stronger, instill in them a sense of self-control, patriotism, and respect for authority, and provide the country with a better option than maintaining a large standing army.[18] The movement faded soon after the Spanish–American War, but the idea of militarily training the country's boys and young men at educational institutions endured.[19]

When the debate resurfaced in the mid-1910s as part of the calls for preparedness, the introduction of military training to schools was debated in several states.[20] The state of New York discussed a set of bills that provided for physical training for all male students in public and private schools more than eight years old and compulsory military training for all men between ages sixteen and nineteen (excluding those regularly employed.)[21] Opponents argued that children should not be "conscripted" for military training before adult men were and that gymnastics in the open air and games like baseball, football, and basketball would "do more for the physical youth of America in a year than military training will do in half a century."[22] The supporters, on the other hand, contended that military training would not only build boys physically and foster loyal citizens but would have a character-building effect – it would "supply an outlet for their animal spirits which if not properly directed may cause them to 'go bad.'"[23] The supporters won out, with the bills being signed into law in May 1916, and working men of the same age range were soon made applicable to the law. Moreover, an amendment to this Act of September 1918 stipulated that "physically sound" men

---

[17] "Patriotism in Schools," *NYT*, January 18, 1895; "Military Drill in Schools," *NYT*, January 19, 1895; "To Make Boys Soldiers," *NYT* January 26, 1895; "A Schoolboy Army," *Saint Paul Daily Globe*, February 4, 1895.
[18] "Teach 'em to Murder!" *Kansas Agitator*, February 8, 1895; "School Directors on 'the Spirit of Militarism,'" *The Sun* (New York), March 1, 1895; "Military Education, Why Not?" editorial, *NYT*, February 20, 1896.
[19] Marvin A. Kreidberg and Merton G. Henry, *History of Military Mobilization in the United States Army, 1775–1945* (Washington, DC: Department of the Army, 1955), 210; "The Military Convention," *NYT*, February 10, 1899; "Urge Military Training and Rifle Practice for Boys in Public Schools," *The Sun* (New York), April 6, 1913.
[20] See, for instance, "Society of Friends Oppose Reid's Plan of War Training" and "Reid's Military Training Plan for Schools Receive Notice through State," both in *Richmond Palladium* (Richmond, IN), November 27, 1915; "Pass Military Training Bill," *Perth Amboy Evening News* (Perth Amboy, NJ), March 9, 1916; "Favor Military Training," editorial, *Perth Amboy Evening News*, March 13, 1916.
[21] "Schoolboy Army Ready by Autumn," *NYT*, May 17, 1916.
[22] P. Hollingsworth Wood, letter to the editor, *NYT*, April 3, 1916; "Five Preparedness Bills Signed by the Governor," *The Sun* (New York), May 16, 1916.
[23] D. A. Wilcox, letter to the editor, *NYT*, April 5, 1916.

between ages sixteen and nineteen, both those in school and at work, who failed to comply with the law could not be educated or employed in the state.[24]

Although civilian supporters of these measures expected that military training would benefit national security, social order, and youth discipline, the military was not willing to encourage any move that did not directly help build stronger armed forces. For a brief period before the U.S. entry into World War I, the War Department showed some interest in the local calls for military training in high schools, but such interest waned with the country's entry into the war, as it was faced with a more pressing need to train men of military age.[25] In response to school officials' requests for advice on how schools could best serve the war effort, the U.S. Bureau of Education issued a leaflet in April 1918, approved by the Secretaries of War, Navy, Agriculture, Labor, and a few other relevant federal departments and which stated that the "Army and Navy do not want, and can not [sic] use, boys under 18 years of age, nor boys nor men of any age who are not strong and well-developed physically."[26] As such, it suggested that high schools should emphasize physical education to prepare boys for future military service along with technical training for both girls and boys to prepare them for war work.[27] The discrepancy between the expectations of civilian supporters of military training for the training to advance broad social and educational goals, in addition to military preparedness, and military leaders' focus on military needs would continue into the following decades.

The Origins of ROTC

While military training of boys was being debated in various communities, the idea of offering military training in higher education institutions also emerged. The idea originated in the early nineteenth century. After West Point was founded in 1802 as the first federal military academy, the American Literary, Scientific, and Military Academy (today Norwich University) was founded in 1819 as a private

---

[24] "Schoolboy Army Ready by Autumn"; "Military Training in New York," editorial, *NYT*, March 7, 1917; "Boys Must Train, Says Military Law," *NYT*, September 9, 1918; "Training the Boys," editorial, *NYT*, September 10, 1918.
[25] Kreidberg and Henry, *History of Military Mobilization*, 211–13.
[26] Department of the Interior, Bureau of Education, *Government Policies Involving the Schools in War Time* (Washington, DC: GPO, 1918), 3, filed in Folder 8, Charles Riborg Mann Papers, #1048, Southern Historical Collection, The Wilson Library, University of North Carolina at Chapel Hill (online collection) (hereafter cited as Mann Papers).
[27] Ibid., 3–4.

military college, offering military training to produce militia officers. Thomas Jefferson introduced compulsory military training to the University of Virginia the next year for the same purpose, while a few other civilian universities also began offering military training during this period.[28]

The federal government's involvement in military training in colleges and universities began with the Land Grant Act, or the Morrill Act, of 1862. Under this Act, the government was to offer individual states public lands or land scrip, and with the funds derived from the sale of the lands or land scrip, each state was to establish a college where "the leading object shall be, without excluding other scientific and classical studies, *and including military tactics*, to teach such branches of learning as are related to agriculture and the mechanic arts, in such manner as the legislatures of the states may respectively prescribe, in order to promote the liberal and practical education of the industrial classes."[29] Based on this law, each state either formed a new institution or designated an existing university as a land-grant institution, except for Massachusetts, which divided Morrill Act funds between two schools, the Massachusetts Institute of Technology (MIT) and Massachusetts Agricultural College. In the segregated South, land-grant institutions for African Americans would be later established (as discussed later in this chapter.) Except for a few private universities such as MIT and Cornell, all land-grant institutions were public institutions supported by federal and state government funds, as well as tuition and donations.[30] This law founded many of the state universities that exist today.

Supporters of land-grant institutions emphasized that the establishment of the institutions marked a new chapter in the history of higher education in the United States, in that they were publicly funded, geared toward technical, practical subjects, and intended to make higher education accessible to Americans who had not previously seen it as a possibility. They stressed this last factor in particular: the institutions' accessibility. For example, Arthur J. Klein, director of a study of land-grant institutions conducted in the 1920s and professor of school administration at Ohio State University, positioned the institutions as the final component of the public education system in the United States. He stated that the "original conception of the land-grant colleges was

---

[28] John Whiteclay Chambers II, *To Raise an Army: The Draft Comes to Modern America* (New York: Free Press, 1987), 31; Neiberg, *Making Citizen-Soldiers*, 18–19.

[29] Emphasis mine. *An Act Donating Public Lands to the Several States and Territories Which May Provide Colleges for the Benefit of Agriculture and the Mechanic Arts*, U.S. Statutes at Large 12 (1863): 504.

[30] Arthur J. Klein, "The Rise of the Land-Grant Colleges and Universities," *School Life* 16, no. 5 (1931): 83.

that they were to be a part of the free public-school systems of the States, the child being able to pass from the common school to the high school and finally to the State land-grant college or university, exempt from the payment of tuition or the equivalent charges in fees," although the institutions introduced tuition and fees later.[31] *School Life*, a monthly publication of the U.S. Office of Education, boasted in 1931 that these institutions "brought higher education within reach of the masses for the first time," and that they had "made higher education democratic" in the United States since.[32] In the 1930s, however, public debates over mandatory ROTC in land-grant institutions would highlight the tensions between access to public colleges and the obligations of youth in national security.

It is noteworthy that the Morrill Act made "military tactics" one of the subjects to be taught at land-grant institutions. In fact, the original Land Grant bill introduced in 1857 had made no mention of it. The outbreak of the Civil War in 1861, however, convinced Northern legislators of the need for schools that taught military knowledge. By the time of the bill's passage in 1862, military training in civilian educational institutions was conceived as a measure to secure adequately trained reserve officers without expanding West Point or other military institutions.[33]

The Act required that military personnel be sent to educational institutions as "professors of military science and tactics" to oversee military training programs. Supplementary Acts passed in the late nineteenth and early twentieth centuries provided that the War Department should send arms and other equipment and funds to educational institutions for the maintenance of the programs. Until the early twentieth century, however, the military was not particularly interested in training civilian college students, and the program remained low-key in most institutions and likely consisted of mere drilling.[34]

---

[31] Ibid., 83–84.
[32] *School Life* 16, no. 5 (1931), cover page. See also Klein, "The Rise of the Land-Grant Colleges and Universities," 83; Arthur J. Klein, *Survey of Land-Grant Colleges and Universities*, vol. 1, U.S. Department of the Interior, Office of Education, Bulletin, 1930, no. 9 (Washington, DC: GPO, 1930), 1.
[33] Hansen, "A History of the Reserve Officers' Training Corps," n.p. (p. 6 of "Introduction"); Gene M. Lyons and John W. Masland, *Education and Military Leadership: A Study of the R.O.T.C.* (Princeton, NJ: Princeton University Press, 1959), 30; Neiberg, *Making Citizen-Soldiers*, 20–21.
[34] Kreidberg and Henry, *History of Military Mobilization*, 206–207; Elbridge Colby, "Military Training in Land Grant Colleges," *Georgetown Law Journal* 23, no. 1 (1934): 3–6; *The Oxford Companion to American Military History*, ed. John Whiteclay Chambers II, s. v. "ROTC," by John Whiteclay Chambers II, www-oxfordreference-com.libproxy1.nus.edu.sg/view/10.1093/acref/9780195071986.001.0001/acref-9780195071986-e-0796 (accessed September 1, 2023); Lyons and Masland, *Education and Military Leadership*, 31.

72   The Age of Youth

The early twentieth-century move toward military modernization brought the courses into the public spotlight. Military preparedness advocates came to see military training in land-grant colleges as a useful system of producing reserve officers and propagating the need for preparedness among the broader public. The War Department General Staff developed courses for officer training in colleges and universities and plans to establish junior units in military schools of the secondary level. Representatives of land-grant institutions also actively assisted the military in developing such courses.[35]

These moves led to the establishment, by the National Defense Act of 1916, of ROTC in civilian educational institutions, including the land-grant institutions that had provided military instruction under the Morrill Act.[36] Section 40 of the Act authorized the U.S. President to "establish and maintain in civilian institutions a Reserve Officers' Training Corps, which shall consist of a senior division organized at universities and colleges requiring four years of collegiate study for a degree" and a "junior division organized at all other public or private educational institutions," essentially schools below the college level. The Act authorized the Secretary of War to prescribe military training courses and the U.S. President to detail the number of officers and other military personnel for duty on campuses.[37] No ROTC unit was to be established until an Army officer was detailed to the institutions as a professor (or assistant professor) of military science and tactics and the institution maintained at least 100 "physically fit" male students under military instruction. The Secretary of War was also authorized to provide the institutions with funds, arms, equipment, and other materials necessary

---

[35] Lyons and Masland, *Education and Military Leadership*, 33–39; "Report and Recommendation of Civilian Committee Appointed to Study Junior R. O. T. C.," n.d. [December 1920], p.2, "Junior R. O. T. C. Conference FY 1921" folder, General Correspondence of the Advisory Board, 1919–1925, Operations and Training Division (G-3), Records of the War Department General and Special Staffs, RG 165, NACP; W. O. Thompson, "The Reserve Officers' Training Corps: Historical Statement," in *Proceedings of the Thirtieth Annual Convention of the Association of American Agricultural Colleges and Experiment Stations*, ed. J. L. Hills (Burlington, VT: Free Press, 1917), 143–44; Edward Orton Jr., "The Land-Grant Colleges and Their Part in the National Defense," *Proceedings of the Thirtieth Annual Convention*, ed. Hills, 163.

[36] A Navy ROTC program was established in 1926, but it remained comparatively a small program throughout this period. This chapter focuses on the Army program. Lyons and Masland, *Education and Military Leadership*, 51.

[37] *An Act for Making Further and More Effectual Provision for the National Defense, and Other Purposes*, Public Law 64-85 (hereafter cited as *National Defense Act of 1916*), *U.S. Statute at Large* 39 (1915–1916): 191; Colby, "Military Training in Land Grant Colleges," 7–8.

for the maintenance of ROTC units, and students with uniforms or uniform allowances.[38]

As mentioned earlier, ROTC in higher education institutions consisted of two courses. Students in the basic course devoted three hours per week to military training, during which they were taught rudimentary military tactics and theory. Students in the advanced course were required to devote five hours per week, during which they engaged in practical and technical training in leadership and command. Those who completed all four years of the program, attended a six-week training camp during the summer following their junior year, participated in further training after graduation as prescribed by the Secretary of War, and had reached age twenty-one were offered a chance to become a reserve officer of the U.S. Army.[39] In August 1918, ROTC was replaced by the Student Army Training Corps, which, as discussed in the previous chapter, established the role of educational institutions as military training sites during wartime. After the armistice, ROTC was reestablished at the request of the Committee on Education and Special Training (CEST) and with authorization by the National Defense Act of 1920.[40]

ROTC after World War I

The debates over military training of young men in peacetime, including ROTC, were halted during World War I, but after the war, Americans concerned with national defense resumed their discussion on the topic. Statistical data acquired from selective service during World War I provided the basis for calls for military training programs. Army data suggested that 46.8 percent of the men whose health was examined by the Selective Service System during the war had been deemed physically "defective." Moreover, many of those "defects" were deemed preventable or curable.[41] Additionally, according to the Army, approximately

---

[38] *National Defense Act of 1916*, 191–92.
[39] Ibid., 192–93; Ralph Chesney Bishop, *A Study of the Educational Value of Military Instruction in Universities and Colleges*, U.S. Office of Education Pamphlet No. 28 (Washington, DC: GPO, 1932), 1–2.
[40] CEST Advisory Board, *Committee on Education and Special Training*, 33, 143–44; Carl S. Gruber, *Mars and Minerva: World War I and the Uses of the Higher Learning in America* (Baton Rouge: Louisiana State University Press, 1975), 248–49; *An Act to Amend an Act Entitled "An Act for Making Further and More Effectual Provision for the National Defense, and for Other Purposes," Approved June 3, 1916, and to Establish Military Justice*, Public Law 66-242 (hereafter cited as *National Defense Act of 1920*), U.S. *Statutes at Large* 41 (1919–1921): 776–79.
[41] [Conference on Training,] *Special Report of the Secretary of War*, 11.

one-quarter of young draftees of World War I, half of whom were foreign-born, could not read or write simple English, and many draftees had "only the vaguest ideas of why this Nation was fighting."[42] Military training, its supporters contended, would be beneficial for both national defense and producing patriotic, educated citizens. Preparedness advocates thus emphasized its supposed educational value more than they had before the war.[43]

While preparedness advocates called for the establishment of expansive military–educational programs in peacetime run by or assisted by the military, the military leadership overall was not as enthusiastic about being involved in programs that did not directly contribute to strengthening the military. This was due, in part, to declining human and material resources from which they suffered after the war, but also to what they described as "a peculiar dilemma" that they faced – national security was under the purview of the federal government, but education was within the jurisdiction of local and state governments. Although the experience of World War I had raised military leaders' interest in the "mental, moral, and physical fitness" of American people, therefore, they expected that civilian educational institutions would address vocational training, citizenship, and other related subjects that were not directly military but which would help the military in the long run.[44]

As previously stated, the National Defense Act also established a "junior division" of ROTC in secondary schools. The minimum age for this program was fourteen, and the four-year training corresponded to the basic course of senior division units in higher education institutions.[45] However, after the war, public interest in military training at schools below the college level declined. Significantly, the number of secondary schools offering military training fell from its peak during the

---

[42] Ibid., 13.
[43] Chambers, *To Raise an Army*, 242–43; Newton D. Baker, "Universal Military Service of Immense Benefit to Youth of America and to National Interests," *Harvard Crimson*, April 2, 1920.
[44] [Conference on Training,] *Special Report of the Secretary of War*, 3, 6–7; C. R. Mann, "War Department's Conference on Training for Citizenship and National Defense," *Educational Record* (January 1923): 26, filed in "Report of the Conference" folder, Records of the Conference on Training the Youth of the Country for Citizenship and National Defense, October 1922–June 1923, Operations and Training Division (G-3), Records of the War Department General and Special Staffs, RG 165, NACP.
[45] "2,500 Juniors Enrolled in Local R.O.T.C.," *Indiana Daily Times* (Indianapolis, IN), April 4, 1921. The National Defense Act of 1916 had assumed that the establishment of junior ROTC units would be limited to private military academies, but after the war, the Act was interpreted more liberally to make public high schools eligible. "Report and Recommendation of Civilian Committee Appointed to Study Junior R. O. T. C.," pp. 2–3.

war, when it had increased fifteenfold from 82 in 1914 to 1,286 in 1918.[46] Supporters of military training in these schools argued that junior ROTC would assist the country in removing the alleged "personnel obstacles" to rapid mobilization displayed during World War I, such as a low level of physical fitness and technical skills among the country's youth, illiteracy, and a lack of a systematic classification of men according to ability.[47]

Contrary to their enthusiasm, junior ROTC was unlikely to significantly benefit the military because high-school students were typically too young for military service. With the limited funds and personnel that can be allotted to the ROTC programs, the military channeled their efforts into maximizing the efficiency of the ROTC units at the college level. Schools below the college level that wished to maintain military training units were thus encouraged to do so under Section 55c of the National Defense Act of 1920, which allowed local school cadet corps to apply to the federal government for minor assistance. The chief difference between this program and ROTC was that, in this program, participating schools still needed to rely primarily on the community for support, financial or otherwise.[48]

Consequently, military training in secondary schools was dealt with thereafter primarily as a local issue, unlike that in higher education institutions which attracted nationwide attention. In various localities,

---

[46] Charles F. Howlett and Ian M. Harris, *Books, Not Bombs: Teaching Peace Since the Dawn of the Republic* (Charlotte, NC: Information Age Publishing, 2010), 137; Edwin C. Johnson, "Main Issues in the Junior R. O. T. C. Controversy," *Harvard Educational Review* 9, no. 4 (1939): 470n13, a reprint filed in "Military in General Corres. 1936–40" folder, Box 68, NSGC Records.

[47] "The Problem of R.O.T.C. in Secondary Schools," a statement attached to C. R. Mann, memorandum to the Director, War Plans Division, April 1, 1920, "Director, War Plans Division" folder, Operations and Training Division (G-3), General Correspondence of the Advisory Board, 1919–1925, Records of the War Department General and Special Staffs, RG 165, NACP.

[48] *National Defense Act of 1920*, 776–77; Hansen, "A History of the Reserve Officers' Training Corps," n.p. (pp. 1, 7–8 of "Chapter VII – The Section 55C [National Defense Act] Schools" and pp. 22–25 of "Chapter VIII – Critique of Training Accomplished"), and "R.O.T.C. Conference Committee: Question No. 1," November 16, 1922, pp. 3–4, both in "Report of the Conference" folder, Records of the Conference on Training the Youth of the Country for Citizenship and National Defense, October 1922–June 1923, Operations and Training Division (G-3), Records of the War Department General and Special Staffs, RG 165, NACP. That twelve-year-old Paul Brinkman, whom we met at the beginning of this chapter, was forced to take ROTC training is possibly another example of the federal government's lack of interest in ROTC in secondary schools and consequent lack of federal direction to schools that maintained a unit. Although the Augusta school compelled him to take it, the National Defense Act stated that only boys fourteen years old or older were eligible for the training. *National Defense Act of 1916*, 192; *National Defense Act of 1920*, 780.

supporters of military training of boys continued to promote their cause, through such moves as holding annual drilling competitions by high-school cadet corps, many of which dated back to the late nineteenth and early twentieth-century movement to make American boys healthy and manly, and trying to establish new military training units in local schools. These attempts met with considerable opposition from such people as parents, teachers' unions, pacifists, and others who protested them as militarism and regimentation of students.[49] The fact that debates over military training in schools below the college level remained largely a local issue affected students who resisted the training in various ways, as will be discussed later in this chapter.

Meanwhile, ROTC in higher education institutions diverged paths from its secondary school counterpart. By this time, higher education had undergone a significant transformation from its original purpose of educating upper-class men in the liberal arts and piety. The establishment of land-grant institutions had signaled one such change, but students were still largely from the upper class and upper middle class. As discussed in Chapter 1, it was during World War I that higher education institutions enthusiastically promoted their social value to the public, spreading the idea that college education was useful for vocational and practical training and economic advancement, and that it was beneficial not only to elite youth but also to other Americans. The decline of apprenticeships and other informal on-the-job training traditions went hand in hand with the growth of the college. In 1922, a college professor wrote for the *New Republic* that "The old jibe of futility no longer holds against our colleges; their training pays in cash and power, and their influence is compounding at usurious rates."[50] Another academic noted that "the time is past when a youth is initiated into business by sweeping out the office."[51]

---

[49] "Intermediate School Cadets Hold Their Competitive Drill," *Boston Daily Globe*, May 18, 1928; "Central High Cadets Win Regimental Drill," *Washington Post* (hereafter cited as *WP*), May 1, 1928; Andrea P. Sckoppeglia, "School Cadet Drill Will Be Tomorrow," *WP*, June 5, 1932; "City High Schools to Hold R. O. T. C. Exercises Today," *Atlanta Constitution*, May 2, 1928; "Oppose Military Training," *NYT*, December 28, 1928; "United Parents Vote against School Drill," *NYT*, February 12, 1929; "Board Halts Action on Military Drill," *NYT*, February 15, 1930; "School Army Drill Stirs Bitter Debate," *NYT*, February 27, 1930; "Dr. O'Shea Defends Military Course," *NYT*, March 31, 1930; "Military Drill Ended in Brooklyn School," *NYT* April 9, 1930; "School Drill Unit Approved by Board," *NYT*, January 15, 1931; "High School R.O.T.C. Fought," *NYT* February 3, 1936; "Military Training Upheld in Schools," *NYT*, October 6, 1936.

[50] Quoted in David O. Levine, *The American College and the Culture of Aspiration, 1915–1940* (Ithaca, NY: Cornell University Press, 1986), 24.

[51] Quoted in ibid., 48.

In the years between the two world wars, enrollment in higher education surged from 250,000 to 1.3 million, raising the percentage of Americans between the ages of eighteen and twenty who attended college from less than 5 percent in 1917 to 15 percent twenty years later.[52] As military training in secondary schools was cut off from federal support, and as more and more young people wished to pursue a college education, ROTC at higher education institutions became the focus of the nationwide debates over military training in educational institutions.

The central issue in these debates was whether training should be compulsory for all male students. At some institutions, it was entirely optional, while at others, it was made compulsory for two years by university regulation, charter provisions, or state legislation. The exception was land-grant institutions, which had long assumed that the 1862 Morrill Act had made military training compulsory at their institutions. The War Department appears to have thought so as well. After the passage of the National Defense Act of 1916, for example, the land-grant college of Connecticut applied to the War Department for an ROTC unit with a two-year elective course only; the War Department replied that the two years of military training at land-grant institutions had to be compulsory.[53]

However, this assumption was shaken in 1923 when the Wisconsin State Legislature ordered that military training for first- and second-year students at the University of Wisconsin, a land-grant institution, be made voluntary. The U.S. Department of the Interior, which determined whether each state was entitled to receive federal funds for land-grant institutions, decided that Wisconsin did not lose those benefits by making military instruction optional.[54]

The news seems to have spurred movements by students, pacifists, and others to speak out against military training, provoking heated debates on college campuses over whether ROTC should be elective or compulsory. To a large degree, these debates pitted institutional authorities, including chancellors and presidents, against students, with faculty members largely on the former's side but wavering between the two camps.

---

[52] Thelin, *A History of American Higher Education*, 205.
[53] Colby, "Military Training in Land Grant Colleges," 3, 7–8; Hill, *Proceedings of the Thirtieth Annual Convention*, 150; Gene M. Lyons and John W. Masland, "The Origins of the ROTC," *Military Affairs* 23, no. 1 (1959): 10; Lyons and Masland, *Education and Military Leadership*, 38, 45.
[54] "For Optional Military Training," *NYT*, May 25, 1923; "Military Drill Issue Stirs Many Colleges," *NYT*, May 2, 1937; James H. Hawkes, "Antimilitarism at State Universities: The Campaign against Compulsory ROTC, 1920–1940," *Wisconsin Magazine of History* 49, no. 1 (1965): 41–42; Colby, "Military Training in Land Grant Colleges," 12.

At the City College of New York, for example, 2,000 students voted against compulsory drill in 1925, while 300 voted in favor of it. However, the college president despised the students' movement, claiming that they were merely trying to escape military training because of its heavy load and that students were simply being instigated by the movement's student leader, whom the president said contemptuously was "popular" among students and had "handled his case well."[55] The faculty seemed to have wavered between the two positions. At first, it voted overwhelmingly in favor of continued compulsory military training for first- and second-year students, but in a surprising turn, it announced the following year, under a new acting president, that students could now take a course in "civilian drill" directed by the college's Hygiene Department as an alternative to the compulsory military training course.[56] In 1926, at Ohio State University, a faculty committee investigating the merits of compulsory and optional military training concluded that the former was preferable, while a student referendum indicated a slight majority for the latter.[57] At Cornell University, a petition signed by 1,796 male students against compulsory military training was rejected by the faculty.[58] Others, such as conservative politicians, veterans' associations, and patriotic groups, pushed for military training while liberal intellectuals, religious and labor union leaders, and pacifists were against it.[59]

A conspicuous absence in these debates was historically Black colleges and universities (HBCUs). In 1925, the *New York Times* reported that at Howard University, one of the few HBCUs that maintained a military training unit, 400 students went on strike against compulsory military training.[60] However, such an appearance of Black Americans on this issue in major media outlets was rare. Rarely did white Americans, who led the debate, mention HBCUs. They often stated that *all* land-grant institutions before the 1923 University of Wisconsin decision maintained

---

[55] Savel Zimand, "Military Training in Schools Is Again Debated," *NYT*, November 29, 1925.

[56] "Student Military Training," editorial, *NYT*, December 12, 1925; "'Civilian Drill' at City College," *NYT*, September 24, 1926. Students at City College continued their fight against military training by requesting that the college either make it wholly optional (meaning that no alternative should be required) or eliminate it entirely from the curriculum. "Want City College to Revise Courses," *NYT*, May 8, 1929; "Drill at City College Starts 'Circular War,'" *NYT*, December 17, 1930.

[57] "Ohio Faculty for Drill," *NYT*, May 14, 1926.

[58] "Cornell Rejects Protest on Drills," *NYT*, February 13, 1927.

[59] The debates over military training in secondary schools revealed a similar pattern of groups for and against military training. Johnson, "Main Issues in the Junior R. O. T. C. Controversy," 470–71.

[60] "Howard Students Strike," *NYT*, May 8, 1925.

compulsory military training.⁶¹ However, although the government in this period seems to have not kept a record of the number of ROTC units in HBCUs, sources indicate that most – or even all – Black land-grant institutions did not have ROTC units. War Department data from August 1935, for example, suggests that of seventeen Black land-grant institutions that existed then, none had an ROTC unit. In fact, according to the data, only two HBCUs in the entire country (Howard and Wilberforce) had ROTC units at the time.⁶²

The invisibility of HBCUs in this issue resulted from the systematic discrimination against Black people in both education and the military, as well as American society more broadly. Consider, for instance, the impact that economic and social injustice and inequality in the Jim Crow South had on Black youth's access to postsecondary education in the region. As of 1939, Washington, D.C. and seventeen Southern states, a region where 81 percent of all Black people in the country lived, legally mandated complete segregation of educational institutions. During the 1933–1934 school year, in these seventeen states, which were falling behind the rest of the country in higher education enrollment rates, 6 percent of white youth aged eighteen to twenty-one were enrolled in public higher education institutions, compared to only 1.2 percent of Black youth of the same age range.⁶³

With the passage of the 1862 Land Grant Act, four Southern states set aside funds for the establishment of separate institutions for Black students. In 1871, Mississippi's Alcorn University became the first of these

---

⁶¹ John M. Thomas, "'And Including Military Tactics,'" in *Proceedings of the Forty-Third Annual Convention of the Association of Land-Grant Colleges and Universities*, ed. Charles A. McCue (Burlington, VT: Free Press, [1930]), 426; "Report of Committee on Military Organization and Policy," in *Proceedings of the Association of Land-Grant Colleges and Universities, Fifty-Second Annual Convention*, ed. William L. Slate (New Haven, CT: Quinnipiack Press, [1939]), 271.

⁶² *Congressional Record*, March 18, 1936, pp. 3930–31. See also Chart 2.1. It is difficult to determine how many Black land-grant colleges had ROTC units. According to one source, as of April 1, 1919, seven Black land-grant institutions were selected for ROTC training (although it is unclear if it was made compulsory at these schools). However, a U.S. Army study of Black troops published after World War II indicates that outside of Howard and Wilberforce, Black students were rare in ROTC units during the interwar years. These and other sources on ROTC in HBCUs collectively indicate that there was likely never a time during this period when *all* Black land-grant institutions had an ROTC unit, which suggests that white Americans engaged in the debates over mandatory ROTC training largely ignored HBCUs. Emmett J. Scott, *Scott's Official History of the American Negro in the World War* ([United States]: [publisher unidentified], 1919), 341–42; Ulysses Lee, *The Employment of Negro Troops* (Washington, DC: GPO, 2001 [1963]), 29–30.

⁶³ Doxey A. Wilkerson, *Special Problems of Negro Education*, Staff Study No. 12, prepared for the Advisory Committee on Education (Washington, DC: GPO, 1939), xv, 63.

institutions. The Second Morrill Act of 1890 established land-grant institutions for Black Americans in the rest of the segregated South – while the 1862 Morrill Act did not address racism in higher education, this second Act specifically required "a just and equitable" distribution of federal funds received by the Act between Black and white land-grant colleges in the Jim Crow states.[64] However, these colleges were severely underfunded, their facilities and curriculum were greatly limited in comparison to their white counterparts, and their sites were unevenly spread. There were more than a dozen permanent funds through which land-grant institutions received federal support, but only funds from the 1890 Morrill Act and its extensions were allocated proportionally to the Black population. As a result, in the years between the two world wars, only 5 percent of all federal funding for land-grant institutions in the South went to Black land-grant colleges, although Black Americans made up one-quarter of the region's college-age population. Furthermore, due to the limited public education below the college level accessible to Black Americans in these states, these colleges had to provide subcollegiate education to prepare students for college, and the enrollment of high-school and elementary students in these colleges often outnumbered the enrollment of college-level students.[65]

The same could be said of secondary education. Although no data has been found on the number of Black Americans who went through military training in secondary schools, it is likely the number was very small. Secondary-school enrollment for white youth experienced a rapid increase from the 1880s through the 1930s, making secondary schools a near-universal institution sometimes referred to as the "people's college."[66] However, for Black people, especially those in the South, secondary education was not as accessible. In 1930, 46.6 percent of the country's children of high-school age (defined here as ages fourteen to seventeen) were enrolled in public secondary schools, and by 1934, the

[64] Klein, *Survey of Land-Grant Colleges and Universities*, vol. 2, 838–41; J. F. Drake, "The Negro Land Grant College and Public Education," in Conference of the Presidents of Negro Land Grant Colleges, *Proceedings of the Fourteenth Annual Conference of the Presidents of Negro Land Grant Colleges, November 10–11, 1936* (publisher unidentified, n.d.), 10.
[65] Wilkerson, *Special Problems of Negro Education*, 72–86; Klein, *Survey of Land-Grant Colleges and Universities*, vol. 2, 880–83.
[66] James D. Anderson, *The Education of Blacks in the South, 1860–1935* (Chapel Hill: University of North Carolina Press, 1988), 187. On the popularization of high schools in this period, see Reed Ueda, *Avenues to Adulthood: The Origins of the High School and Social Mobility in an American Suburb* (New York: Cambridge University Press, 1987); Edward A. Krug, *The Shaping of the American High School, Volume 2, 1920–1941* (Madison: University of Wisconsin Press, 1972).

proportion had increased to 60 percent, or 64 percent adding private high-school enrollments. However, in the same year, only 19 percent of Southern Black children of high-school age were enrolled in public high schools.[67]

In addition, the racial segregation and discrimination in the U.S. military, in which Black Americans were forced to serve in separate units, confirmed that only white men were qualified to serve as officers and were therefore eligible for ROTC. Even segregated Black soldiers were led by white officers. Prior to 1940, only four Black Americans graduated from West Point.[68]

The nationwide debates over ROTC in the years after World War I, therefore, largely proceeded as those concerning the link between white men's access to education and national security. A leading voice in the campaign against military training in educational institutions was the Committee on Militarism in Education (CME), established in New York City in 1925, which aimed to eliminate compulsory military training from civilian higher education institutions and all military training from secondary schools through legislative and public relations means. Educators, religious leaders, journalists, and others who were sympathetic to the cause supported the committee. Prominent public figures like reformer Jane Addams, philosopher John Dewey, and Nebraska Senator George W. Norris were among them. Its officers included Episcopalian priest and peace activist John Nevin Sayre, journalist Oswald G. Villard, and George A. Coe, a religious education professor at Teachers' College, Columbia University.[69] The CME even sought supporters internationally. A manifesto the committee issued in 1930 calling for the abolishment of conscription and military training of youth from the entire world listed internationally renowned signers such as Albert Einstein, Sigmund Freud, Thomas Mann, Bertrand Russell, Rabindranath Tagore, and H.G. Wells.[70] The adults who ran or supported these campaigns against military training in educational

---

[67] Wilkerson, *Special Problems of Negro Education*, 35–37; Grayson N. Kefauver, et al., *The Secondary School Population*, U.S. Office of Education, Bulletin, 1932, No. 17, National Survey of Secondary Education, Monograph No. 4 (Washington, DC: GPO, 1933), 4; Anderson, *The Education of Blacks in the South*, 193.

[68] Lee, *Employment of Negro Troops*, 29n26.

[69] "Move to Abolish Military Training," *NYT*, December 7, 1925; Edwin C. Johnson, "1939 Report of Committee on Militarism in Education," n.d., p. 1, "Military in General Corres. 1936–40" folder, Box 68, NSGC Records; Hawkes, "Antimilitarism at State Universities," 42; Howlett and Harris, *Books, Not Bombs*, 135–37; Winthrop D. Lane, *Military Training in Schools and Colleges of the United States: The Facts and Interpretation* (New York: Committee on Military Training, n.d.), 3–4.

[70] "Urge World to End Military Training," *NYT*, October 12, 1930.

institutions were united by the conviction that having military training in educational institutions was incongruous with the nature of education.

Counteracting these groups were individuals who firmly believed that military training had an important place in higher education in the United States. The War Department, however, was not a major player here. In response to the establishment of the CME and the growing movement against ROTC, the War Department did make clear that it "stands squarely in favor of military training for the greatest possible number of students."[71] However, it refrained from directly combating its opponents. Instead, it counteracted them primarily through its civilian allies, such as legislators, civilian offices of the federal government, patriotic groups, and educators. Among them was Republican legislator James Wadsworth Jr. of New York (Senator, 1915–1927, Representative, 1933–1951), who was a long-time UMT advocate, the chairman of the Senate Military Affairs Committee in the 1920s, and who would go on to sponsor the 1940 Selective Training and Service Act (Chapter 4). The Veterans of Foreign Wars, the Daughters of the American Revolution, the American Legion, and other patriotic organizations were the military's allies as well.[72]

Another strong supporter of military training was the Association of Land-Grant Colleges and Universities (ALGCU).[73] Founded in 1887 to serve colleges established under the 1862 Morrill Act and the 1887 Hatch Act (which provided for the creation of agricultural experiment stations for scientific research), the ALGCU worked ardently for the promotion of military training on college campuses. As early as 1913, it went on record insisting on a larger use of land-grant colleges by the federal government for military instruction.[74] The association represented the land-grant colleges' faithful endeavors to fulfill their obligations to the federal government in return for the support they received and their preference to maintain military education as a required

---

[71] "Move to Abolish Military Training."
[72] Ronald Schaffer, "War Department's Defense of ROTC, 1920–1940," *Wisconsin Magazine of History* 53, no. 2 (1969–1970): 111–14; "Wadsworth James Wolcott Jr. (1877–1952)," *Biographical Directory of the United States Congress, 1774–Present*, https://bioguideretro.congress.gov/Home/MemberDetails?memIndex=W000012 (accessed December 23, 2023).
[73] Since its founding in 1887, the association has altered its name several times. To avoid confusion, this chapter consistently employs the name Association of Land-Grant Colleges and Universities (ALGCU). The Black land-grant institutions joined the ALGCU in 1954. Association of Public and Land-Grant Universities, "History of APLU," www.aplu.org/about-us/history-of-aplu/ (accessed December 23, 2023).
[74] Thompson, "The Reserve Officers' Training Corps," 143–44.

course.⁷⁵ When Wisconsin made ROTC voluntary in 1923, the ALGCU's Committee on Military Organization and Policy harshly criticized the move, stating that it "deplore[s] any tendency of our time to weaken our traditional sense of obligation or to impair our spirit of patriotic service."⁷⁶ The association would remain an ardent promoter and defender of mandatory ROTC.

The debates over mandatory ROTC requirements in the 1920s highlighted a significant division in opinion about the relationship between military training and higher education. A popular argument for ROTC was that under federal law, military training was, in fact, optional – schools could decide whether they should give military instruction and students could decide what school to attend. The opponents of ROTC, on the other hand, argued that attending a public institution such as a land-grant college with mandatory ROTC tended to be more affordable than enrolling at a private institution that did not maintain a military course. As long as military training was made compulsory in public institutions, these people argued, a male student without financial means would be forced to go through the training while the son of a rich family could escape it.⁷⁷

A related argument in favor of compulsory ROTC held that it was as compulsory as any other academic subject or civic duty. When, as the CME's first major legislative action, a bill prohibiting any course of military training from being made compulsory in schools and colleges was introduced to Congress in 1926, Republican Representative John Philip Hill of Maryland asked the bill's supporters whether it would be a mistake to urge his six-year-old daughter to learn to read if she strongly objected.⁷⁸ Similarly, an ALGCU representative argued that there were "practically no electives in the first two years in any standard college or university in the United States," requiring all students to take basic courses in mathematics, physics, history, and other major subjects, and therefore, military training stood "exactly on par" with those subjects.⁷⁹ To a *New York Times* subscriber, military training was "just as much a civic duty as the payment of taxes," while another reader of the newspaper maintained that "there are moral advantages in a command,

---

⁷⁵ Klein, *Survey of Land-Grant Colleges and Universities*, vol. 2, 306.
⁷⁶ W. H. Heal, ed., *Proceedings of the Thirty-Eight Annual Convention of the Association of Land-Grant Colleges* (Burlington, VT: Free Press, 1925), 437.
⁷⁷ U.S. Congress, House, Committee on Military Affairs, *Abolishment of Compulsory Military Training at Schools and Colleges: Hearings before the Committee on H.R. 8538*, 69th Cong., 1st sess. (Washington, DC: GPO, 1926), 12, 193–94.
⁷⁸ Ibid., 11. ⁷⁹ Ibid., 155.

whether to compulsory drill or compulsory dish-washing. 'You may not like it, but do it you must.'"[80]

Additionally, ROTC supporters, like UMT advocates, emphasized its educational value. For example, the University of Illinois president stressed that "No other subject of study in the curriculum trains a boy so well to carry himself as a man among men, to handle men as a leader, to have a sense of responsibility for those he is working with." He added: "in an unusual degree this training teaches good order, cleanliness of body and mind, integrity and truthfulness." In short, he maintained, military training was more than simply "carrying the gun or mere physical training."[81]

Some supporters of mandatory ROTC argued that the choice of whether to take military training should not be left to students as they were too immature to make the "right" decision. This reflects an idea widespread at that time that colleges should act *in loco parentis* to supervise minors.[82] Ironically, then, while ROTC supporters contended that the program was "optional" since students could choose which school to attend, they also assumed that students were not mature enough to recognize the value of military training and would naturally want to escape it. Seen from such a perspective of youthful immaturity, ROTC was a "character builder." The *Chicago Daily Tribune* reported how, in just a month of military drilling, freshmen began to "appear better, to handle themselves better, to wear their clothes better, and to take better care of their clothes." According to this article, at the beginning of the semester, a freshman looking for a military training instructor would ask, "Say, where'll I find Nevins?" but after three weeks of military training, he would learn to reshape the question: "Can you direct me, sir, to Capt. Nevins?"[83]

Finally, the experience of World War I inspired ROTC supporters to advance their arguments on the grounds of military preparedness. In this context, ROTC was needed so that "we would not sacrifice men through

---

[80] Robert S. Allyn, "Defenses Still Necessary," letter to the editor, *NYT*, April 29, 1926; William Stearns Davis, "Objections to Drill," letter to the editor, *NYT*, December 27, 1925.

[81] Quoted in House Committee on Military Affairs, *Abolishment of Compulsory Military Training*, 178.

[82] Ibid., 247; Scott M. Gelber, *Courtrooms and Classrooms: A Legal History of College Access, 1860–1960* (Baltimore: Johns Hopkins University Press, 2015), 1; Christopher P. Loss, *Between Citizens and the State: The Politics of American Higher Education in the 20th Century* (Princeton, NJ: Princeton University Press, 2012), 34–38.

[83] James O'Donnell Bennett, "College Youths Made Fit by Military Drill," *Chicago Daily Tribune* (hereafter cited as *CDT*), October 26, 1925.

ignorance, as we have in the past."[84] The ALGCU argued that land-grant colleges were "the most economic means" of supplying reserve officers with the least possible disturbance to the industries.[85] Labeling the protests against military training as "agitation," it insisted that it was "ridiculous" to assert that ROTC bred militarism or "Prussianized" the United States.[86]

By the late 1920s, the basic arguments for the maintenance of ROTC units were well laid out: ROTC was not meant to be imposed upon youth, as youth could choose to attend an institution with military training, it was good for youthful discipline and education, and it was useful for military preparedness. While people opposed to ROTC struggled to refute such claims and persuade the public that military training did not belong to American campuses, ROTC graduates began to replace elder men, including many World War I veterans, in organized reserve units. By the early 1930s, approximately half of the officers in reserve divisions were men commissioned from colleges.[87]

Military Training and Access to Higher Education in the 1930s

The uncertainty over whether land-grant institutions should require military training for male students persisted into the 1930s. In 1930, in response to the U.S. Secretary of the Interior's question of whether these institutions should make military training compulsory, Attorney General William D. Mitchell concluded that the federal statutes did not specifically require it to be compulsory. Yet most of these institutions continued to operate it on a mandatory basis. Some institutions even expelled or suspended students who refused to undergo military training.[88] As a result, in the 1930s, the tension between students' access to public higher education and mandatory military training became central to the debates over ROTC. A related question was whether military training in colleges could be considered a national defense policy, and thus under federal

[84] Robert S. Allyn, letter to the editor, *NYT*, April 29, 1926.
[85] An ALGCU committee report reprinted in House Committee on Military Affairs, *Abolishment of Compulsory Military Training*, 153–54.
[86] "Report of the Committee on Military Organization and Policy," in *Proceedings of the Fortieth Annual Convention of the Association of Land-Grant Colleges and Universities*, ed. S. B. Haskell (Northampton, MA: Metcalp, 1927), 400–401.
[87] Colby, "Military Training in Land Grant Colleges," 7.
[88] In 1933 (or, June 1934, according to some sources), the University of Minnesota made military training elective. Ibid., 12–14; "Military Drill Held Optional by Mitchell," *NYT*, June 26, 1930; Edwin C. Johnson, letter to the editor, *NYT*, April 14, 1935; "Ohio State Suspends Student Objectors," *NYT*, January 12, 1934.

jurisdiction, or an educational policy, and therefore the realm of state and local governments. This second question reflected a broader political debate of the time when American society faced the drastic expansion of the federal government under President Franklin D. Roosevelt's New Deal programs.

How mandatory military training increasingly became an issue concerning access to *public* education can be observed from statistics regarding the increase in the number of higher education institutions in the 1920s and the 1930s, as well as the number of institutions with ROTC units. In 1921, 124 higher education institutions had an ROTC unit, out of a total of 1,162 higher education institutions.[89] By comparison, in 1938, out of the 1,690 institutions of higher education in the country, 137 institutions had a ROTC unit.[90] While the number of higher education institutions grew by 45 percent during this period, therefore, the number of those with ROTC units only grew by 10 percent.

Although higher education expanded in the 1920s and the 1930s, these statistics suggest that ROTC training remained concentrated in land-grant institutions, as most of the newly established institutions did not adopt ROTC. The concentration of mandatory military training at land-grant institutions is illustrated in Chart 2.1. The impact of this concentration on young men wishing to pursue higher education was significant, as land-grant institutions tended to have a larger student population than other institutions. According to a three-year survey (1927–1930) conducted by the U.S. Office of Education at the request of the Association of Land-Grant Colleges and Universities, there were sixty-nine land-grant institutions in the country. There was one per state (except for Massachusetts, which split the Morrill funds for two institutions), one each in Alaska, Hawaii, and Puerto Rico, and a separate

---

[89] The number of higher education institutions in the country is derived from data collected by the U.S. Department of Education. However, according to a report from a 1922 conference between the War Department and educational institutions on national security, the number was approximately 670 that year. [Conference on Training,] *Special Report of the Secretary of War*, 17; Thomas D. Snyder, *120 Years of American Education: A Statistical Portrait* (Washington, DC: U.S. Department of Education, Office of Educational Research and Improvement, 1993), 80. See also Lyons and Masland, *Education and Military Leadership*, 42. According to another War Department document from 1922, the number was 526. "R.O.T.C. Conference Committee: Question No. 1," November 16, 1922, p. 1, "Report of the Conference" folder, Records of the Conference on Training the Youth of the Country for Citizenship and National Defense, October 1922–June 1923, Operations and Training Division (G-3), Records of the War Department General and Special Staffs, RG 165, NACP.

[90] Snyder, *120 Years of American Education*, 80; Hansen, "A History of the Reserve Officers' Training Corps," n.p. (p. 7 of "Chapter III – Training Program: Administration").

University of California, Berkeley	Creighton University	University of Arkansas	Cornell University	Norwich University
University of California at Los Angeles		Clemson Agricultural College	Drexel Institute	Pennsylvania Military College
Colorado State College of Agriculture and Mechanic Arts	University of Dayton	University of Delaware	Lehigh College	University of Puerto Rico
Colorado School of Mines	University of Illinois	University of Florida	University of Maine	Virginia Military Institute
University of Idaho	Indiana University	Georgia School of Technology	Massachusetts State College	
Montana State College of Agriculture and Mechanic Arts	Iowa State College of Agriculture and Mechanic Arts	State University of Iowa	Massachusetts Institute of Technology	
University of Montana		Howard University (HBCU)	University of New Hampshire	
University of Nevada	Kansas State College of Agriculture and Applied Science	University of Georgia	New York University	
New Mexico College of Agriculture and Mechanic Arts	Missouri School of Mines	University of Kentucky	Pennsylvania State College	
North Pacific College of Oregon, School of Dentistry	University of Missouri	Louisiana State University	Rhode Island State College	
Oregon State College	University of Nebraska	University of Maryland	Rutgers University	
University of Oregon	North Dakota Agricultural College	Mississippi State College	University of Vermont and State Agricultural College	
Utah State Agricultural College	University of North Dakota	North Carolina State College of Agriculture and Engineering		
Washington State College	Ohio State University	North Georgia College		**Historically-Black land-grant institutions without ROTC**
University of Washington	Purdue University	Oklahoma Agricultural and Mechanical College		(A.) State Agricultural and Mechanical Institute for Negroes
University of Wyoming	Ripon College	University of Oklahoma		Arkansas Agricultural, Mechanical & Normal College
	St. Louis University School of Medicine	Ouachita College		(OD) State College for Colored Students
	South Dakota State College of Agriculture and Mechanic Arts	Presbyterian College		Florida Agricultural and Mechanical College for Negroes
	University of South Dakota	University of Tennessee		Georgia State College
	Wilberforce University (HBCU)	Texas College of Agriculture and Mechanic Arts		Kentucky State Industrial College for Colored Persons
		Virginia Agricultural and Mechanical College and Polytechnic Institute		Southern University
		Western Maryland College		Princess Anne Academy
		West Virginia University		Mississippi State College
				Lincoln University
				Negro Agricultural and Technical College of North Carolina
		Davidson College	Boston University	(OK) Colored Agricultural and Normal University
Elective	Pomona College	Johns Hopkins University	University of Buffalo	Colored Normal Industrial Agricultural and Mechanical College of South Carolina
	Stanford University	Medical College of Virginia	Carnegie Institute of Technology	Tennessee Agricultural & Industrial State College
	University of Utah	Western Kentucky State Teachers College	College of City of New York (mandatory until 1929)	Prairie View Normal and Industrial College
		Knox College	Fordham University	Virginia State College for Negroes
		Michigan College of Mining and Technology	Georgetown University	West Virginia State College
		Michigan State College of Agriculture and Applied Science (see footnote)	George Washington University Medical School	
		University of Michigan	Gettysburg College	
		University of Minnesota (mandatory until 1933)	Harvard University	
		Northwestern University Dental School	Lafayette College	
		Rose Polytechnic Institute	University of Pennsylvania	
		Municipal University of Wichita	University of Pittsburgh	
		University of Wisconsin (mandatory until 1923)	Princeton University	
			Syracuse University	
			Yale University	

Chart 2.1 A list of ROTC institutions by region as of 1935 (land-grant institutions are in bold). Chart created by author.

Source: "Higher Educational Institutions Having Courses in Military Training," a list provided by the War Department printed in the *Congressional Record* at the request of Senator Lynn Joseph Frazier (ND), speaking on H.R. 11035, March 18, 1936, 74th Cong, 2nd sess., *Congressional Record* 80, pt. 4: 3930–31; "Land-Grant Colleges and Universities Map," https://nifa.usda.gov/resource/land-grant-colleges-and-universities-map (accessed October 10, 2020); Conference of the Presidents of Negro Land Grant Colleges, *Proceedings of the Fourteenth Annual Conference of the Presidents of Negro Land Grant Colleges*, November 10–11, 1936 (publisher unidentified, n.d.), 1.

It is unclear when – or, if – military training at Michigan State College of Agriculture and Applied Science became optional. In this chart, I have classified the college as one of the few land-grant universities that offered military training as an elective course, using data from a War Department list of institutions with military training units presented to Congress in 1936. According to other sources, however, the only land-grant institutions that had made military training voluntary by the late 1930s were the universities of Wisconsin and Minnesota and North Dakota Agricultural College (which made the training voluntary in 1937). For different line-ups of land-grant colleges that made military training elective, see Lyons and Masland, *Education and Military Leadership*, 47n23; Associated Students of the University of California Peace Committee, "Survey of Compulsory R. O. T. C., Summary of Report," p. 1, n.d. [1939], attached to Edwin C. Johnson to friend [Richard Welling], February 27, 1940, "Military in General Corres. 1936–40" folder, Box 68, NSGC Records; "Military Drill Issue Stirs Many Colleges."

institution for African Americans in each of the seventeen states in the segregated South.[91] These institutions enrolled a total of 296,276 students, of which 104,992 were women. This suggests that while the number of land-grant institutions was only 5 percent of the total number of higher education institutions in the country (1,409), they enrolled more than a quarter of all higher education students (1,101,000, with 620,000 men and 481,000 women).[92]

The relationship between access to public education and military training, as well as whether ROTC was a national defense or educational program, was highlighted in the early 1930s, when student conscientious objectors, supported by the CME, challenged the compulsory ROTC requirement in court. In December 1934, the U.S. Supreme Court affirmed the decision of the University of California, a public land-grant university, to suspend two Methodist students who refused to participate in military training on religious and conscientious grounds. The appellants presented their case on multiple grounds. First, they underlined that they were denied access to *public* education and couldn't afford other universities in the state. Second, they argued that since the War Department provided the study programs, uniforms, and other equipment for ROTC and because ROTC trained students to become reserve officers in the U.S. Army, it should be treated as a federal issue, not a state one; after all, ROTC was "a part of the military forces of the United States," not "part of the military establishment of the State [of California]." As such, they contended that mandatory military training violated "the privileges and immunities of appellants as citizens of the United States, in violation of the Fourteenth Amendment" to the U.S. Constitution, and deprived religious and conscientious objectors of the "liberty" guaranteed by the same amendment's due process clause.[93] Thus, the appellants defined ROTC as a military program under federal jurisdiction and maintained that the university's suspension of the students was a violation of their constitutional rights.

The court acknowledged that the appeal could not be dismissed for lack of a substantial federal question, but it placed ROTC in a hazy, confusing position in which it could not be readily identified as either a

---

[91] Klein, "The Rise of the Land-Grant Colleges and Universities," 83. According to this study, three land-grant institutions were classified as military colleges (degree-granting institutions "in which students are habitually in uniform and constantly under military discipline") by the War Department. The rest of the institutions were classified as "not essentially military." Klein, *Survey of Land-Grant Colleges and Universities*, vol. 2, 303.

[92] Klein, "The Rise of the Land-Grant Colleges and Universities," 83; Snyder, *120 Years of American Education*, 76, 80; Loss, *Between Citizens and the State*, 57.

[93] *Hamilton et al v. Regents of the University of California et al*, 293 U.S. 245 (1934).

federal (thus military) or state (thus educational) program. It stated that the involvement of the War Department in the program did not imply that the Department was exclusively in charge of it. Rather, military instruction in land-grant institutions was founded on "the long-established voluntary cooperation between federal and state authorities," and "every State has authority to train its able-bodied male citizens of suitable age appropriately to develop fitness" to serve in the U.S. Army and state militia, making the state "the sole judge" of the means and content of the training to be exacted. Furthermore, regarding the appellants' claim that the "privileges and immunities" guaranteed by the Fourteenth Amendment were infringed, the court ruled that the "privilege" of attending a state university did not fall under the protection of the amendment because it was not granted by the federal government but by the state. The fact that the students could not afford to attend any other university in the state was therefore deemed irrelevant. The "liberty" was also deemed uninfringed because "California has not drafted or called them to attend the university," and the "liberty" did not confer the "right to be students in the state university free from obligation to take military training as one of the conditions of attendance."[94] Overall, the court upheld the university's decision without specifying whether ROTC was an educational or a national defense program.[95]

This case illuminates the uneasy relationship between access to public higher education and youth's obligations in national security, as well as how ROTC stood at the intersection of military preparedness and education, a vague, murky position that allowed for multiple interpretations of whether ROTC was a national defense program or an educational one. The ROTC supporters, when supporting the program on the grounds of its alleged educational values, argued that their opponents' strategy of asking the federal government to interfere in ROTC issues was incongruent with the principle of the state and local control of education.[96] To counter such an argument, the opponents of ROTC argued that it was ROTC, which they considered to be a national defense measure under the jurisdiction of the federal government, that infringed on the

---

[94] Ibid.; "Compulsory Drill in Colleges Upheld," *NYT*, December 4, 1934.
[95] The court's ruling followed the general pattern of college access litigation in this period, which favored colleges over students. The rising view among judges that college governance should be left to college administrators who specialized in the "highly technical" area of higher education led to this deference. Gelber, *Courtrooms and Classrooms*, 27–30.
[96] Senate Subcommittee of the Committee on Military Affairs, *Compulsory Military Training*, 6, 254.

states' right to control education.[97] They also countered ROTC supporters' claim that ROTC had educational value by arguing that military training was not pedagogically sound. A representative of the Progressive Education Association argued that if "we want obedience without question, the blind following of orders, the concept of organization that is predetermined," then military training would certainly give it. However, "If we want intelligent and resourceful leadership," other types of training would be more useful.[98] A professor at Teachers College, Columbia University, argued that all the benefits ROTC claimed it bestowed on youth – technical skills, team playing, "vitality and vigorous manhood" and the like – could be just as easily acquired through a good physical education program.[99]

Student activism against mandatory ROTC in the 1930s may also have distressed ROTC supporters and turned them to emphasizing the disciplinary merits of ROTC. The 1930s is generally known as a time in which college student activism flourished, but the degree of student interest in political activism, in fact, varied between campuses and across regions, rendering it difficult for observers at that time and historians alike to draw a cohesive national portrait of student activism.[100] Individual students' attitudes toward military training varied as well. At Stanford University, where military training was optional, the average student's attitude toward such issues was indifference, according to the *Stanford Daily*.[101] On the other hand, a survey conducted in the early 1930s by a pro-ROTC author unsurprisingly concluded that college graduates who had completed four years of ROTC work generally believed that ROTC had a definite educational value, especially in the areas of leadership, orderliness, and discipline.[102] The diminishing number of students taking ROTC courses at the University of

---

[97] Ibid., 174–76; "Want Schools Free of Army Education," *NYT*, February 2, 1932.
[98] Senate Subcommittee of the Committee on Military Affairs, *Compulsory Military Training*, 24.
[99] Ibid., 5.
[100] An educational correspondent for the *New York Times* observed that the antiwar view among college students was generally strongest in the East and weakest in the South. Eunice Fuller Barnard, "Students Lay a Barrage against War," *NYT*, April 29, 1934. Historians have not agreed on the scale of college students' activism in the 1930s. Some argue that students remained largely conservative, while others disagree. Loss, *Between Citizens and the State*, 71; Levine, *American College*, 205–207; Cohen, *When the Old Left Was Young*, xviii.
[101] "Daily News Presents Consensus of Editors' Opinions on Reserve Officers' Training Corps," *New York University Daily News*, March 5, 1931, reprinted in Senate Subcommittee of the Committee on Military Affairs, *Compulsory Military Training*, 95.
[102] Bishop, *Study of the Educational Value of Military Instruction*, 7, 14.

Chart 2.2 *The number of students taking the basic and advanced ROTC courses at the University of Wisconsin, 1921–29.*

	1921	1922	1923	1924	1925	1926	1927	1928	1929
Basic	1,466	1,383	933	906	607	595	537	562	555
Advanced	121	145	193	218	197	126	91	83	112

Chart adapted from John M. Thomas, "'And Including Military Tactics,'" in *Proceedings of the Forty-Third Annual Convention of the Association of Land-Grant Colleges and Universities,* ed. Charles A. McCue (Burlington, VT: Free Press, [1930]), 431.

Wisconsin after the university switched to elective military training in 1923, however, suggests that many male students in the compulsory military training era may have been taking it reluctantly (Chart 2.2). Likewise, according to an Army memorandum in March 1945, 86 percent of all basic course enrollment before World War II was in the institutions that had the basic course compulsory for male students. In such institutions, 37 percent of all male students were enrolled in the basic course, but in the institutions that did not require students to take the basic course, only 8 percent of all male students were enrolled in it.[103]

Although it is difficult to obtain a nationwide portrayal of students' opinions about ROTC, it was the students who turned against ROTC who became most visible in public, and their activism intensified in the 1930s. The Intercollegiate Student Council of the League for Industrial Democracy circulated a petition in 1931 declaring that military training "idealize[s] war and inculcate[s] a spirit of unquestioning military obedience which is an emotional armament of war" and asked Congress to outlaw compulsory training at colleges and universities. A student delegation gathered in Washington, D.C. to present the petition, signed by 10,000 students from fifty-five colleges and universities throughout the country, to President Herbert Hoover and members of Congress.[104]

[103] Hansen, "A History of the Reserve Officers' Training Corps," n.p. (p. 12 of "Chapter III – The Training Program: Administration").

[104] "Ask Hoover to Outlaw Army Drill in College," *NYT*, February 28, 1931; "Requests Senators to Oppose R. O. T. C.," *NYT*, March 1, 1931. The same name as one of the student appellants in the University of California case appears in a 1935 newspaper article as the chairman of the executive committee of the Student League for Industrial Democracy, although it is unclear if this is the same person and if he was active in this capacity during the case. [An article on plans for a one-day strike by college students protesting war and Fascism,] *San Bernando Daily Sun*, April 2, 1935.

When the Oxford Union, Oxford University's renowned debating society, pledged in February 1933 that "this House will in no circumstance fight for its King and country," college students in the United States praised it and created similar pledges that declared their opposition to military service.[105] In 1935, the annual congress of the National Student Federation of America voted for the abolition of compulsory military training and demanded the reopening of the University of California case.[106]

In the 1930s, some universities reconsidered whether compulsory military training should be continued. At Cornell University, a land-grant institution that had made military training compulsory for first- and second-year students since its founding, faculty voted 81 to 38 in 1931 in favor of making it elective.[107] Even at Princeton University, where ROTC was maintained only as an elective course that one-third of its students took, in 1934, eighty-four faculty members responded negatively to the question "Do you approve of R. O. T. C. training as given here?" while sixty-six answered positively.[108] A few land-grant institutions followed the lead of the University of Wisconsin and relaxed the military training requirement. For example, in the fall of 1937, MIT, where military training had been mandatory for over seventy years, decided to start a two-year trial period in which students with religious or moral objections to military training could instead take alternative courses such as international law, history of arbitration, and diplomacy. The measure was to be retroactively applied to the situation of a recent graduate who had graduated with a certificate because he had forfeited his degree by refusing to complete the military training requirement on religious grounds. This arrangement made it possible for him to earn his degree if he successfully completed the substitute courses as specified by the university.[109]

Overall, however, the land-grant college authorities' strong support of military training remained unaltered. They complained about administrative inconveniences concerning the maintenance of ROTC and the lukewarm support they received from the War Department but not the maintenance of compulsory ROTC on their campuses.[110] At the University of California, where students had long been engaging in a

---

[105] Cohen, *When the Old Left Was Young*, 79–80; Levine, *American College*, 206; "Student Pacifism Revealed by Vote," *NYT*, May 2, 1933; "Student War Poll Strongly Pacifist," *NYT*, May 25, 1933.
[106] Eunice Barnard, "Student Heads Hit Military Training," *NYT*, January 2, 1935.
[107] "Urges Cornell End Compulsory Drill," *NYT*, May 15, 1931.
[108] "Faculty Opposes Princeton R.O.T.C.," *NYT*, May 22, 1934.
[109] "Military Drill Issue Stirs Many Colleges."
[110] Charles A. McCue, ed., *Proceedings of the Forty-Ninth Annual Convention of the Association of Land-Grant Colleges and Universities* (Wilmington, DE: Gann Bros., [1936]), 324; William L. Slate, ed., *Proceedings of the Fifty-First Annual Convention of*

campaign against compulsory military training, a 1938 student peace committee delegated some of its members to study the issue of compulsory military training at the university's Berkeley and Los Angeles branches. The 71-page report, made public in October 1939, recommended that the training be made voluntary, a peace education course be established, and that the intramural athletic program at the university be expanded as a solution to the University Board of Regent's contention that compulsory military training was desirable as physical training.[111] The students' campaign ended in March 1940, however, with a Regents' vote to retain military training on a compulsory basis, ignoring the report as well as a student poll that indicated that 75 percent of the students favored voluntary training.[112]

Issues concerning military training in secondary schools at the local level also persisted throughout the 1930s. Toward the late 1930s, worried about calls for additional military training programs in secondary schools, a number of organizations worked to oppose such a requirement. In New York City in October 1935, at CME's initiative, representatives of groups opposing military training – including the Teachers Union, the United Parents Associations of New York City, the American League against War and Fascism, the War Resisters' League, and the Women's International League for Peace and Freedom – all worked together to establish the United Committee Against Militarism in New York City Schools to counter the increase of military training units in the city's schools.[113]

While anti-ROTC groups like them struggled to abandon military training in local schools, however, how to deal with conscientious objector students in secondary schools with military training requirements continued to depend on local authorities. In November 1939,

---

the *Association of Land-Grant Colleges and Universities* (New Haven, CT: Quinnipiack, [1938]), 259; William L. Slate, ed., *Proceedings of the Association of Land-Grant Colleges and Universities, Fifty-Third Convention* (New Haven, CT: Quinnipiack, [1940]), 271; William L. Slate, ed., *Proceedings of the Association of Land-Grant Colleges and Universities, Fifty-Fourth Convention* (New Haven, CT: Quinnipiack, [1941]), 293.

[111] Associated Students of the University of California Peace Committee, "Survey of Compulsory R. O. T. C., Summary of Report," p. 1.

[112] "California Regents Vote to Retain Compulsory Drill," *News Bulletin of the Committee on Militarism in Education* (March 1940), 1, filed in "Military in General Corres. 1936–40" folder, Box 68, NSGC Records.

[113] United Committee against Militarism in New York City Schools, "Minutes of Meeting of October 14, 1935," pp. 1–2, attached to Irving Alder to All Organizations Interested in Eliminating Militarism from New York Schools, November 1, 1935, "United Committee against Militarism in N.Y.C. Schools" folder, Box 69, NSGC Records; Edwin C. Johnson, "The Junior R.O.T.C. Knocks at the High-School Door," *Clearing House* 11, no. 8 (1937): 460–64.

Gloucester High School in Massachusetts granted exemption from compulsory military courses to a junior who had submitted a petition for exemption under a section of Massachusetts law that provided that no pupil in public schools "shall be required to take part in any military exercises if his parent or guardian is of any religious denomination conscientiously opposed to bearing arms, or is himself so opposed, and the school committee is so notified in writing."[114] On the other hand, there were students like Paul Brinkman, discussed in this chapter's opening paragraphs, who were not as fortuitous. The persistence of military training in secondary schools, despite being largely cut off from federal support, demonstrates the enduring belief among civilian leaders in various communities in the character-building effect of military training, which can be traced back to the nineteenth century as previously mentioned and proclaimed by the UMT movement in the early twentieth century. By this time, the country had faced a new world war, and the debates over the relationship between youth, education, and military training would enter a new phase, which will be explored in Chapter 4.

Situated at the intersection of education and national security, ROTC in the years between the two world wars solidified a new role for higher education: the education of young men for national security in peacetime. The fact that many universities made the first two years of ROTC mandatory for all male students, even though completion did not qualify them for reserve officers, demonstrates how ROTC in this period drew on the UMT and the Plattsburg idea of viewing military training as beneficial for broad social goals – such as character building and social order, as well as military preparedness. Meanwhile, the continued calls for military training in secondary schools by civilian supporters, despite the War Department's indication that it was not militarily useful, once again suggests how military training was expected to achieve goals other than those purely military. Additionally, the fact that many institutions kept military training as an educational option from which students could choose, rather than abandoning it entirely when the compulsory course was discontinued or not adopting ROTC in the first place, signifies how military training had come to be considered an acceptable course to be offered at civilian educational institutions.[115] It is also important to note that in a period in which racial segregation and discrimination were deeply embedded in the U.S. education and military, many young

---

[114] "Conscientious Objectors and Compulsory Drill," 3.
[115] The University of Wisconsin reverted back to compulsory military training after World War II. Lyons and Masland, *Education and Military Leadership*, 46n20.

Black Americans were not even given the option of choosing whether or not to enroll in military training courses.

Furthermore, the establishment of ROTC in public educational institutions raised the question of the relationship between access to public education and mandatory military training, as those who refused to participate in the training for religious or conscientious reasons could be denied the opportunity to receive the education. Indeed, as this chapter has shown, students who could not afford to attend a private college without the training were likely to be forced to choose between undergoing the training at a public institution or giving up their education if no public institution without the requirement was available. The debates over mandatory ROTC thus involved the relationship between social class, national security, and education, which was also evident in military-educational programs during World War I, as discussed in the previous chapter, and would become more prevalent in World War II.

Finally, although it was not a key actor in the debates over the program, the military would eventually find ROTC beneficial as well, as ROTC provided over 100,000 reserve officers for the Army in 1941.[116] George Marshall, Chief of Staff during World War II, reported that "without these officers the successful rapid expansion of our Army... would have been impossible."[117]

While ROTC served to legitimate the link between national security and higher education during this time, the Great Depression sparked an even broader reconsideration of the link between youth, education, and national security. The next chapter will explore how this unfolded.

---

[116] Lyons and Masland, "Origins of the ROTC," 12.   [117] Quoted in Ibid.

3 The Great Depression, National Security, and the Redefinition of Youth

Fort Devens, a U.S. Army installation in Massachusetts established in 1917 as a reception center for World War I draftees, had been quietly maintained after the war as a summer training camp site for New England-based National Guard troops, Reserve Units, Reserve Officers' Training Corps (ROTC) cadets, and candidates of the Citizens' Military Training Camp (CMTC), a training camp program for young men that originated in the "preparedness" movement of the mid-1910s. In June 1933, it was once again busy as an "induction center," receiving hundreds of young men every day. The men who arrived at Fort Devens in 1933 were there to join the Civilian Conservation Corps (CCC), a newly established federal program aimed at assisting unemployed young men in their late teens and early twenties affected by the Great Depression by providing them with food, clothing, a salary, and shelter in rural camp settings, as well as opportunities for temporary work and vocational training in forestry and conservation. Young men from across the country joined the CCC at one of these facilities near their homes, where they were screened by the Army and then transferred to the camps where they would live and work for a few months.[1]

The camps to which the enrollees were taken were likewise reminiscent of wartime. These camps were administered by the Army, whose members served as camp administrators. Each camp housed about 200 enrollees who lived in barracks and wore uniforms. The enlistees followed a strict daily schedule that began with reveille and the raising of the U.S. flag at 6 a.m., and that divided their day into work, sleep, and

---

[1] "History," *USAG Devens RFTA*, https://home.army.mil/devens/index.php/Misson%20and%20Vision/history (accessed September 5, 2023); "Work of Putting Youth in Forests Moves Forward," *Christian Science Monitor* (hereafter cited as *CSM*), June 1, 1933; Charles E. Heller, "The U.S. Army, the Civilian Conservation Corps, and Leadership for World War II, 1933–1942," *Armed Forces and Society* 36, no.3 (2010): 446; Garrett Gatzemeyer, *Bodies for Battle: US Army Physical Culture and Systematic Training, 1885–1957* (Lawrence: University Press of Kansas, 2021), 118.

Figure 3.1 CCC enrollees performing "review" and "colors" routines. "CCC Boys – Camp Sanders – General View of Boys at Evening Review and 'Colors,' Mt. Hermon, Louisiana," circa 1938, NAID: 276537984. Courtesy of the U.S. National Archives.

leisure (Figure 3.1). In addition to receiving vocational training, they were to learn to "discipline" themselves by washing their clothes, making their beds, and adhering to health and safety requirements they had never heard of before. Within a few years, educational sessions involving not only vocational training but a wide range of subjects – from basic literacy and citizenship to college-level academic subjects – would also be introduced to the camps. In the 1930s, Americans referred to the CCC as "Roosevelt's tree army" due to President Franklin D. Roosevelt's (FDR) strong support for the initiative.[2]

---

[2] Kenneth Holland and Frank Ernest Hill, *Youth in the CCC* (Washington, DC: American Council on Education, 1942), 7, 37–42; Heller, "The U.S. Army, the Civilian Conservation Corps, and Leadership," 446–47; American Youth Commission (AYCM), "Civilian Conservation Corps," ([Washington, DC: AYCM, 1940]), 8–9, "Education: Administrative Organization of CCC Educational Programs" folder, Records Relating to the CCC Educational Program, 1933–1942, Selection Division, Records of the Civilian Conservation Corps, Record Group (hereafter cited as RG)

The CCC's attempts at addressing not only youth unemployment but also their discipline and education reflect a wider attempt by American adults during the Great Depression to solve what they referred to as the "youth problem," a catchphrase that quickly spread across the United States in the 1930s and identified young people in their mid-teens to mid-twenties as a distinct age group with economic, educational, and cultural problems. The "youth problem" was primarily economic, stemming from the fact that this age group had the highest unemployment rate of all age groups of working age, but also evolved into one with cultural and educational dimensions. As undemocratic regimes rose to power in other countries and mobilized their youth politically and militarily, some Americans claimed that American youth could also be susceptible to such ideologies if left unattended, and they were not only worried about unemployed youth but also other young people who challenged their authority, such as student activists. Moreover, many adults came to believe that the federal government should take the lead in addressing the "youth problem," and supported the establishment of New Deal agencies for youth, such as the CCC and the National Youth Administration (NYA). This chapter explores the intersection of youth, education, and national security during the Great Depression, which many adults viewed as a national security emergency comparable to war. Building on earlier debates over young people's role in a national emergency, such as those regarding universal military training (UMT) and selective service in World War I, American adults performed a sweeping reinterpretation of youth, their relationship with the government, and their role in national security.

During the 1930s, American adults wrote extensively on "youth" and their "problem." "The discovery of youth is one of the by-products of the depression," stated Jerome H. Bentley, the program director of the Young Men's Christian Association of the City of New York, in 1937. His analysis mirrored what many other Americans had come to believe – that there was now a general awareness that youth, "officially identified as comprising the age range of 16–25 years," had a special set of vocational, personal, and social adjustment problems and that "society is not facilitating a smooth, easy, and natural transition for its members from childhood into settled and happy adult life."[3] A sociologist at the University of Pennsylvania likewise stated in the same year that the generation in question was "the first adolescent Americans to be called collectively

---

35, U.S. National Archives at College Park, College Park, MD (hereafter cited as NACP); Gatzemeyer, *Bodies for Battle*, 118–19.

[3] J. H. Bentley, "The Vocational Guidance of Youth," *Annals of the American Academy of Political and Social Science* 194 (Nov. 1937): 34.

'Youth.'" They were physically larger, stronger, and healthier; wealthier, and "more colorful" than their predecessors; and they were better educated and "more sophisticated," he observed. In other words, "youth" now signified the emergence of a "distinct population element" consisting of people between ages sixteen and twenty-five who were "no longer children and are not yet adults."[4] Young people mattered because, as another observer said, they were "the trustees of posterity" on which the future of the crisis-ridden nation depended.[5] Young people themselves were aware of this rise in discussions about "youth." In January 1933, a young journalist writing to FDR introduced himself to the incoming U.S. President as "one of the millions of young men forming the so called [sic] 'Youth' of the nation." He wrote down his age ("age 22") next to his signature.[6]

Adults thus came to think of young men and women as still requiring adult supervision, education, and guidance even after they reached the age of majority, and the "problem" they saw in these young people led to the grouping of these people as a distinct age group, while downplaying the diversity and inequality among them. The blurred connection between majority and maturity not only shaped adults' response to youth unemployment during the Great Depression but would shape the debates over selective service in World War II (Chapter 4.)

Historians have long recognized that FDR and other New Dealers frequently likened the Great Depression to war to legitimize the New Deal, which expanded the size, jurisdiction, and function of the federal government on a scale that was unprecedented in American society during peacetime. They have also noted how New Dealers drew on the nation's experiences during World War I to combat the Great Depression, modeling New Deal agencies after wartime agencies or appointing individuals with experience leading wartime agencies to head New Deal agencies.[7]

However, the impact of World War I on the New Deal went beyond rhetoric, analogy, or institution. The idea that adults should discipline young people at the federal government's initiative, which had driven the

---

[4] W. Wallace Weaver, "Modern Youth – Retrospect and Prospect," *Annals of the American Academy of Political and Social Science* 194 (Nov. 1937): 1.
[5] Maxine Davis, *The Lost Generation: A Portrait of American Youth Today* (New York: MacMillan, 1936), 3.
[6] John William Tinnea to FDR, January 4, 1933, Folder: OF 58b Youth Movements 1934, Official File (hereafter cited as OF) 58b (Box 3), Franklin D. Roosevelt Library, Hyde Park, NY (hereafter cited as FDRL).
[7] William E. Leuchtenburg, "The New Deal and the Analogue of War," in *Change and Continuity in Twentieth-Century America*, ed. John Braeman, et al. (Columbus: Ohio State University Press, 1964), 81–143; Ira Katznelson, *Fear Itself: The New Deal and the Origins of Our Time* (New York: Liveright Publishing, 2013), 120–22.

UMT movement and the Student Army Training Corps (SATC) in the World War I period, reverberated around adults' various proposed remedies to the "youth problem." For example, it gave the CCC a paramilitary image and prompted some people to urge the introduction of military training in the CCC. The idea of using a national emergency as a "plastic juncture" for change resonated across debates about the "youth problem" as well. Educational leaders once again played a major role in redefining youth and their relationship with the government in national security. Furthermore, as the urgent focus on World War II dominated U.S. policy decisions in the late 1930s, the New Deal programs for young people were converted into national defense programs, revealing the deep link between the Great Depression and war. The 1930s were a pivotal period that connected the two world wars and reshaped how Americans viewed the relationship between youth, education, and national security.

The Rise of the "Youth Problem"

Young people, like any other age group, included a wide range of individuals. However, the significance of the invention of the "youth problem" rests in the way adults grouped them into a single category. The invention was driven primarily by the mass unemployment of young people. No definitive figure of the number of unemployed people in the age range labeled as "youth" exists because the ages surveyed and the definition of unemployment varied from study to study. Moreover, the Great Depression lasted for over a decade, during which the unemployment rate fluctuated. Nevertheless, study after study confirmed the ongoing seriousness of youth unemployment. According to the National Unemployment Census of 1937, for example, people aged eighteen to twenty-five constituted approximately one-third of all unemployed workers.[8]

In 1939, the Works Progress Administration (WPA), a federal public works agency created in 1935 as part of FDR's New Deal, issued a report

---

[8] Works Progress Administration, Division of Research, *Urban Youth: Their Characteristics and Economic Problems. A Preliminary Report of the Survey of Youth in the Labor Market Prepared by the Urban Surveys Section, Division of Research at the Request of the National Youth Administration*, WPA Research Monograph Series I, no. 24 (Washington, DC: Works Progress Administration, Division of Research, 1939) (hereafter cited as WPA, *Urban Youth*), 28–30; Harry Zeitlin, "Federal Relations in American Education, 1933–1943, a Study of New Deal Efforts and Innovations" (PhD diss., Columbia University, 1958), 189; John E. Bryan, "Youth Learn Manual Skills: Alabama NYA Out-of-Work Youth Program," *Education* 61, no. 2 (1940): 78, filed in "Correspondence with Office of Director CCC Camp Education 1940" folder, Correspondence with Office of Director CCC 1933–41 Camp Education, Records Relating to CCC Educational Program, 1933–1942, Selection Division, RG 35, NACP.

analyzing the rise of the "youth problem" as one of the country's most pressing economic problems. In this report, the WPA stated that the "basic problem confronting youth, particularly in a period of depression, is that of getting and keeping a job."[9] The Great Depression had put millions of people out of work, and, as this report made very clear, the impact on young people was particularly devastating. Just as young men and women, fresh out of schools but still at an age when they required encouragement and guidance, the WPA argued, young people were bluntly told by the society that they were not needed, evaporating any hope they'd had during their years in school about their future. This mass unemployment and dissatisfaction caused "the so-called 'youth problem,'" the report explained.[10]

The massive youth unemployment was caused partly by the fact that both public and private sectors prioritized hiring and retaining older male workers, namely fathers and husbands, but people also blamed the schools for not properly preparing young people for work. A 1934 study of Pennsylvania youth under the age of twenty and looking for a job found that 71 percent of them had never held a paying job, confirming that few jobs were open to young people without vocational skills.[11] Young people themselves named a lack of previous work experience as the most important factor that made it difficult for them to obtain a job, but some also believed that they would have found employment more easily if they had taken vocational training courses in school.[12]

Moreover, even as educational attendance rose, the Great Depression brought into sharp relief the great extent to which social class, schooling, and employment intertwined. The statistics that showed a growth in school attendance did not illuminate the gap in the quality and amount of education that children and young people across the country received and unsurprisingly, students in the 1930s tended to come from families that could afford the education even at the depth of the Depression. Out of the 1,727,000 young urbanites between ages sixteen and twenty-five on financial relief in May 1935, only 45 percent had attended school beyond the grade school level, and less than 3 percent had attended college. College students dropped out of college because they could not afford the tuition and high-school students left school primarily because their parents could not pay the expenses.[13] The withdrawal of

---

[9] WPA, *Urban Youth*, 1.   [10] Ibid., 1–2.
[11] Homer P. Rainey, *How Fare American Youth?* (New York: Appleton-Century, 1938), 35–36; Zeitlin, "Federal Relations in American Education," 68.
[12] WPA, *Urban Youth*, 17–19.
[13] Federal Security Agency, War Manpower Commission, *Final Report of the National Youth Administration, Fiscal Years 1936–1943* (Washington, DC: GPO, 1944) (hereafter cited as FSA, *Final Report of the NYA*), 44; David Tyack, Robert Lowe, and

young people from school not only troubled them but also worsened the already overcrowded labor market. The "youth problem" thus became a labor and educational problem of keeping young people in school and training them for work.

Some adults also believed that unemployed, unsupervised youth were prone to psychological issues. In 1936, journalist Maxine Davis called youth the "lost generation" of the 1930s. People who came of voting age in 1935 had been born in 1914, she pointed out, and therefore their earliest memories were of war, followed by memories of the booming economy of the 1920s. Then, the Depression suddenly struck them. The Depression, according to Davis, had made many young people foster an attitude that was "cynical of constructive effort, barren of faith in society and government, innocent of any sense of obligation, and animated only by a blind and unreasoned hope that times will be better – that something will turn up."[14]

Images of this "lost generation" out of work, wandering the streets, or becoming transients appeared regularly in the press. They were gendered, too, with approximately 90 percent of the young transients being men.[15] Such images easily fueled public fear that youth were prone to criminality. In the spring of 1933, a Republican senator submitted an Act to Congress that proposed to house unemployed young men between the ages of seventeen and twenty-four in military camps to monitor and prevent their immoral and criminal activities for the safety of American society.[16] The *New York Times Magazine* published a report by the director of the United States Bureau of Prison in 1935 which stated that, according to crime reports by the Federal Bureau of Investigation and the Census Bureau, an increasing number of young men were becoming involved in crime since the mid-1920s and that age nineteen seemed to be the "favorite age for crime."[17] Some academics argued that the

---

Elisabeth Hansot, *Public Schools in Hard Times: The Great Depression and Recent Years* (Cambridge, MA: Harvard University Press, 1984), 125.

[14] Davis, *The Lost Generation*, 4, 321; Obituary, Maxine Davis McHugh, *Washington Post* (hereafter cited as *WP*), May 23, 1978.

[15] Kriste Lindenmeyer, "New Opportunities for Children in the Great Depression in the United States," in *The Routledge History of Childhood in the Western World*, ed. Paula S. Fass (London: Routledge, 2013), 441; Kingsley Davis, *Youth in the Depression* (Chicago: University of Chicago Press, 1935), 1–8.

[16] The Act was shelved partly because of the military's opposition to the plan. Holly Allen, *Forgotten Men and Fallen Women: The Cultural Politics of New Deal Narratives* (Ithaca, NY: Cornell University Press, 2015), 71.

[17] Sanford Bates, "The Young Criminal," *New York Times Magazine*, August 4, 1935; Zeitlin, "Federal Relations in American Education," 68.

popular image of young people as susceptible to crime lacked evidence.[18] Yet, the discourse connecting young people with crime prevailed.

The "youth problem" became educational in a different sense as well, and this was primarily due to the rise of dictatorships elsewhere in the world. Concerns over its implications for American democracy became widespread in American society with the rise of Adolf Hitler, and Americans strived to distinguish their society from them.[19] As historian Alan Brinkley has pointed out, by the eve of World War II Americans would come to define their country "as the antithesis of dictatorship" and defend "their own government to themselves and to others as a nation admirable above all for *not* being a totalitarian state."[20] In the 1930s, newspapers published sensational photos of young Germans, Russians, and Italians marching in uniform, and reported that Adolf Hitler emphasized the importance of the indoctrination of youth for Nazi rule by frequently stating that "Who has youth has the future."[21] American youth "[had] been living through the same dark days that caused their foreign brothers to see Mussolini and Hitler and Lenin appear as leaders bathed in light," Maxine Davis argued. Hitler gave young Germans work, a reason for existence, and "a reservoir into which they could pour their energy and their devotion. They *are* the Third Reich," she wrote.[22] Many adults thus saw the problems of American youth and foreign youth as comparable, and they sought ways to keep the former on the democratic path.

Adults proposed various answers to what they saw as a psychological and educational problem among American youth. Some of them, for example, organized "youth movements" to align young people to causes they considered appropriate. In September 1933, Edward A. Filene, the department-store magnate, philanthropist, and chairman of the Massachusetts State Recovery Board, wrote to FDR about a "Youth

---

[18] J. P. Shalloo, "Youth and Crime," *Annals of the American Academy of Political and Social Science* 194 (Nov. 1937): 79.

[19] Benjamin L. Alpers, "This Is the Army: Imagining a Democratic Military in World War II," *Journal of American History* 85, no. 1 (1998):132–35.

[20] Emphasis in original. Alan Brinkley, *The End of Reform: New Deal Liberalism in Recession and War* (New York: Vintage Books, 1995), 155.

[21] "Schooling for Young Totalitarians," *New York Times* (hereafter cited as *NYT*), October 2, 1938; "Boys of Europe Trained for War," *NYT*, September 30, 1934; "Farewell to Youth," editorial, *NYT*, September 20, 1936; James Wechsler, "Europe's Youth Calmly Surveys a 'Next War,'" *NYT*, October 3, 1937; Alice Hamilton, "The Youth Who Are Hitler's Strength," *NYT*, October 8, 1933. The phrase "who has youth has the future" predates Hitler in German history. See Derek S. Linton, *"Who Has the Youth, Has the Future": The Campaign to Save Young Workers in Imperial Germany* (Cambridge, UK: Cambridge University Press, 1991).

[22] Emphasis in original. Davis, *The Lost Generation*, 5, 37.

Movement" that his board had initiated. He explained that he had come up with the idea while traveling to Europe the previous year, during which he had witnessed children and young people being enlisted by governments for ideological ends. He was especially horrified by the situation he had observed in Germany, where "tens of thousands of boys and girls from eight years to maturity, organized in military fashion, proudly marched through the city." European youth had a political impact not only through their direct action but through influencing their parents and other adults, he argued. He found it imperative that the United States organize and direct its youth "along constructive lines" to avoid a similar fate. His "Youth Movement" intended to mobilize American youth for the support of the National Recovery Administration, a major New Deal agency, through the coordination of the Boy Scouts, the Campfire Girls, and other youth and religious organizations. He hoped that, with FDR's recognition, it would become a national program.[23]

Likewise, the president of an organization named the National Youth Movement of Pennsylvania wrote to FDR in August 1934, insisting that American youth had become "a fertile field for the reddest kind of radicalism" whose agents capitalized on young people who were frustrated because of unemployment but full of energy. He asked FDR to address youth on the radio, deputizing every one of them as "an agent to help you combat this menace." This would "boost up their courage," give them meaning in life, and reroute their energy away from radicalism, because FDR was "the hero, of the American Youth, Oh Yes, far more, than Babe Ruth ever was."[24]

Other adults supported the rise of youth activism led by young people themselves, and they included prominent liberal leaders such as First Lady Eleanor Roosevelt and Henry A. Wallace, U.S. Secretary of Agriculture and later Vice President under FDR.[25] And in the 1930s, youth activism did become prevalent, as noted in Chapter 2. The youth activist groups had different goals but were united by an antiwar cause and supported the move to eliminate compulsory military drills in educational institutions, opposed military budget increases, and urged

---

[23] Edward A. Filene to FDR, September 7, 1933, Folder: OF 58 Youth 1933–35, OF 58 (Box 1), FDRL.
[24] J. L. Megahan, to FDR, August 22, 1934, Folder: OF 58b Youth Movements 1934, OF 58 (Box 3), FDRL.
[25] "Mrs. Roosevelt Asks a Chance for Youth," *NYT*, November 11, 1938; "Browder Is Chided by Mrs. Roosevelt," *NYT*, November 22, 1939; "First Lady's Plea Ignored by Youth," *NYT*, May 27, 1940; Henry A. Wallace, "The Potentialities of the Youth Movement in America," *Educational Record* 15 (1934): 3–9.

neutrality. Furthermore, the American Youth Congress (AYC), founded to coordinate the lobbying and activist efforts of the various student and youth groups that had been established across the country, succeeded in getting an "American Youth Act" introduced to U.S. Congress and received congressional committee hearings in 1936 and 1938. Although it never became law, the Act, driven by the AYC's criticism of the NYA for not doing enough for youth, stipulated the creation of "a program of vocational training and employment for youth between the ages of sixteen and twenty-five, and full educational opportunities" for high school, college, and graduate students.[26] Eunice Barnard, an educational reporter for the *New York Times*, wrote at the end of 1935 that youth "as a class has become more vocal than ever before," as unemployed youth spoke out about their hardship while students engaged in antiwar movements.[27]

The significant public attention given to a student group with a different tone than these activist organizations indicates how sensitive some adults were to young people's political views. In March 1936, a group of undergraduates at Princeton University organized the Veterans of Future Wars (VFW) satirizing World War I veterans who had won early bonus payments through vigorous lobbying.[28] The public awareness of veterans' economic hardships had been raised by the 1932 veterans' march in Washington, D.C., where they demanded early payment of the bonus promised by the government for their wartime service. The students, however, questioned the federal spending of two billion dollars for the bonus when the entire country was devastated economically. They also satirized the fact that many veterans eligible for the bonus had never seen actual combat, as well as the veterans' and their supporters' militant patriotism.[29] In doing so, they sarcastically declared that as soon-to-be soldiers, they demanded the payment of one thousand dollars to each "future" veteran, due June 1, 1965, but because "it is customary to pay

[26] Thomas F. Neblett, "Youth Movements in the United States," *Annals of the American Academy of Political and Social Science* 194 (Nov. 1937): 147–48; Robert Cohen, *When the Old Left Was Young: Student Radicals and America's First Mass Student Movement, 1929–1941* (New York: Oxford University Press, 1993), 189–92; Zeitlin, "Federal Relations in American Education," 236–37.
[27] Eunice Barnard, "Plight of Youth Main Problem of Educators during Past Year," *NYT*, December 29, 1935.
[28] For the history of the veterans' lobby in the interwar years, see Stephen R. Ortiz, *Beyond the Bonus March and GI Bill: How Veteran Politics Shaped the New Deal Era* (New York: New York University Press, 2010); William Pencak, *For God and Country: The American Legion, 1919–1941* (Boston: Northeastern University Press, 1989).
[29] Chris Rasmussen, "'This Thing Has Ceased to Be a Joke': The Veterans of Future Wars and the Meanings of Political Satire in the 1930s," *Journal of American History* 103, no. 1 (2016): 84, 89, 97.

bonuses before they are due we demand immediate cash payment, plus three per cent [sic] compounded annually for thirty years back from June 1, 1965 to June 1, 1935."[30]

Historians disagree on whether or to what extent these Princetonians were motivated by an antiwar cause, but the group attracted many antiwar student activists as well as other students around the country, with as many as 60,000 applying for VFW membership.[31] The *New York Times* obituary of the VFW's "national commander" six decades later called him the "most famous collegian in America who did not actually play football."[32]

Adults were divided in their reactions to the movement. Some saw it as an excellent piece of political humor, including First Lady Eleanor Roosevelt, who was so amused she said "I think it's just as funny as it can be!" Others, however, were incensed at how the group made fun of war veterans, referring to the VFW students as "war profits babies" born into wealthy families who could afford to send them to prestigious universities like Princeton and criticizing higher education institutions for not teaching students patriotism properly.[33] The national commander of the Veterans of Foreign Wars (the original "VFW" whose members were real veterans of past wars) castigated the students, calling them "monkeys" and "insolent puppies" who would "never be veterans of a future war, for they are too yellow to go to war."[34]

The VFW movement vanished from the public eye just a few months later when the founding members finished their undergraduate degrees and disagreements over the movement's course grew among student members across the country.[35] However, the case suggests how it was not only young unemployed people who were deemed problematic and in need of adult guidance. Young people's many challenges to adult authority and to the boundaries some adults considered to be appropriate for American democracy rendered even wealthy students who were least likely to have been impacted economically by the Depression problematic "youth."

In the 1930s, then, adults increasingly looked at young people in their late teens to mid-twenties as a distinct age group with shared

---

[30] Quoted in Rasmussen, "This Thing Has Ceased to Be a Joke," 85. See also Donald W. Whisenhunt, *Veterans of Future Wars: A Study in Student Activism* (Lanham, MD: Lexington, 2011), 4–5.
[31] Rasmussen, "This Thing Has Ceased to Be a Joke," 85, 94–95, 103.
[32] "Lewis J. Gorin Jr., Instigator of a 1930's Craze, Dies at 84," obituary, *NYT*, January 31, 1999.
[33] Rasmussen, "This Thing Has Ceased to Be a Joke," 98, 101.
[34] "'Future Veterans' Change War Views," *NYT*, March 4, 1944.
[35] Rasmussen, "This Thing Has Ceased to Be a Joke," 104–105.

characteristics and problems. Unemployed, out-of-school youth were primarily considered to be prone to economic and psychological problems, while students who challenged adult authority were considered to be prone to political ones. As adults sought different solutions to the "youth problem," they looked to two sectors of society: education and the federal government.

The Educational Elite and the Great Depression

Because the "youth problem" was considered an educational problem to a great extent, educators emerged as some of the most vocal participants in the debates over it. At the end of 1935, Eunice Barnard of the *New York Times* noted that "For the first time perhaps since the founding of Latin schools in early New England, the child has been eclipsed by the adolescent in the view of educators." By "adolescent," she meant young people in their twenties as well as teens. "What to do with the millions of unemployed youth between the ages of 16 and 25, whether walking the streets, or overcrowding the high schools, or looking wistfully toward college" had become a major educational problem, she observed.[36] Academic literature on "youth" flourished in the 1930s. The *Annals of the American Academy of Political and Social Science* devoted its November 1937 issue to "The Prospect for Youth." The editors acknowledged that "much of our social concern seems to have shifted in the thirties from the problems of childhood to those of youth."[37]

Although the federal government had previously been involved in young people's education through programs such as the SATC and ROTC, its involvement in education during the New Deal was unparalleled in scale and affected a greater spectrum of individuals and institutions. Some educational organizations, such as the National Education Association (NEA), which largely serviced elementary and secondary education, saw New Deal measures like the CCC and the NYA as a major threat to local and state control of education and remained skeptical of them throughout the 1930s.[38] The American Association of School Administrators demanded that the work of New Deal agencies for young people, such as the NYA and the CCC, be transferred to the

---

[36] Barnard, "Plight of Youth."
[37] James H. S. Bossard and W. Wallace Weaver, "Foreword," *Annals of the American Academy of Political and Social Science* 194 (Nov. 1937): xi.
[38] Zeitlin, "Federal Relations in American Education," 295–96, 298; Paula S. Fass, *Outside In: Minorities and the Transformation of American Education* (New York: Oxford University Press, 1989), 120; "N.E.A. Report Cites Danger to Free Speech," *New York Herald Tribune* (hereafter cited as *NYHT*), June 27, 1938.

states. Additionally, it criticized the FDR administration for setting up "two public school systems in this country, one controlled by Washington and the other controlled by the localities and the States."[39]

At the same time, other educators saw the Depression as a national emergency equivalent to a state of war, and the educational sector's cooperation with the federal government in times of emergency was not new, as programs like the SATC make clear. Recognizing that an economic crisis of this magnitude could only be overcome through federal intervention, these educational leaders embraced the government's role in addressing the "youth problem." In other words, even though they, too, were largely opposed to the federal *control* of education, they welcomed federal initiatives and financial assistance in tackling the problem.

The most prominent of this group was the American Council on Education (ACE), which originated in the World War I period (Chapter 1) and represented higher education institutions as well as other institutions of learning. In April 1934, the U.S. Commissioner of Education George F. Zook (head of the U.S. Office of Education within the Department of the Interior) urged FDR to publicly demonstrate that he fully recognized the hardship young people were going through and express his intention to help.[40] Within a few months of making this suggestion to FDR, Zook resigned as Commissioner of Education to become the director of ACE, succeeding Charles R. Mann.[41] Under Zook, the ACE created the American Youth Commission (AYCM) in 1935 to study the "youth problem," and the commission soon established itself as a leading authority on the topic.

Members of the AYCM changed from time to time, but they included a wide array of representatives from the government, industry, social work, and education, and many of them would go on to serve the federal government in World War II. Among them were John Studebaker, who succeeded Zook as U.S. Commissioner of Education, and Floyd W. Reeves, professor of administration at the University of Chicago who would lead FDR's Advisory Committee on Education in 1938. Reeves would go on to serve the presidential advisory committee on selective service during World War II. Clarence A. Dykstra, the president of the University of Wisconsin, who would become the first director of the Selective Service System for World War II in 1940 and subsequently

---

[39] "State Control of U.S. School Projects Sought," *WP*, March 1, 1939.
[40] George F. Zook to Stephen Early, April 24, 1934, Folder: OF 58b Youth Movements 1934, OF 58b (Box 3), FDRL.
[41] "Favors Extension of School System," *Baltimore Sun*, May 29, 1934. For Mann's involvement in the military training of young men, see Chapters 1 and 2 of this book.

chair the National Security Resources Board's Post War Committee on Readjustment of Civilian and Military Personnel during the war, also joined. Newton Baker, the Secretary of War during World War I, was the first AYCM chairman, and Owen Young, the namesake of the Young Plan that helped Europe recover from World War I and a retired chairman of the General Electric Co., was the second chairman.[42] Until it closed its doors in 1942, the AYCM studied and raised public awareness of the problems and needs of young people. Topics discussed were wide-ranging, including health, employment, education, juvenile delinquency, and the needs of African American and rural youth.[43]

The members of the AYCM, much like the American public in general, never agreed on a single definition of the "youth problem." However, they did agree that the federal government should take the lead in solving it with the aid of educational specialists. The AYCM worked closely with federal agencies established to help needy youth during the Depression, including the NYA and CCC, and produced statistical and analytical studies of youth.[44] The AYCM continued to support federal policies for young people and would become a major participant in the debates over the draft of young men for World War II (Chapter 4).

---

[42] AYCM, *Youth, Defense, and the National Welfare: Recommendations of the American Youth Commission of the American Council on Education* (Washington, DC: American Youth Commission of the American Council on Education, [1940]), 12; "The American Youth Commission," memorandum, October 9, 1940, p.1, Records of the American Council on Education (hereafter cited as ACE Records), Box 188, folder 9, Hoover Institution Library & Archives, Stanford, CA (hereafter cited as Hoover Institution Archives); Tyack et al., *Public Schools in Hard Times*, 102; Louis B. Hershey, *Selective Service in Peacetime: First Report of the Director of Selective Service, 1940–41* (Washington, DC: GPO, 1942), 11; Floyd W. Reeves, "Youth in Defense and Postdefense Periods," *Journal of Educational Sociology* 15, no. 2 (1941): 108; George F. Zook to Newton D. Baker, December 16, 1935, ACE Records, Box 171, folder 4, Hoover Institution Archives; American Youth Commission press release, n.d., ACE Records, Box 171, folder 5, Hoover Institution Archives. Even though Studebaker joined the ACYM and rose to the position of U.S. Commissioner of Education, he was also known for being in favor of local control of education. Although it may seem odd that a person with such a belief became the U.S. Commissioner of Education, he appears to have sought to implement this ideal from the top down. On Studebaker, see Christopher P. Loss, *Between Citizens and the State: The Politics of American Higher Education in the 20th Century* (Princeton, NJ: Princeton University Press, 2012), ch. 3.

[43] AYCM, *Youth, Defense, and the National Welfare*, 10; Floyd W. Reeves, "Planning for Youth – Past and Future," April 18, 1941 (draft prepared for the ACE annual meeting on May 2, 1941), ACE Records, Box 190, folder 15, Hoover Institution Archives; Bruce Clayton Flack, "The Work of the American Youth Commission, 1935–1942" (PhD diss., Ohio State University, 1969), 67; Floyd W. Reeves, "The Program of the American Youth Commission," *High School Journal* 23, no. 3 (1940): 101–105.

[44] "The American Youth Commission," 1–5.

The New Deal Programs for Youth

The rise of the "youth problem" as a cultural, educational, and economic issue, as well as the emergence of an educational leadership prepared to work with the federal government to find a solution, drove the creation of the New Deal's initiatives for young people. The urging for the federal government's intervention in youth matters came from young people themselves as well. In April 1933, a young man from Indianapolis wrote to FDR's advisor Louis Howe, suggesting that the President appoint a "junior secretary" of about twenty-five years of age whose duty would be to "act as a 'contact man' for the President in sounding out the opinions of the young voters." He insisted that youth should have a voice in federal policymaking: "We young people have grave responsibilities in times of stress. We must be the first to give our lives in defense of our country in times of war; we are the first to lose our positions in economic depression." Despite these sacrifices and responsibilities that young people shouldered, he argued, he did not recall a single President who had consulted or recognized their ideas and opinions.[45]

The President did not adopt this proposal, but he did launch two New Deal work programs for young people: the NYA and the CCC. Of the two, the NYA, created in 1935 to provide part-time work to students in need of financial assistance to continue their education, and to unemployed, needy youth out of school, cast a wider net.

The NYA administered several programs. Its student–work program provided part-time employment to students from ages sixteen to twenty-four, inclusive.[46] The types of work students performed varied widely. Examples included academic research, laboratory assistance, library services, construction and automotive repair projects, clinical and nursery assistance, reforestation and soil conservation, and menial jobs that the NYA called the "leaf raking" type. Additional funds were allocated in 1936 for Black students in college and graduate school. During its eight years of operation, the student–work program supported over two million students.[47]

The NYA's out-of-school work program offered work opportunities to young people out of school and employed nearly three million young men and women. Enrollment was limited to people ages eighteen to twenty-four, inclusive, for most years of operation.[48] Additionally, in

---

[45] B. Nelson Deranian to Louis Howe, April 8, 1933, Folder: OF 58 Youth 1933–35, OF 58 (Box 1), FDRL.
[46] FSA, *Final Report of the NYA*, 49.   [47] Ibid., 51–53, 58–60, 235.
[48] Ibid., 234–35. Congress lowered the minimum age to seventeen for the 1941 fiscal year and then to sixteen for the 1943 fiscal year. Ibid., 85.

1936, the NYA opened "resident work centers" as part of this program to aid young people located in sparsely populated areas of the country where it was difficult to secure the same work projects, adequate equipment, and proper adult supervision as the ordinary out-of-school work program. These centers, typically housing fifty to two-hundred young people, initially offered agricultural training to boys and handicrafts, sewing, and home-economics training to girls, and from 1937 on, larger industrial-type resident centers were established for mechanical production projects.[49] The products they made were utilized through local agencies that cosponsored the projects. For example, they produced playground equipment for public parks, hospital supplies for local hospitals, mechanical supplies for municipal and state governments and later for national defense agencies.[50] The NYA thus offered a variety of work opportunities, but as will be discussed later in this chapter, as the country shifted its gear from the Depression to war in the late 1930s, the emphasis would shift from financial assistance and work relief to national defense, such as training in automobile and aviation mechanics as well as in radio, electrical, and welding work.[51]

While the NYA offered job and training opportunities in a broad range of fields and for both young men and women, FDR's favorite was the CCC. In fact, he had already expressed the idea of establishing the CCC when he accepted the Democratic nomination for the U.S. presidency in July 1932.[52] On March 21, 1933, he asked U.S. Congress for authority to create "a civilian conservation corps to be used in simple work, not interfering with normal employment, and confining itself to forestry, the prevention of soil erosion, flood control and similar projects." Beyond these material gains, however, he also highlighted the "spiritual and moral stability" that such work, assumed to be performed in "healthful surroundings," would bring the unemployed. On March 31, 1933, Congress authorized the establishment of the CCC, and FDR established the Corps on April 5.[53]

---

[49] NYA, *NYA Resident Work Centers* (Washington, DC: Federal Security Agency, NYA, [1941?]), 1–4; filed in "N.Y.A." folder, Documents File Health (cont'd) – Recreation, Records of Youth and Education Units, 1939–1942, Records of Division A, Records of the National Security Resources Board, RG 187, NACP; Tom L. Popejoy to Marvin H. McIntyre, February 2, 1939, Folder: OF 444d National Youth Administration 1939, OF 444d (Box 19), FDRL.

[50] FSA, *Final Report of the NYA*, 181.

[51] Zeitlin, "Federal Relations in American Education," 222–23, 225.

[52] Holland and Hill, *Youth in the CCC*, 9.

[53] Message from the U.S. President to Congress on unemployment relief, March 21, 1933, reprinted in 73rd Cong., 1st sess., *Congressional Record* 77, pt. 1: 877–78; "House Passes

Despite the popular image of the CCC as a program for unemployed youth, neither FDR's message to Congress urging the establishment of the CCC nor the Act or executive order creating the CCC mentioned any age restrictions. However, the planned work demanded manual labor and living in camps in remote locations, and young, unmarried men, who would have less settled habits of life, were assumed to be more adaptable to the life of the camps, and physically strong enough for the work.[54] Accordingly, eligibility for the first selection of enrollees went to unemployed, unmarried men, eighteen to twenty-five years of age, who agreed to send a substantial part of their cash allowance to their families and dependents.[55] The age limit changed several times during the lifespan of the CCC, but the upper limit never went above twenty-eight (except for war veterans and Native American men, for whom separate camps were established).[56] The CCC was soon known as a program for

---

Bill for Forestry Jobs," *NYT*, March 30, 1933; Holland and Hill, *Youth in the CCC*, 7. Residential camps for young unemployed women were also established, partly inspired by the CCC. With the support of the First Lady and the Secretary of Labor Frances Perkins, a pilot program was introduced in August 1933, followed by a nationwide launch in 1934. The camps relied heavily on state and local agencies, both private and public, for financial and administrative support, as the federal government and the American public remained unwilling to fund residential relief projects for women. The initiative was discontinued in 1937 because it was unable to convince the public of its importance or find solutions to its logistical and financial problems. Joyce L. Kornbluh, "The She-She-She Camps: An Experiment in Living and Learning, 1934–1937," in *Sisterhood and Solidarity: Workers' Education for Women, 1914–1984*, ed. Joyce L. Kornbluh and Mary Frederickson (Philadelphia: Temple University Press, 1984), https://temple.manifoldapp.org/read/sisterhood-and-solidarity-workers-education-for-women-1914-1984/section/18e4570c-6f18-495d-980d-834d81a8793c (accessed March 15, 2023); "Girl Camp Mapped by Mrs. Roosevelt," *NYT*, June 2, 1933; "Camp for Needy Women Will Be Enlarged to Give Summer Vacations to 200 at Once," *NYT*, April 15, 1934.

[54] *An Act for the Relief of Unemployment through the Performance of Useful Public Work, and for Other Purposes*, Public Law 73-5, *U.S. Statutes at Large* 48 (1933–1934): 22–23; "Executive Order 6101–Relief of Unemployment through the Performance of Useful Public Work," *The American Presidency Project*, www.presidency.ucsb.edu/documents/executive-order-6101-relief-unemployment-through-the-performance-useful-public-work (accessed October 7, 2023); Holland and Hill, *Youth in the CCC*, 13–14. See also Allen, *Forgotten Men and Fallen Women*, 72–73.

[55] Statement issued by CCC Director Robert Fechner, April 6, 1933, Folder: OF 268 CCC Apr 1933, OF 268 (Box 1), FDRL. Enrollees earned a dollar a day for their work, and twenty-five dollars a month of their pay was to go to their families. "CCC Is the Rebuilder of Youth's Morale," *WP*, August 19, 1934.

[56] Holland and Hill, *Youth in the CCC*, 14. Up to one-tenth of CCC enrollment slots were reserved for war veterans selected by the Veterans Administration. Additionally, a separate program for Native Americans was run by the Office of Indian Affairs of the U.S. Department of the Interior. Ibid., 28–29.

young men and was popularized as a solution for "a serious problem in American Life, viz., the Youth Problem."[57]

Several federal agencies were involved in the operation of the CCC. The U.S. Department of Labor supervised the selection of enrollees, the War Department constructed and administered the camps, and the Departments of the Interior and Agriculture administered the work projects in which the enrollees engaged.[58] By July 22, 1933, the CCC already had 301,230 members scattered throughout more than 1,500 camps across the country. This meant that the program had enrolled more men than the National Socialist Labor Service of Germany, an unemployment camp program the Nazi government had established to serve youth in the same age range.[59] Black Americans made up a maximum of roughly 10 percent of all enrollees, most of whom were placed in segregated camps.[60] Enrollment in the CCC ranged from around 240,000 to over 500,000.[61] (Figure 3.2)

Adults portrayed CCC enrollees in ways that reflected the broader perception of "youth" at the time; that is, adults saw them as either unfortunate victims of the Depression or potential threats to social order, and regardless of whether or not each individual enrollee had reached legal adulthood, they saw all CCC enrollees as requiring adult supervision. For instance, the AYCM's depiction of a "typical" white enrollee in its 1941 study of the CCC exemplifies the perspective of youth held by adults sympathetic to their plight. While recognizing the limitations of any attempt to generalize about CCC participants due to the wide range of their social, cultural, racial, and educational backgrounds, the AYCM described a typical white CCC participant as being between the ages of seventeen and eighteen (the average age of enrollees had dropped somewhat by this time due to the transition of older men into the military and defense industries), weighing 145 pounds (65.8 kilograms), and standing at five feet, six inches (167.6 centimeters). His health was "fairly good, but he is a little underweight, probably from insufficient food of the right kind." Before entering the CCC, he had lived with his parents and five siblings. The home had no telephone, refrigerator, or running water, but

---

[57] Fred E. Lukens, "The CCC and the Schools," *Education* 61, no. 2 (1940): 82, filed in "Correspondence with Office of Director CCC Camp Education 1940" folder, Records Relating to CCC Educational Program, 1933–1942, Selection Division, Records of the Civilian Conservation Corps, RG 35, NACP.

[58] Holland and Hill, *Youth in the CCC*, 27–28, 30–31. State and local agencies also took part in the project. For example, while the U.S. Department of Labor supervised the selection of enrollees, the actual work of selection was done by state relief agencies. Ibid., 30.

[59] Ibid., 14n12, 28.   [60] Ibid., 111–12.

[61] FSA, *Final Report of the NYA*, 23; Holland and Hill, *Youth in the CCC*, 45.

Figure 3.2 CCC enrollees at work.
Federal Security Agency, *The CCC at Work: A Story of 2,500,000 Young Men* (Washington, DC: GPO, 1941), 12. In the public domain.

had a radio. His father was an unskilled worker but had been unemployed for some time, and the family was on local relief rolls. He had received more education than his parents, but it took eleven years for him to complete eight and three-quarter school grades. While somewhat dissatisfied with his experience in schools, he held a "vague conviction that schooling helps people to get jobs." Before entering the CCC, he had worked for pay for a total of two months at unskilled, poorly paid jobs. He hoped that the CCC would teach him "how to work hard and like it."[62] According to the report, "[y]outh, poverty, inexperience, parents with little formal education – such characteristics are all but universal" among CCC members.[63]

The discourse of young "gangsters," immature "boys," and "idle" youth roaming the country being turned into socially responsible, mentally and physically healthy citizens (i.e., adult men) through disciplined

---

[62] Holland and Hill, *Youth in the CCC*, 57–58.   [63] Ibid., 60.

living in a natural setting, far away from irresistible temptations that the cities presumably offered, remained widespread throughout the 1930s.[64] The idea that having young men in healthy surroundings and training them would help strengthen them physically and mentally had a long history that dated back to early in the century, during which it developed as an alternative to the military training programs for young men and boys discussed in earlier chapters of this book. A famous articulation of such an idea was by the philosopher William James in his 1910 essay, "The Moral Equivalent of War," in which he proposed the "conscription" of young men for peaceful activities. Although FDR did not credit his CCC idea to James's essay, his proposal nevertheless reminded many people of it.[65] In this essay, James proposed the "conscription of the whole youthful [male] population to form for a certain number of years a part of the army enlisted against *Nature*," in which they would engage in a variety of activities such as road building, tunnel making, dishwashing, and window washing. He hoped that such public service would serve as an alternative to the widespread idea of toughening young men through military service. Under this scheme, confrontation with nature was to have the same effect as training men militarily – it would "get the childishness knocked out" of young men, instill in them a sense of manliness and public service, and send them back into society with "healthier sympathies and soberer ideas."[66]

Many people expected that the CCC would serve a similar purpose. As an AYCM study of the CCC summed up, American adults hoped

---

[64] Uncle Dudley, "Continue the C.C.C.," editorial, *Boston Daily Globe* (hereafter cited as *BDG*), December 3, 1933; "Work of Putting Youth in Forests Moves Forward"; "Worth Trying," editorial, *NYHT*, April 1, 1933; Osgood Nichols, "CCC – The Scientific Solution of Two Conservation Problems," *WP*, March 31, 1935; "Six Months of the CCC," editorial, *CSM*, November 7, 1933. Although the CCC was popularly seen as helping urban youth, allowing them to live under healthy conditions in the open air while receiving subsistence and work experience, the CCC, in fact, helped more young men from rural areas than those from cities. The proportion of rural youth in the CCC in April 1937 was 59.2 percent, although only 43.8 percent of the total population of the United States lived in rural areas of the country. Robert Fechner, "The Civilian Conservation Corps Program," *Annals of the American Academy of Political and Social Science* 194 (Nov. 1937): 137.

[65] George Philip Rawick, "The New Deal and Youth: The Civilian Conservation Corps, the National Youth Administration, and the American Youth Congress," (PhD diss., University of Wisconsin, 1957), 41. For references to James in descriptions of the CCC at the time, see Raymond Moley, "C. C. C. Bolstered Youth during Slump, Says Moley," *NYHT*, August 27, 1933; "A Permanent CCC," editorial, *NYT*, April 6, 1937; "Poor Young Men," *Time*, February 6, 1939; Aubrey Williams to FDR, June 20, 1940, "OF 58b Youth Movements 1939–40" folder, OF 58b (Youth) Box 4, FDRL.

[66] Emphasis in original. William James, "The Moral Equivalent of War," in *Memories and Studies* (New York: Greenwood Press, 1968 [1911]), 290–91.

that through the CCC "not only would men be given jobs, but they would be fortified and perhaps be rebuilt as men."[67] In assessing the first six months of the CCC, the *Christian Science Monitor* stated that the "greatest improvement was made in the men," rather than in the forests. According to this article, CCC boys arrived in the camps "frightened, bewildered and disorderly," looking underfed and undernourished. After six months of camp life, however, they were "in good spirits," and were physically stronger, cleaner, and neater.[68] The *Washington Post* also called the program a "job worth doing," arguing that the program successfully made young men, who had been roaming the streets and considered social and police problems, healthier and happier.[69] The *New York Times* published a letter from a CCC member that referred to the corps as "The greatest event of the depression." Thanks to his place in the CCC, he wrote, he was earning his way, no longer worrying about being on charity, and that to him, that was "a grand and glorious feeling."[70] The public's high hopes for the Corps to perform the dual roles of economic relief and improving young men's behavior lasted until the agency was closed in 1942.

The positive views of the CCC cut across party lines. *Time* magazine wrote in 1939 that "More continuously than any other New Deal experiment, CCC has had the respect of foes as well as friends of Franklin Roosevelt."[71] When the media reported negatively on the CCC, it was likely due to disobedient or immature behavior on the part of some of its members, rather than any flaws they found in the agency. The ratio of CCC enrollees who left the camps midterm was, in fact, high. By the end of 1941, out of 2,750,000 enrollees, more than 500,000 had left by desertion or for disciplinary reasons.[72] Yet, media coverage of the CCC, as well as the public view of the CCC, remained overwhelmingly positive.

It was not just the mass media that praised the CCC for putting young men back on the right track; government representatives did so, too.

---

[67] Holland and Hill, *Youth in the CCC*, 13.   [68] "Six Months of the CCC."
[69] "A Job Worth Doing," *WP*, December 2, 1933.
[70] William Frazier, letter to the editor, *NYT*, August 1, 1933. For positive views of the CCC's effect on young men in its initial years, see also "Real Reconstruction," editorial, *Baltimore Sun*, August 20, 1933; "Father of C. C. C. Boy Who Gained 24 Pounds Thanks the President," *BDG*, October 8, 1933; "Praise for CCC," editorial of the *Detroit News* reprinted in *NYT*, September 30, 1934; "CCC Is the Rebuilder of Youth's Morale".
[71] "Poor Young Men." See also George Gallup, "Both Parties Approve Conservation Project," *WP*, July 5, 1936.
[72] Holland and Hill, *Youth in the CCC*, 127. For more on why enrollees left the CCC, see Rawick, "The New Deal and Youth," 134–36; "Three Discharged Youth Criticize C. C. C. Food," *BDG*, June 4, 1933.

In 1936, the chairman of the Attorney General's Advisory Committee on Crime claimed that the CCC was likely contributing to the fight against youth criminality by replacing "the unhealthy recreational pursuits of the cities – gambling, drinking, immoral movies, etc. – with organized programs, to suit any taste."[73] The CCC was "largely responsible for the 50 per cent reduction in Chicago's crime record during the last four years," maintained a judge of the Chicago Boys' Court in 1936. *Happy Days*, a weekly newspaper that carried information about the CCC and was approved by the agency, interpreted the judge's statement to mean that "many of the men who have made up the CCC undoubtedly would have gained criminal tendencies if it hadn't been for the CCC."[74] J. Edgar Hoover, the director of the Federal Bureau of Investigation, stated before a House committee in 1938 that the CCC had been one of the most important factors in the reduction of crime among youth.[75]

Adults thus hoped that the CCC would not only assist in reducing youth unemployment but also make young men better citizens. Public expectations for the CCC's character-correcting role, as well as the belief that a lack of education was a significant cause of youth unemployment, prompted calls for broad educational programs in the CCC that went beyond training in forestry and conservation. These expectations, as well as the Army's involvement in managing the CCC, converged with the long-standing UMT idea of transforming youth into adult men through military training and spurred calls for the introduction of military training in the CCC as well.

Education and Military Training in the CCC

From the beginning, there were public expectations for the CCC to serve broader educational ends that ranged from teaching illiterates how to read and write, vocational training and academic education, to character building. Some enrollees wanted education as well. Robert Fechner, who headed the CCC from its beginning until his death in 1939, reported in October 1933 that a "strong interest in education is evinced" in the enrollees as many of the enrollees had never had the opportunity to complete their schooling beyond or through grammar school. However, there was no centralized plan for an educational program in the CCC at that moment, so educational work was conducted voluntarily in each camp at the discretion of the camp's officers and based on the interest of

---

[73] Quoted in Fechner, "The Civilian Conservation Corps," 138.
[74] "A 'Citizen' Is Not a Criminal," editorial, *Happy Days*, October 3, 1936.
[75] Zeitlin, "Federal Relations in American Education," 315.

the enrollees and available resources in the camp. The work ranged from literacy education, vocational training, advanced education related to the forestry work enrollees were engaging in, and academic education of various kinds. In some camps, local educational institutions welcomed enrollees to their evening school courses.[76]

In the meanwhile, George F. Zook, the U.S. Commissioner of Education who would become the ACE director in 1934, Army Chief of Staff General Douglass MacArthur, and Fechner worked out a plan to formally establish an education program in the CCC, and FDR approved it in December 1933. The program was voluntary and was to be conducted after work hours so that it would not interfere with the CCC's primary purpose of conservation and forestry work. Clarence S. Marsh, Dean of the Evening Session at the University of Buffalo, became the first national Educational Director of the CCC (he would resign in early 1935 to become an associate director of the ACE), and civilian educational advisors (who were mostly experienced teachers) were assigned by the U.S. Office of Education to each camp to administer the program. The program included a wide range of subjects, each dealing with either vocational training, basic literacy, or academic study, and intended to help make CCC youth employable and better citizens.[77] The CCC educational advisors in Columbus, Ohio, hailed the education in the CCC as the "blue denim university" in which young men who had lost opportunities for schooling because of the Depression could receive them.[78] In June 1937, U.S. Congress made education compulsory for CCC enrollees.[79]

The public perception of youth as being in need of adult guidance and the expectation that youth-serving agencies should not only help young people financially but also build them up morally also led to calls for the introduction of military training to the CCC and sparked both support and opposition. When the bill to establish the CCC was being discussed in 1933, some people had voiced concern over the plan of having the War Department play a major part in its operation. A legislator worried, for

---

[76] Robert Fechner, "Study Hour in the CCC," *NYT*, October 1, 1933.
[77] "The CCC Educational and Job-Training Program," memorandum, April 20, 1938, p. 1, "Education: Administrative Organization of CCC Educational Program" folder, Records Relating to CCC Educational Program, 1933–1942, Selection Division, RG 35, NACP; Calvin W. Gower, "The Civilian Conservation Corps and American Education: Threat to Local Control?" *History of Education Quarterly* 7, no. 1 (1967): 60–61; C. S. March, "New Outlooks in the CCC," *NYT*, June 3, 1934.
[78] "'Blue Denim' University Deans Plan CCC Studies," *Columbus Citizen* (Columbus, OH), November 11, 1935, filed in "Education Publicity" folder, Records Relating to CCC Educational Program, 1933–1942, Selection Division, RG 35, NACP.
[79] Zeitlin, "Federal Relations in American Education," 88–89.

example, that the Act looked too similar to the draft Act of 1917. The President of the American Federation of Labor attacked the bill as a means for "regimenting" labor.[80] Responding to the allegations that through the CCC young men were being mobilized in peacetime for military purposes, Fechner emphasized that the CCC was "fundamentally a relief program" whose enrolment was purely voluntary.[81]

The Army's involvement in the CCC's administration gave the program a military air, but the involvement was primarily motivated by necessity; logistically, it was the only federal agency capable of establishing the camps and enrolling a large number of young men in a short amount of time. Indeed, Army leaders were hesitant to participate in the CCC. As mentioned in Chapter 2, the Army's size and budget had dropped significantly after World War I, and they grumbled that serving with the CCC interfered with their usual peacetime duties, which they had to carry out with limited resources.[82] Initially, Regular Army officers served in leadership roles at the camps, but within a few years, the majority of them were replaced by officers of the Organized Reserve Corps and CCC enrollees trained in managerial skills.[83] Despite the Army's complaints about its role in the CCC, however, the public soon praised the Army for its effective handling of the corps. For example, the *Rockford Register-Republic* (Rockford, IL) wrote that the Army's work in the CCC "has been a striking demonstration of what rigid discipline, combined with quiet, orderly efficiency, may accomplish in an amazingly short time."[84]

The Army's efficient administration of the CCC and the CCC's focus on peaceful purposes thus alleviated initial concerns that the CCC was militaristic; however, politicians and military men occasionally proposed introducing military training into the CCC, generating headlines in the newspapers. These men saw in the CCC a potential akin to the UMT – toughening and disciplining young men while enhancing military preparedness. In February 1934, for example, Senator David A. Reed of Pennsylvania, speaking at a meeting of the National Defense Council of

---

[80] U.S. Congress, Senate Committee on Education and Labor and House Committee on Labor, *Unemployment Relief: Joint Hearings before the Committees on S. 598, A Bill for the Relief of Unemployment through the Performance of Useful Public Work and for Other Purposes*, 73rd Cong., 1st sess. (Washington, DC: GPO, 1933), 41, 45.
[81] "Fechner Defends Conservation Corps," *BDG*, May 19, 1933.
[82] Heller, "The U.S. Army, the Civilian Conservation Corps, and Leadership," 441–42; "The Army's Extra Work," editorial, *WP*, August 20, 1933; "Army Weakened, Says M'Arthur," *NYT*, November 27, 1933.
[83] Gatzemeyer, *Bodies for Battle*, 118.
[84] "The Army Carries On," editorial of the *Rockford Register-Republic* (Rockford, IL) reprinted in *Chicago Daily Tribune* (hereafter cited as *CDT*), June 5, 1933.

Philadelphia, proposed that the CCC and the CMTC be combined to "teach the CCC to drill and march and obey commands, or teach the young men in the CMTC to build roads and trails." He saw such an arrangement as "a step in the right direction and a distinct contribution to the national defense."[85] Others, including a Massachusetts governor, the national commander of the Veterans of Foreign Wars, and American Legion members, publicly proposed military training programs for the CCC with either character-building or national defense goals, or both.[86]

These proposals were sometimes bolstered by occasional claims by those who thought that the CCC's nonmilitary features could be valuable for national defense. The CCC director Fechner, for example, extrapolated in 1937 that CCC-trained men "could be turned into first-class fighting men at almost an instant's notice," because the CCC had taught the men discipline, living together, and hygiene, all of which were transferrable abilities to military life.[87] An Army officer assigned to the CCC asserted that CCC-trained youth could become effective soldiers in a month in the event of war because they had been taught to "obey orders, how to get along with other men in a camp, personal sanitation, and how to handle themselves in group activities."[88]

The proposals to introduce military training to the CCC, however, sparked intense opposition.[89] When bills, one of which was proposed by MacArthur, were introduced in Congress in 1935 to require CCC men to undergo two months of training in preparation for a five-year enrollment in an auxiliary reserve force, 156 prominent individuals signed a petition to FDR urging him to oppose the measures and demanding the termination of the War Department's involvement in the CCC. The signers included representatives of major pacifist and civil liberties organizations such as Roger Baldwin of the American Civil Liberties Union,

---

[85] "Militarism vs. Conservation," editorial, *CSM*, February 26, 1934.
[86] "Military Work in C. C. C. Urged," *BDG*, June 2, 1936; "Soldiers or Civilians?" editorial, *CSM*, August 15, 1936; "C.C.C. Arms Study Asked," *LAT*, July 21, 1936; "Legion to Study Militarization of CCC Camps," *WP*, August 27, 1936; "The CCC and Defense," editorial, *WP*, September 9, 1936.
[87] "2,300,000 CCC Youths Ready for War; 'First-Class Fighting Men,' Says Fechner," *NYT*, December 21, 1937. This not only shocked pacifists but also aroused criticism from people with military expertise who believed that the training in the CCC by no means readied young men for immediate service in the military. "CCC Soldiers?," *CSM*, December 23, 1937.
[88] "Emergency Army Is Pictured in CCC," *NYT*, March 21, 1938.
[89] "Militarism vs. Conservation"; "Soldiers or Civilians?"; E. B., "Youth and Compulsory Military Training – Guidance for Boys," *NYT*, August 16, 1936; "Military Training in All CCC Camps Is Proposed by Fourth Corps Area General," *Happy Days*, September 12, 1936; "'Not Militaristic,'" editorial, *Baltimore Sun*, September 15, 1936; "Subversive Forces," editorial, *WP*, September 15, 1936.

clergies such as Harry Emerson Fosdick and Reinhold Niebuhr, academics such as John Dewey, and publishers and editors such as George Soule of the *New Republic* and Oswald Garrison Villard of the *Nation*. The petition argued that there was no imminent threat, both external and internal, that could justify the increase in military forces, that the measure would heighten other countries' suspicion of U.S. foreign policy, and that the opposition was "wholly consistent with the historic traditions of American democracy," which had always viewed extensive military institutions and the attitudes of the military caste with suspicion. The Committee on Militarism in Education, which was campaigning against military instruction in educational institutions (Chapter 2), was likely behind this effort.[90]

Until the late 1930s, editorials in major newspapers were also generally against the idea of the CCC offering military training, frequently referencing the Nazis to argue that it was un-American. In 1936, for instance, the *Washington Post* criticized it by stating that the CCC's educational program, which taught young men to read and write, was more important than military training in safeguarding democracy "in a world fast abandoning the ballot box for the concentration camp." As the editors put it, "the pen is mightier than the sword."[91]

Despite these objections being voiced, public opinion polls revealed that the majority of respondents supported the idea of giving the CCC military training. A Gallup poll taken in July 1936, for example, indicated that roughly three-quarters of the American population supported it.[92] Respondents stated they favored the idea not only because it was good for national defense but also because military training in the CCC would teach men discipline and be good for their health. These reasons resonate with those given in support of other military–educational programs, such as the SATC and ROTC, discussed in earlier chapters of this book. Respondents who opposed the idea argued that implementing such a measure would undermine the CCC's mission of providing relief and employment to young men, that a large military would jeopardize democracy, and that if a larger army was required, the military should recruit volunteers rather than training CCC men for military service.[93]

---

[90] "Petition Opposes Drill by the CCC," *NYT*, March 13, 1935; Edwin C. Johnson, "1939 Report of Committee on Militarism in Education," n.d., p. 1, "Military in General Corres. 1936–40" folder, Box 68, National Self Government Committee Records, New York Public Library, New York, NY.
[91] "The CCC and Defense". See also "American Strom Troopers?" editorial of the *Cincinnati Enquirer*, reprinted in *WP*, May 5, 1935.
[92] Institute of Public Opinion, "Voters Reject Steiwer's CCC View," *WP*, July 5, 1936.
[93] Ibid.

In another Gallup poll conducted in December 1938, the approval rate of military training in the CCC remained unchanged. This time, however, the survey also included the question of whether "every able-bodied American boy 20 years old [should] be required to go into the army or navy for one year," which essentially asked if respondents favored UMT. Sixty-three percent of respondents said they were against this idea, while 37 percent indicated they were in favor of it. Opponents contended that such a move could lead to war, would be undesirable in times of peace, and would be "too much like foreign nations." On the other hand, the most common reason for support was that it would provide "good training and discipline" for young men. The second most frequent argument for support was that it would improve national defense, which was followed by one indicating that it was a "good solution for unemployment." Young people were the most likely to oppose the plan, with a 30 percent approval rate among those aged nineteen to twenty-two. The rate was 34 percent for those under the age of thirty, 39 percent for those between the ages of thirty and forty-nine, and 36 percent for those aged fifty and above.[94]

The contrast between the public's strong support for military training in the CCC and its rejection of UMT is striking. The discussions about the right style of military training for young Americans was overshadowed by the tension between coercion and voluntarism, which reflected broader U.S. efforts to distinguish American society from Nazi Germany. When a major general of the U.S. Army proposed in 1936 that the CCC be transformed into a UMT-like program, requiring all eighteen-year-old men in the country to complete a "six-months' course in work, education, and military training," it received much criticism along those lines.[95] The Baltimore *Sun* harshly criticized it, calling it "quite misleading" and argued that it would lead to universal service, which would then be "followed by all of the evils of militarism as they have been experienced in Europe."[96] The executive secretary of the American Peace Society stated that "I can see such a thing growing into a vast militaristic movement like Hitler's." The president of the Washington, D.C. Board of Education said that although he believed "very strongly in preparedness," he did not want to "see us converted into a nation of militarists."[97]

---

[94] George Gallup, "The Gallup Poll: Military Training for CCC Favored by Large Majority in Survey," *WP*, December 16, 1938. See also Institute of Public Opinion, "Nation's Voters Approve CCC," *WP*, April 17, 1938.
[95] "Army Training in CCC Assailed by War Foe," *NYT*, September 15, 1936.
[96] "'Not Militaristic'."
[97] "War Training for CCC Boys Opposed Here," *WP*, September 14, 1936.

This paralleled the debates over the ROTC discussed in Chapter 2. As we have seen, opponents of ROTC frequently accused it of being militaristic. The ROTC supporters, on the other hand, argued that ROTC actually prevented the United States from developing a large standing army and becoming militaristic. The key here is that ROTC and the CCC, unlike UMT, were not mandatory for all male youth. In theory, young men could choose to avoid attending a college with an ROTC requirement or joining the CCC if they did not wish to go through military training, even if in reality those from economically disadvantaged backgrounds may have had no options. Americans thus linked mandatory military training to Nazi Germany, while emphasizing that voluntary training was American and democratic. They would reassess this link in a few short years, however, as they entered a nationwide discussion over activating selective service once again, this time in anticipation of the deterioration of – and possible U.S. involvement in – World War II (Chapter 4).

From Unemployment Relief to Preparedness

While the debates over introducing military training to the CCC raged in American society, the FDR administration was careful not to make the CCC appear as an institution for military training. In January 1934, when Assistant Secretary of War Harry H. Woodring suggested that the CCC be put under military control and proposed to "organize the veterans of the World War, the C. C. C. men, and through them the administration of the emergency relief, into a system of economic storm troops that could support the Government's efforts to smash the depression," he was reported to have been called to the White House to be confirmed that FDR firmly believed that the CCC "should be devoted solely to conservation."[98]

While striving to distinguish its youth programs from those of Nazi Germany, the government also carefully studied youth policies in other countries, notably Germany, to gather ideas for creating effective policies for American youth. This became increasingly significant as the probability of mobilizing young people for another national emergency loomed toward the end of the decade. In August 1938, Assistant Secretary of War Louis Johnson wrote to FDR that a shortage of skilled workers, especially airplane mechanics, for national defense was

---

[98] "200 Professors Demanded that F. D. Fire Harry Woodring for Saying This," *BDG*, January 28, 1934; "CCC Militarization Proposal Arouses Storm of Objection," *CSM*, September 15, 1936.

anticipated both in civilian manufacturers and in the armed forces. He argued that the private industry, trade schools, and federal aid in vocational training through programs like the CCC and NYA would not be enough to meet this need. Therefore, he argued, the War Department should be directed to prepare a plan for establishing and operating an apprentice school of a size sufficient to graduate approximately five thousand air mechanics annually. "It is well known that foreign governments have gone to great lengths to set up adequate systems of apprentice training, particularly as a resource to their airplane industries," he explained, referring to examples of Germany and England. Franklin D. Roosevelt forwarded the letter to his advisor Harry Hopkins. Expressing his willingness to study the possible development of the federal youth agencies into a technical training system for national defense, FDR also forwarded a study of the German work camps conducted by the U.S. Embassy in Berlin.[99] The study reported how effective work camps for youth in Germany were in combining work and education and bridging the gap between the time youth left school and their employment in the industry, while cautiously noting that the camps' main functions included the education of youth in the philosophy of National Socialism.[100]

Whether FDR and Hopkins discussed these plans is unknown, but as the country shifted gears from combating the Depression to military preparedness in the late 1930s, the youth agencies were increasingly incorporated into work for the latter. The CCC's annual report for the fiscal year of 1938–39 explained that the original purpose of the CCC had been to "relieve the acute condition of widespread distress and employment," but the agency now had a different objective; that is, the CCC "as a monetary relief and job-giving agency has been replaced by the CCC as a work-training agency."[101] This shift signaled the agency's incorporation into the swiftly expanding national defense effort that occupied the FDR administration. In May 1940, 500 CCC enrollees

---

[99] Louis Johnson to FDR, August 12, 1938, and FDR to Harry Hopkins, August 15, 1938, in Folder: OF 58b Youth Movements 1938, OF 58b (Box 4), FDRL. See also Kiran Klaus Patel, *Soldiers of Labor: Labor Service in Nazi Germany and New Deal America, 1933–1945*, trans. Thomas Dunlap (New York: Cambridge University Press, 2005), 278.

[100] Henry P. Leverich, "Memorandum for the Ambassador: The Reichsarbeitsdienst (Reich Labor Service)," 25–28 (main text), Folder: OF 58b Youth Movements 1938, OF 58b (Box 4), FDRL.

[101] CCC, *Activities of the Civilian Conservation Corps, July 1, 1938–June 30, 1939* (Washington, DC: GPO, 1940), 10. Initially, only men from families on public relief were eligible. From June 1935 to June 1937, enrollment was restricted to men whose family was receiving or in need of public relief or other assistance. Holland and Hill, *Youth in the CCC*, 49.

were transferred to the Merchant Marine to be trained as marine radio men and apprentice seamen. Attention was paid to not making this arrangement look like the militarization of the CCC – it was made purely on a voluntary basis and the volunteers were given an honorable discharge from the CCC before being transferred.[102] At the end of the same month, a bill was introduced to Congress, with FDR's approval, for the training of CCC enrollees in "non-combatant" defense-related work in such fields as radio, truck operation and repair, construction, and aviation ground operations. This training began in September 1940.[103]

The President also announced that vocational training in the NYA would be utilized to train "non-combatant" workers for national defense.[104] In August 1940, the NYA instructed the state administrators to provide greater opportunities in mechanical production work for youth on NYA resident projects, on the grounds that "the increasing demands for experienced workers in the vital and mechanical fields would provide greater employment opportunities for young people."[105] By December 1940, the NYA operated 595 resident projects, located in forty-five states and Puerto Rico, employing a total of 33,780 young men and women. This was a massive increase from the 4,242 participants in March 1938. The number would continue to climb to an average of 38,607 in the fiscal year of 1942. The NYA boasted that the practical work experience that the agency was providing young people in these resident projects was "one of the contributions that this agency is making to national defense."[106]

Finally, in August 1941, military drilling was introduced to the CCC, although the CCC director emphasized that this move did not signify the incorporation of the CCC into the military.[107] While emphasizing that these measures did not represent a militarization of the youth agencies and downplaying the links to the military with terminology like "non-combatant," therefore, the FDR administration gradually incorporated the agencies into military preparedness work.

With this shift in national priorities, the tone of the opinions expressed in the media on military training in the CCC changed. A Gallup poll taken in September 1939 once again revealed a public majority in favor of

---

[102] "Guns for the CCC?" editorial, *WP*, May 28, 1940.
[103] FDR to Jennings Randolph, June 8, 1940, Folder: OF 268 CCC 1940–1941, OF 268 (Box 6); FDRL; "Asks Military Aid of 300,000 in CCC," *NYT*, May 31, 1940.
[104] "Asks Military Aid of 300,000." [105] NYA, *NYA Resident Work Centers*, 3.
[106] Ibid., 2; Zeitlin, "Federal Relations in American Education," 226.
[107] "Military Drill Is Ordered for CCC Men," *WP*, August 17, 1941; "Military Training for the C.C.C.," editorial, *LAT*, September 8, 1941; Heller, "The U.S. Army, the Civilian Conservation Corps, and Leadership," 450.

it, with 90 percent of respondents supporting the idea of introducing voluntary military training to the CCC.[108] Commenting on the poll results, the *Atlanta Constitution* criticized pacifists who continued to oppose the measure as unrealistic, claiming that if military training was introduced to the CCC, enrollees would be "more fortunate than those of other groups who do not have the advantage of the training." The editors went on to argue that many American soldiers lost their lives in World War I because they had not received adequate military training, and that the CCC should be made available to all young men in the country to avoid a repeat of that tragedy and "make men" out of them.[109] In June 1940, Bailey Millard, a renowned editor and a special writer for the *Los Angeles Times*, argued that military training in the CCC had been a "neglected opportunity." If the measure had been adopted, he continued, the country would then have had a few million young men ready for military duty.[110]

Educational leaders around the AYCM were cooperative in turning the federal youth agencies' focus from economic relief to military preparedness. For example, a policy statement prepared by the AYCM in October 1939 in response to the outbreak of war in Europe demonstrates how the commission sought to advance their educational goals and ensure a better future for young Americans by using the sacrifices the youth would be required to make during the crisis as leverage. Although the AYCM believed that the United States "should not become involved in the present war unless its territories are invaded or the vital interests of the nation are attacked," it acknowledged the need for preparedness and emphasized the importance of education in it: "the primary motive of any program of national defense is to protect our freedom and our democratic institutions. In this respect, education is established in public policy, not as a secondary interest, but as *the first line of defense* against that internal breakdown which in many nations has proved to be even more dangerous than external attack."[111] The statement thus infers the ideological dimension of the "youth problem" to insist on the importance of education to national security. Additionally, it stated that "No part of the population is affected more vitally or occupies a more essential

---

[108] Institute of Public Opinion, "Voluntary Military Training for C.C.C. Backed by Public," *LAT*, October 1, 1939.
[109] "CCC Military Training," *Atlanta Constitution*, October 14, 1939.
[110] Bailey Millard, "Can We Arm the C.C.C.?" *LAT*, June 23, 1940.
[111] Emphasis added. AYCM, *A Program of Action for American Youth* (Washington DC: AYCM, [1939?]), 3, 17, attached to Floyd W. Reeves to Stephen Early, February 12, 1940, Folder: OF 58 Youth 1939–40, OF 58 (Box 2), FDRL.

position in time of war or world crisis than youth."[112] To young people, democracy "must seem to be worth every sacrifice and to offer the brightest opportunities for happiness and the good life," and therefore, the survival of the nation depended on the improvements in the fields of employment, education, and health of youth. The commission urged the government at all levels, schools, and "all organizations concerned with the welfare of youth to expand their programs and redouble their effort."[113]

The involvement of ACE/AYCM leaders in the national preparedness effort accelerated in the period that followed. The U.S. Commissioner of Education John W. Studebaker stated in May 1940 that trade and engineering schools of the country stood ready to train 1,500,000 "non-combatant" workers a year if requested.[114] Floyd W. Reeves, a professor at the University of Chicago and the AYCM director, suggested that the federal government train unemployed youth in the defense industries and that the CCC and the NYA, as well as vocational schools around the country, should be greatly extended with federal funding for this purpose. He anticipated that these and other national defense projects would help reduce youth unemployment.[115] Owen D. Young, retired chairman of the General Electric Co. and the second chairman of the AYCM, was appointed by FDR in June 1940 to a position in the newly created National Defense Advisory Commission to aid national defense work in the NYA and the CCC. In December 1940, the AYCM proposed that the CCC and the NYA be merged to better serve the preparedness effort.[116] The AYCM's integration of preparedness and educational policy, as well as its seeing the war emergency as leverage to advance its educational agenda, was also evident in its support of selective service for World War II, which was being discussed in American society around this time (Chapter 4.)

Americans reshaped the relationship between youth, education, and national security during the New Deal period. The "youth problem" they found stemmed primarily from massive unemployment of people in their late teens to mid-twenties, but they considered it not only an economic problem but an educational and cultural one as well, and one that required federal intervention. The CCC demonstrates this broad shift that took place in American society. Many adults projected their view of youth as naïve and immature onto CCC participants, hoping that the program would not only assist them financially but also strengthen them

---

[112] Ibid., 3.   [113] Ibid., 5, 14–15.   [114] "Asks Military Aid of 300,000 in CCC."
[115] "Skilled Training for Youth Is Urged," *NYT*, June 4, 1940.
[116] "Owen D. Young Takes Post on Defense Board," *NYHT*, June 30, 1940; "Youth Commission Urges Merger of CCC and NYA," *WP*, December 8, 1940.

mentally and physically and make them better citizens. Furthermore, the debates over the inclusion of military training into the CCC demonstrate the lasting impact of the idea, which evolved in the early twentieth century and World War I, that young men should be physically and mentally toughened by military training. The debates also illuminate how efforts to distance youth agencies in the United States from those in Nazi Germany affected ideas about what forms of military training were appropriate in a democracy.

The debates about youth during this period both built on previous ideas about youth and diverged significantly from them. Both the continuities and discontinuities served to establish the New Deal as a pivotal period in the history of youth, education, and national security. The UMT concept of viewing military training as an opportunity to transform "boys" into "men" formed expectations of what the CCC might achieve for young men, and it would continue to shape discussions over selective service during World War II. Additionally, key educational leaders, particularly those in the AYCM circle, supported federal intervention in the "youth problem," as they saw the Depression as a national emergency equivalent to a state of war. As a result, the ties that had begun to form between educators and the federal government during World War I were strengthened during the Great Depression; they would be solidified during World War II. On the other hand, the connection between legal age, maturity, and military obligations that had defined selective service in World War I became muddled as the term "youth" came to refer not only to minors but also to young people in their twenties; the public discussions on the role young people should play in World War II would both expand upon and redefine the notion of "youth" that was prevalent during the Great Depression. The major developments that took place in the 1930s about the relationship between youth, education, and national security, therefore, drew on and developed previous ideas about this relationship, and they would serve as the foundation for American conversations about it during World War II.

This chapter began at a bustling Fort Devens in 1933. In the fall of 1940, the fort was once again functioning as a reception center for draftees, as a new Selective Service System had recently been set up to meet the war emergency.[117] How young people, once considered a problem, were conscripted in World War II and what effects this had on their education, their relationship with the government, and the image of the "youth problem" will be discussed in the next few chapters.

---

[117] "History," *USAG Devens RFTA*.

4 Conscripting Youth for World War II

World War II was a young man's war. Soldiers on both sides of the war were younger than those of World War I and included many teenagers. In the 1930s, Americans had attacked Nazi Germany for regimenting youth, positioning American democracy as the ideological opposite of such regimes. In doing so, they associated voluntarism with Americanism and coercion with militarism and dictatorship, supporting military training in the Civilian Conservation Corps (CCC) while opposing universal military training (UMT). Nonetheless, by the autumn of 1942, the U.S. government had begun to draft teenagers and had established conscription as fundamentally democratic and American.

This chapter examines American debates over establishing the draft as "democratic" and "American" during World War II. Although selective service had been implemented in World War I and was considered "democratic" at the time as well, the one in World War II differed in a few ways: first, it was established in September 1940, more than a year before the United States entered the war, and second, it eventually conscripted a disproportionate number of young men aged eighteen to twenty-five. As a result of nationwide debates over creating a "democratic" draft and disproportionately drafting young men, the image of "youth," which had been regarded as problematic in the 1930s, was transformed into what would later be known as the "Greatest Generation," a generation that bravely fought for their country during the war and remained strongly committed to community service, democratic politics, and economic prosperity in the postwar United States.[1]

During World War II, this change in the perception of youth was noted throughout American society. Figure 4.1 shows a photograph taken by photographer Joe Rosenthal in February 1945, during the battle between the United States and Japan on Iwo Jima, that became a sensation in the United States and remains an iconic image of brave U.S. soldiers in the

---

[1] Tom Brokaw, *The Greatest Generation* (New York: Random House, 1998).

Figure 4.1 Flag raisers on Iwo Jima, 1945.
Joe Rosenthal, "Flag Raising on Iwo Jima," February 23, 1945, NAID: 520748. Courtesy of the U.S. National Archives.

war. All six of the U.S. servicemen depicted here would have been considered "youth" in the 1930s. From left to right, Ira H. Hayes was twenty-two years old, Harold H. Schultz had just turned twenty, Michael Strank was twenty-five, Franklin R. Sousley was nineteen, Harold P. Keller was twenty-three, and Harlon H. Block was twenty.[2]

The iconizing of the young flag-raisers on Iwo Jima during World War II illustrates how American society had come to associate the image of a typical American soldier with young men – no longer problematic, but

---

[2] "Joe Rosenthal, Photographer Who Captured the Flag-Raising at Iwo Jima, Dies at 94," obituary, *New York Times* (hereafter cited as *NYT*), August 22, 2006; Ross E. Phillips and Annette Amerman, "Biographical Sketches of Key Personnel," in *Investigating Iwo: The Flag Raisings in Myth, Memory, and Esprit de Corps*, ed. Breanne Robertson (Quantico, VA: Marine Corps Historical Division, 2019), 322–30. Two of the names of the flag-raisers listed in the above obituary for Rosenthal do not correspond to the names listed here, as they were misidentified until 2016 and 2019, respectively. Breanne Robertson, "Iwo Jima and the Struggle for Historical Truth: An Introduction," in *Investigating Iwo*, ed. Robertson, xv–xvi, xxii–xxiv.

Figure 4.2 The Rough Riders on San Juan Hill, 1898.
"Colonel Roosevelt and His Rough Riders at the Top of the Hill Which They Captured, Battle of San Juan," Library of Congress Prints and Photographs Division, Reproduction Number: LC-USZC4–7934. In the public domain.

rather innocent, brave, and spirited. Compare this to a photo of Theodore Roosevelt posing triumphantly on San Juan Hill, Cuba, for the iconic Rough Rider photo in July 1898, which brought him national fame (Figure 4.2). He was thirty-nine years old when this photograph was taken, and while we cannot identify the ages of all the Rough Riders around him, many of them appear older than the young men on Iwo Jima.

There are certainly limitations to comparing these two photos. First, these iconic figures do not represent all U.S. service people who fought in U.S. wars – they do not reflect the racial, ethnic, and gender diversity of the service people, nor their age diversity. Those praised for their service in World War II, for example, included older commanders like Dwight D. Eisenhower, who was fifty-four in August 1945, and Douglas MacArthur, who was sixty-five. Additionally, the majority of U.S.

soldiers who fought in that war were draftees, in contrast to the volunteers who fought in the Spanish–American War. Yet, the Iwo Jima photo captures the transformation that occurred as a result of the mobilization of young people for World War II – they were no longer viewed collectively as a problem, but as laudable individuals who devoted their lives to the country on the battlefields or supported the war effort at home.

The establishment of the Selective Service System, through which 66 percent of the nearly fifteen million Americans who served in the U.S. Armed Forces during World War II were drafted, was crucial to this shift in the perception of youth. There were a few aspects of the new Selective Service System that did not exist during World War I. First, it was established more than a year before the United States entered the war. Second, the progression of the war necessitated the draft of minors shortly after the U.S. entry into the conflict. This stands in striking contrast to the situation in World War I – even though the amendment to draft teens was passed in 1918, the war ended before eighteen-year-olds were drafted. The reshaping of the image of youth was therefore closely related to debates over establishing a Selective Service System before the country's entry into the war and conscripting young men, both in the name of democracy.

In scholarly works, the 1940 Selective Training and Service Act, which established the U.S. Selective Service System for World War II, is frequently referred to as the "first peacetime" conscription Act in U.S. history. This comprehension is demonstrated by the title of one of the representative works on this Act: *The First Peacetime Draft*. Similarly, the Selective Service System's annual report for 1940–1941 is titled *Selective Service in Peacetime*.[3] However, as this chapter reveals, the Selective Training and Service Act became law in 1940, despite strong resistance to UMT in the 1930s, precisely because Americans increasingly felt they were no longer living in peacetime. The terms selective "training" and "service" in the Act's title blur the distinction between wartime "service" and peacetime "training." The debates over the appropriate draft age were based on the neither-war-nor-peace atmosphere and reflected the overlap of the Great Depression and World War II.

The "democratic" system of selective service was not meant to draft men equally from all ages and segments of society. The fact that the lower limit of the draft age was set in 1940 at twenty-one, even though it had been lowered to eighteen in 1918 and had established a precedent

---

[3] J. Garry Clifford and Samuel R. Spencer, Jr., *The First Peacetime Draft* (Lawrence: University Press of Kansas, 1986); Lewis B. Hershey, *Selective Service in Peacetime: First Report of the Director of Selective Service, 1940–41* (Washington, DC: GPO, 1942).

that minors could be conscripted, demonstrates how controversial the conscription of minors remained. Yet, by the end of 1942, the country had decided to draft disproportionally men aged eighteen to twenty-five. Older men were also subject to draft registration, but provisions of the Selective Service law granted deferments to men with families and those with expertise considered useful for war industries on the home front. Many young men were single and had little practical work experience, a situation that had been severely amplified by the massive youth unemployment during the Great Depression. Young men were also considered physically stronger than older men. Through the process of establishing the draft of youth as "democratic," the proponents reinterpreted the characteristics of youth that had been deemed serious problems in the 1930s. That is, a lack of advanced work experience now indicated immediate availability for military service, an unstable lifestyle now meant mobility, and mental malleability now signified adaptability to military discipline.[4]

Youth conscription entailed more than the issue of who should put on the khaki; it was deemed to also affect the educational opportunities of those in the age bracket considered most fit for military service. Young men out of school and with no notable vocational skills were likely to be the first to be called. On the other hand, plans were developed, with higher education elites' involvement, to offer an opportunity to young men considered talented from a military perspective to receive college-level training at the government's expense. This move signaled how a close partnership had been developed by this time between the higher education sector, its representatives, and the government through military–educational programs such as the Student Army Training Corps (SATC) during World War I and the Reserve Officers' Training Corps (ROTC) in the 1920s and 1930s, as well as the New Deal's youth agencies; it also demonstrates the spread of the idea that military training and service could be considered a rewarding educational opportunity. In a period in which schooling had largely replaced apprenticeships and other on-the-job training opportunities as the primary route to employment, the pairing of education and military service implied that the government was in a position to limit or expand the long-term career opportunities for young people.

By the time young men raised the American flag on Iwo Jima, American society had largely embraced the idea that young men were the country's principal source of soldiers in total war and had invented

---

[4] Two-thirds of U.S. servicepeople during World War II were single. Kathleen J. Frydl, *The GI Bill* (New York: Cambridge University Press, 2009), 69.

ways to explain it as "democratic" and "American." Along the way, it accepted the idea that the federal government could determine the educational and career paths of youth in war and peace and that serving the national good was one of the fundamental goals of higher education. The "democratic" mobilization of young Americans for World War II had thus internalized the stratification of youth based on the individual's potential to serve the collective good, which had originated in World War I and evolved in the subsequent decades.

Plans for Conscription after World War I

The selective draft in World War I was terminated soon after the armistice in November 1918, but conscription plans continued to be developed after the war. The American Legion, for instance, began studying conscription as early as 1921. A bill proposed by the Legion in 1928 stipulated the conscription of capital and industrial resources in addition to personnel during times of conflict. It never received congressional support because of its ambitious and expansive scope, but that did not mean legislators were opposed to the idea of drafting civilians. In fact, many of them believed that drafting men was much less controversial than the conscription of material resources. Some said that "There is no trouble about getting the men under the draft act," while others thought that "it is a good thing to have a conscription act."[5] The question was not so much whether to adopt a draft as it was when to do so.

The military also began to formulate plans for a draft system to be implemented in the future soon after the end of World War I, as the National Defense Act of 1920 required the War Department General Staff to prepare plans for the mobilization of personnel and material resources. Based on this Act, the Joint Army and Navy Selective Service Committee (JANSSC) was formed in 1926 to study conscription and train reserve officers, many of whom would be called to duty in 1940 to set up the new Selective Service System.[6] The committee explored a possible age range for future conscription laws that would simultaneously meet military requirements and be acceptable to civilians. Accordingly, the study concluded that even though the military generally

---

[5] U.S. Congress, House, Committee on Military Affairs, *Universal Draft: Conscription of Man Power, Wealth, and Industrial Resources in Time of War: Hearings before the Committee on H.R. 455, H.R. 8313, H.R. 8329,* 70th Cong., 1st sess. (Washington, DC: GPO, 1928), 1–3, 14, 16.

[6] Hershey, *Selective Service in Peacetime,* 9, 11.

believed that young men made for better soldiers, in a future draft Act, the military should request that men aged eighteen through forty-four be subject to registration, but that those aged twenty-one through thirty, which matched the initial registration age during World War I, should be registered first; younger and older men could then be made subject to registration if a military necessity demanded it.[7]

In the 1920s and 1930s, then, military leaders and others concerned with military preparedness conceived of conscription as a means of securing military manpower in wartime. However, they assumed that Washington and the public would only approve it after the country was officially at war.[8] The course of World War II, however, shattered the Americans' distinction between wartime and peacetime, prompting the passage of a selective conscription Act prior to the U.S. entry into the war.

The Selective Training and Service Act of 1940

In May 1940, eight months after German troops invaded Poland and launched Europe into massive armed conflict, a group of a hundred men gathered at the Harvard Club in New York City to discuss a plan to alert Americans to the need to be better prepared militarily and possibly for a new war. These men were members of the Military Training Camps Association (MTCA), a gathering of elite men that had provided voluntary military training programs to civilians since 1915 and had been a major proponent of UMT (Chapter 1.) The group was led by Grenville Clark, the driving force behind the MTCA's preparedness campaigns in the 1910s, and its members included presidents of Harvard and Princeton, as well as other upper-class men in business, politics, and education. These men believed that the United States should further aid the Allies to stop Axis aggression, strengthen military preparedness, and that the draft was the most efficient method of procuring the necessary military force with minimal economic disruption. The MTCA drafted a

---

[7] [R. F. Cox], "Estimate of Manpower," [1933], pp. 3–4, in "200 Cox, Estimate of Manpower, 1930" folder, Files from the Reference Library of the Research and Statistics Division, 1926–1969, Records of the Selective Service System, Record Group (hereafter cited as RG) 147, National Archives at College Park, College Park, MD (hereafter cited as NACP); [R. F. Cox], "Initial and Later Registrations," pp. 6, 17, attached to R. F. Cox, memorandum for the JANSSC, December 28, 1933, "203C Cox, Priority of Age Group 1933," folder, Files from the Reference Library of the Research and Statistics Division, 1926–1969, Records of the Selective Service System, RG 147, NACP.
[8] Mark Skinner Watson, *Chief of Staff: Prewar Plans and Preparations* (Washington, DC: GPO, 1950), 183; John Whiteclay Chambers II, *To Raise an Army: The Draft Comes to Modern America* (New York: Free Press, 1987), 249.

conscription bill of its own while preaching the need for a draft to politicians and the broader public through personal connections in Washington, mass media, and various patriotic and business organizations such as the American Legion and Rotary clubs as well as chambers of commerce. Their campaign soon materialized as the Selective Training and Service Act of 1940, which was introduced by Edward R. Burke (D-NE) in the Senate on June 20 and James Wadsworth (R-NY) in the House on June 21.[9] Wadsworth, as mentioned in Chapter 2, had been a keen UMT advocate and an important ally of the War Department in its effort to defend ROTC in educational institutions against anti-ROTC movements.

As discussed in the previous chapter, public opinion polls in the 1930s had indicated that most Americans were opposed to UMT of young men even while having no issue introducing military training to the CCC. Yet, the tide of the times changed what was acceptable as a "democratic" measure of training young men militarily and pushed the bill through Congress. When the bill was introduced to Congress on June 20, 1940, the Axis powers were on the offensive. France surrendered to Germany two days later, and Britain was suffering heavy losses as well. Although opposition to aiding Britain at the risk of becoming embroiled in the war remained strong, the aggression of the Axis powers swayed public opinion in favor of adopting a military training program. The shift was already evident in a Gallup poll conducted in May 1940, which indicated that 50 percent of respondents supported compulsory military training for all twenty-year-old men, up from 37 percent in December 1938 and 39 percent in October 1939. Moreover, 85 percent of the respondents considered that the U.S. armed forces were not strong enough to keep the country safe from an attack by a foreign power.[10]

The country's future was more uncertain than ever – no one knew how the war would progress, when it would conclude, and most significantly, whether the United States would join it. In light of this uncertainty, there was considerable confusion regarding the precise nature of the issue at hand. People tended to use the terms "military training" and "military

---

[9] George Q. Flynn, *The Draft, 1940–1973* (Lawrence: University Press of Kansas, 1993), 9–11; Grenville Clark to FDR, May 24, 1940, Folder: "Selective Service Legislation, Jan.–May 1940", Official File (hereafter cited as OF) 1413 (Box 4), Franklin D. Roosevelt Library, Hyde Park, NY (hereafter cited as FDRL); Watson, *Chief of Staff*, 189; Clifford and Spencer, Jr., *The First Peacetime Draft*, 14; Wayne S. Cole, *Roosevelt and the Isolationists, 1932–1945* (Lincoln: University of Nebraska, 1983), 376–77; Frank L. Kluckhohn, "Both Parties Back Selective Service," *NYT*, June 22, 1940.

[10] "Military Training Gains Supporters," *NYT*, June 2, 1940.

service" interchangeably, did not differentiate between wartime service and peacetime training, and did not always specify whether the service or training in question would be mandatory or voluntary for all men of a certain age. Indeed, this uncertainty is exemplified by the juxtaposition of "military training" and "service" in the name of the 1940 draft Act. Yet, precisely because of this uncertainty, the public was more willing to embrace some form of military training (or service) even if the country had not declared war. On June 20, 1940, the day the draft bill was introduced in Congress, FDR appointed Republican and interventionist Henry Stimson to replace noninterventionist Harry H. Woodring as Secretary of War, marking the administration's push toward military preparedness and endeavor to establish a bipartisan image of it. As a result, the War Department, which had been doubtful of the possibility of a draft Act being passed before the United States entered a war, worked out changes to the MTCA bill that fulfilled their expectations.[11]

The MTCA had initially envisioned a highly comprehensive system that required the registration of all men between ages eighteen and sixty-five, with those between ages twenty-one and forty-five liable for military training and the rest for "home defense" training.[12] This extensive age range, the MTCA expected, would affect virtually every household and create a "united front for a great national defense effort." The military, by contrast, was interested in creating the most effective fighting force. Firmly believing that young men were better soldiers, it proposed that the age range be twenty-one to thirty-one, with the possibility of expanding it to ages eighteen to thirty-five if Congress declared a national emergency.[13]

Significantly, the debates over the bill, both in and out of Congress, centered on establishing the draft as a "democratic" measure, in contrast to both volunteerism, which had long been considered a U.S. tradition, and Nazi Germany's mobilization of civilians for the war. National security exigencies – that the United States and American democracy were in grave danger of being attacked by Germany – and the inability of the volunteer system to meet the scale and rapidity requirements for mobilization were the primary arguments made by supporters of the bill.

The supporters claimed that selective training and service was truly democratic by drawing on a logic for selective service stated during World War I – that it would draft men equally from all social classes

---

[11] Flynn, *The Draft*, 12–13; Cole, *Roosevelt and Isolationists*, 367–68.
[12] Kluckhohn, "Both Parties Back Selective Service."
[13] John O'Sullivan, "From Voluntarism to Conscription: Congress and Selective Service, 1940–1945" (PhD diss., Columbia University, 1971), 30.

and would be more effective than the volunteer system.[14] Senator Morris Sheppard, chairman of the Senate Military Affairs Committee, explained that in the proposed system, the "burdens of military service will be borne not only by the willing and those compelled to volunteer because of lack of funds – as is true under a volunteer system operating alone – but such burdens will be borne equally by all classes, *regardless of economic means.*"[15] Secretary of War Stimson elaborated on the inefficiency of volunteerism before the House Committee on Military Affairs. According to him, the nation's past war experiences had proved the volunteer system a "costly failure," as it produced much confusion on both the military and the home front. Great Britain had also experienced enormous losses and confusion in World War I and the ongoing war with Germany because the country favored volunteering and delayed the adoption of conscription, he insisted. According to Stimson, in a voluntary system, a man who might be more useful if he stayed home might rush to enlist, while a selective service system compelled each man to serve in the capacity where he was most effective. A selective draft, according to this logic, distributed the duty of national defense to every citizen with minimal disruption to normal civilian life. In short, it was "the only efficient system in the great task of a modern war," and "the only system which is appropriate to a democracy."[16]

An argument that had been repeated by supporters of military training in the previous decades – that military service as specified in the bill would toughen and discipline youth, transforming them into public-minded citizens who understood the obligations of citizenship – was also heard from supporters of the bill, particularly those outside the halls of Congress.[17] A reader of the *New York Herald Tribune* argued that modern technology had turned American youth "soft." According to this writer, who dubbed himself a "Hardboiled Realist," modern youth had "never been obliged to carry in the wood and coal or carry out the ashes. It will not walk a half mile if it can get a ride." He continued that once trained, "the average youngster will return to civil life a more useful citizen,

---

[14] U.S. Congress, House, Committee on Military Affairs, *Selective Compulsory Military Training and Service: Hearings before the Committee on H.R. 10132, A Bill to Protect the Integrity and Institutions of the United States through a System of Selective Compulsory Military Training and Service*, 76th Cong., 3rd sess. (Washington, DC: GPO, 1940), 100–101, 382–84, 387–88, 394, 400.

[15] Emphasis added. Senator Morris Sheppard (TX), speaking on S. 4164, August 9, 1940, 76th Cong., 3rd sess., *Congressional Record* 86, pt. 9: 10092–93.

[16] House Committee on Military Affairs, *Selective Compulsory Military Training and Service*, 382–84. See also pp. 117, 121.

[17] Ibid., 100.

healthier in both body and mind."[18] Writing to the same newspaper, a minister proposed that every young man graduating from high school or upon reaching his eighteenth birthday be required to serve in the military for two years, on the grounds that "In my experience in the ministry I have found very few young men graduating from high school matured enough to enter directly into college, or to go into the business world." Military service, according to him, would succeed in making "a man out of him."[19]

The bill's supporters included educational leaders as well. At the urging of the MTCA, four colleges and universities on the East Coast (Harvard, Yale, Williams College, and Amherst College) held meetings during their commencement period to call for the adoption of the military training program proposed by the MTCA to strengthen national defense. Princeton President Harold W. Dodds, who led this publicity campaign, aired his support for the measure over the radio, arguing that volunteer service was "alien" to the spirit of American democracy and that the concept of noncombatant no longer applied in modern warfare.[20] On June 17, a meeting at Yale of several hundred undergraduates, alumni, and members of the faculty, called by the Yale committee of the MTCA, adopted a resolution advocating universal compulsory military training to protect "the safety and free institutions of the United States." Similar resolutions were also adopted at Brown and Harvard.[21] American Defense, Harvard Group, an interventionist group founded by faculty members at Harvard University after the fall of France in June 1940, sent a poll to faculty members in universities across the country asking whether they supported "universal training in peace and universal service in war, as embodied in such bills as the Burke-Wadsworth Bill"; according to them, within a few days, they received over 300 responses expressing their support and no clearly negative responses.[22]

Other educators, perceiving that the implementation of selective military training and service was unavoidable, advocated for maximal social welfare for young people in exchange for national service. The American

[18] Hardboiled Realist, letter to the editor, *New York Herald Tribune* (hereafter cited as *NYHT*), August 1, 1940.
[19] Rev. Edward J. Bubb, letter to the editor, *NYHT*, August 6, 1940.
[20] "Conscription Aid Seen at 4 Colleges," *NYT*, June 13, 1940; "For Selective Service," editorial, *NYT*, June 15, 1940.
[21] "Yale, Brown Urge Military Training," *NYT*, June 18, 1940; "Military Training Urged at Harvard," *NYT*, June 21, 1940.
[22] "College Teachers Back Defense Call," *NYT*, July 29, 1940; "Records of American Defense, Harvard Group, 1940–1945," *Harvard University Archives*, https://id.lib.harvard.edu/ead/hua12007/catalog (accessed September 18, 2023).

Youth Commission (AYCM) issued a pamphlet titled *Youth, Defense, and the National Welfare* in August 1940 to promote proposals along these lines. Acknowledging the necessity of speedily and efficiently expanding the size of the military, the pamphlet expressed the AYCM's support of the bill.[23] It stated that the obligation to serve in the common defense in time of need was a "universal" and "elementary duty of citizenship, older than civilization, and not absent from any form of organized government, democratic or otherwise." That said, the pamphlet continued, compulsory military service was a "very serious undertaking" in which men would be "trained to kill and to take the risk of being killed in order that the democratic community of free people may continue to exist." As youth would bear most of the burden, the authors insisted that no military conscription bill should be passed without acceptance by the government of full responsibility for the provision of "adequate economic, educational, health, and recreational conditions" for all young people. They stressed that the measures that the government had taken for youth – the National Youth Administration (NYA), the CCC, and other federal aid to in-school programs – were not sufficient to serve the entire youthful population.[24]

The pamphlet stressed that no one be called before reaching the age of twenty-one and that draftees should be chosen by lot and called equally from a wide range of ages to avoid the burdens of military service being concentrated on one age group, especially "the unemployed boys of 18, 19, 20, 21, and 22 who are most willing to volunteer." Furthermore, the number of draftees should be "limited strictly to those needed for military reasons," even though "military training may have certain values as preparation for citizenship."[25] Taken as a whole, the authors asserted that the number of young men called for service must be minimal, but because *some* young men would be asked to risk their lives for the nation, *all* young men and women deserved better welfare.

Opponents of the bill launched a vigorous campaign to prevent it from passing through Congress, and they represented a wide spectrum of political opinions regarding U.S. approaches to foreign policy in general and warfare in particular. For example, some were pacifists who opposed all war, while others agreed that the military must be strengthened to protect national security but disagreed with any action that would

---

[23] "Youth Commission Lists Seven Safeguards for Compulsory Military Service Legislation," *Washington Post* (hereafter cited as *WP*), August 4, 1940; American Youth Commission (AYCM), *Youth, Defense, and the National Welfare* (Washington, DC: AYCM, [1940]), 3.

[24] AYCM, *Youth, Defense, and the National Welfare*, 4–5.   [25] Ibid., 3–4.

indicate active U.S. involvement in the ongoing war, much less the deployment of U.S. soldiers to the front lines. Many of them claimed that a peacetime selective draft was neither democratic nor American, thus building on the earlier distinction between volunteerism and compulsory training that was evident in the debates over military training in ROTC and the CCC and which linked compulsory service to "totalitarianism" and dictatorship. A senator criticized the MTCA for attempting to "regiment American boys," while Senator Robert A. Taft, the leading proponent of anti-interventionism, contended that "[n]o measure considered since I have been in the Senate has sought to change so much the basic theory of American life."[26] Taft continued: "The theory behind it leads directly to totalitarianism." Instead, he argued, the existing volunteer system should be used first. According to him, the volunteer system had become ineffective only because of the popular assumption that the army was an unpleasant occupation that "every boy instinctively avoids." Many men, including millions of unemployed men in CCC camps, would volunteer if it were made more attractive through measures such as increasing pay and making the service period more flexible, and then, "we will have a more earnest, interested, permanent, and enthusiastic force" than one produced by men who were coerced to serve.[27]

Taft was not alone in linking the bill to the unemployment problem the Great Depression had created, reflecting how the Depression and war issues intersected in American society in 1940. A woman critical of the New Deal and opposing the bill wrote to the *New York Herald Tribune*: "Count up our thousands of C. C. C. boys, thousands of unemployed on relief, cut down the many too many [sic] W. P. A. [Work Progress Administration, a New Deal agency that provided temporary work to people out of work] men that are now put on every W. P. A. job. Add all these up, and you will find the government has here a large army of men to put into camps and train at once."[28]

Some supporters of the bill also saw it in light of the New Deal. Senator Robert Rice Reynolds, who would become chairman of the Senate Committee on Military Affairs the following year, contended that if Congress had decided to train the CCC men militarily upon establishing the corps, the country would have already had 1,400,000 trained

---

[26] Frank Kluckhohn, "Clash on Draft," *NYT*, August 7, 1940; Senator Robert Taft (OH), speaking on S. 4164, August 14, 1940, 76th Cong., 3rd sess., *Congressional Record* 86, pt. 9: 10296.
[27] 76th Cong., 3rd sess., *Congressional Record* 86, pt. 9: 10303, 10309, 10311.
[28] Baily Mohlman, letter to the editor, *NYHT*, July 30, 1940. See also Dorothy R. Krouse, letter to the editor, *NYHT*, July 30, 1940.

men.[29] The President of Vassar College in New York argued that "There is much to be said for selective conscription as far more democratic than the securing of an army from the ranks of the unemployed."[30] The interrelations between the issues of unemployment caused by the Great Depression and those concerning military service during World War II in this debate illustrates how American society was neither in "peacetime" nor "wartime."

Some young people, who would likely be called first, also registered opposition, attacking the idea that selective service stipulated in the bill was democratic.[31] One young man pointed out that under the bill, the burden would fall entirely upon young men. He insisted that it was "hardly fair that women, older persons, men with dependents and workers with good jobs in defense industries should escape completely at the expense of the few."[32] The Southern Negro Youth Congress addressed a letter to FDR stating: "Three million Negro Americans, voteless and without representation in congress because of the un-American Poll Tax laws and the flagrant abrogation of the 14th and 15th amendments to the constitution declare their determined opposition" to the Burke-Wadsworth bill, which would "regiment our youth."[33]

The Committee on Militarism in Education (CME), the New York-based organization founded in 1925 to protest military training in civilian schools and colleges and which also opposed military training in the CCC (Chapters 2 and 3), once again took a stand to object to the "militarism" they perceived in the bill. It prepared a document titled "A Declaration Against Conscription," which was signed by 240 educators, writers, religious leaders, and business leaders and published in the *New York Times*.[34] Signers included prominent names such as historian Howard K. Beale, philosopher John Dewey, sociologist Robert S. Lynd, Rev. A. J. Muste, socialist Norman Thomas, and journalist Oswald

---

[29] Senator Robert Rice Reynolds (SC), speaking on S. 4164, August 9, 1940, 76th Cong., 3rd sess., *Congressional Record* 86, pt. 9: 10111.
[30] Henry MacCracken to Edwin C. Johnson, July 1, 1940, Reel 17, *Records of the Committee on Militarism in Education, 1925–1940* (DG 009), Swarthmore College Peace Collection, Scholarly Resources Microfilm Edition (hereafter cited as CME Records).
[31] "Students Fight Training," *NYT*, August 1, 1940; "Girl Scheduled to Arrive Wednesday," *WP*, August 4, 1940; "Students Ask Draft Defeat, Risk Ousting," *Christian Science Monitor*, September 4, 1940; "First Lady Assails Guild on the Draft," *NYT*, September 15, 1940.
[32] David L. Fox, letter to the editor, *NYHT*, August 6, 1940.
[33] "Southern Youth Congress Hits Conscription Bill," *Atlanta Daily World*, August 7, 1940.
[34] "Educators Assail Peacetime Draft," *NYT*, July 9, 1940.

Garrison Villard. The statement declared that military conscription in peacetime "smacks of totalitarianism."[35] It rejected as "transparent sophistry the contention that conscription under the name of 'selective service' is democratic and that voluntary military service is undemocratic." Furthermore, it argued, conscription would result in a widespread dislocation in business, industry, agriculture, and higher education. A volunteer system with a pay sufficiently attractive to induce the required numbers of enrollees would be "vastly preferable" to conscription, it maintained.[36]

Although the statement attracted substantial support, it also faced much opposition from some people who were asked to sign and alienated many who had supported CME's previous campaigns against military training in schools. Some reasons for declining to support the CME's campaign resonated with those supporting UMT in previous decades. A social scientist at Fresno State College in California, for example, argued that he would approve a bill to draft youth because the "lack of any sense of public obligation or duty on the part of our youth is simply appalling."[37] However, others withdrew their support for the CME or declined to support this campaign due to the imminent threat the war posed to American society. Thomas J. Michie, the future judge of the U.S. District Court for the Western District of Virginia and a past contributor to the CME, argued: "It is one thing to oppose militarism in education in times of comparative peace and safety. It is another thing to oppose the only possible means of protecting the independence of this country at a time when it is in imminent danger."[38] President Robert Hutchins of the University of Chicago maintained that "If the United States is going to prepare for defense on a large scale, I favor conscription," while an astronomer at the University of Virginia maintained that "We are *not* living 'in peacetime.'"[39]

This final point – that the United States was "not in peacetime" – was critical to the Act's passage. Although there was still considerable opposition in American society to active military involvement in the war, fewer Americans now opposed military preparedness (assuming it would be a defensive measure.) As a result, the bill's opponents were never able to turn the tide, and the criticism the CME's campaign received

---

[35] "A Declaration against Conscription," n.d., n.p., Reel 16, CME Records. [36] Ibid.
[37] Hubert Phillips to Edwin C. Johnson, September 6, 1940, Reel 17, CME Records.
[38] Thomas J. Michie to Edwin C. Johnson, August 28, 1940, Reel 17, CME Records; Federal Judicial Center, "Michie, Thomas Johnson," *Biographical Directory of Article III Federal Judges, 1789–present*, www.fjc.gov/node/1385086 (accessed December 23, 2023).
[39] Emphasis in original. Robert Hutchins to Edwin C. Johnson, July 2, 1940, Reel 17, CME Records; S. A. Mitchell to the CME, n.d., Reel 17, CME Records.

demonstrates that an increasing number of Americans believed they were no longer living in a time of peace. Unlike in the 1930s, when Americans saw military training in the CCC as acceptable but UMT as objectionable, most Americans agreed on the need for some kind of military preparedness in light of the deteriorating situation in Europe. Moreover, not only FDR, but Republican presidential candidate Wendell Willkie endorsed the bill, giving it bipartisan backing.[40]

The draft age, proposed to be between twenty-one and thirty-one by the Senate and between twenty-one and forty-five by the House, was established by the law to be between twenty-one and thirty-six. The law stipulated the registration of all men in this age range, including both citizens and male resident aliens who declared an intention of becoming U.S. citizens.[41] Men inducted were required to serve for twelve months, after which they were to be placed in the reserves for ten years or until they reached age forty-five, whichever came first. In response to strong opposition to any bill that indicated direct U.S. military involvement in the war in Europe, the law emphasized its limited nature, stipulating that the purpose of the draft was defensive, and therefore, no more than 900,000 men were to be in active training or service at one time and draftees would not be deployed "beyond the limits of the Western Hemisphere except in the territories and possessions of the United States, including the Philippines."[42]

The framing of the bill as a limited, defensive measure – especially the geographical limits on the places draftees would be dispatched and the one-year term of service – reassured many Americans that it was a temporary measure to address the pressing national security threat and it would not institutionalize a permanent military training program nor a program intended to "regiment" American youth.[43] Moreover, non-military reasons – such as the idea that selective service was more "democratic" than other means of securing manpower and the expectations that it would help "toughen" youth or advance social welfare goals – boosted public support for the bill.

At the end of August, Gallup asked young men the following question: "If the draft law is passed, will you, personally, have any objection to spending a year in some branch of military service?" Among men ages twenty-one to twenty-four, 68 percent answered that they had no

---

[40] Cole, *Roosevelt and Isolationists*, 377; Michael S. Sherry, *In the Shadow of War: The United States since the 1930s* (New Haven, CT: Yale University Press, 1995), 48.
[41] Hershey, *Selective Service in Peacetime*, 33–34. Anyone eligible could still volunteer before being called. Volunteers were required to serve for three years. Flynn, *The Draft*, 18.
[42] Hershey, *Selective Service in Peacetime*, 34–35; Flynn, *The Draft*, 18.
[43] Sherry, *In the Shadow of War*, 48.

objection. Among those between ages sixteen and twenty, who would mature to draft age if the "war emergency" lasted long enough, 81 percent had no objection. Some respondents welcomed military training because "it would build me up physically and put me on my own for a while," while others simply regarded it as a duty to fulfill, and still others stated that "If I have to fight, I want to know how." Reasons for objection included obligations to support families and career concerns. These results roughly coincided with those of another poll targeting the general public that the institute conducted in the same week, in which 71 percent responded positively to the question "Do you favor increasing the size of our Army and Navy now by drafting men between the ages of 21 and 31 to serve in the armed forces for one year?"[44]

In essence, the Selective Training and Service Act of 1940 signaled how American society was in a period of enormous uncertainty – neither peacetime nor wartime, but a time when many Americans felt that national security was at risk. It also signifies how the previous associations of voluntarism with American democracy and mandatory military training with dictatorship and totalitarianism were reinterpreted to establish selective service as American and democratic in accordance with the principle of equal service. Franklin D. Roosevelt appointed Clarence A. Dykstra, a political scientist, president of the University of Wisconsin, and an AYCM member, as the director of the Selective Service System. Lieutenant Colonel Lewis B. Hershey, who had played a central role in formulating conscription plans for the JANSSC, was appointed deputy director.[45] On October 29, 1940, Secretary of War Stimson, blindfolded with a cloth taken from a chair used at the signing of the Declaration of Independence, drew the first number for the draft lottery. The lottery bowl from World War I was used to reassure the American public once again that the draft was an American tradition, not a drastic departure from it.[46] Two weeks before this event, the CME announced that it would discontinue its activities, noting how "the spreading war crisis and the enactment by Congress of peacetime conscription" had rendered

---

[44] George Gallup, "The Gallup Poll: Two-Thirds of Young Men Willing to Serve in Army," *WP*, August 30, 1940.

[45] Flynn, *The Draft*, 23; AYCM, *Youth, Defense, and the National Welfare*, 12. Dykstra's tenure as the Selective Service System's director was brief. In April 1941, he resigned in order to become chairman of the National Defense Mediation Board, a position he would occupy for only two months before returning to the University of Wisconsin. In July 1941, Hershey was appointed director of the Selective Service System. Hershey, *Selective Service in Peacetime*, 27, 65; "Dykstra Resigns as Mediation Head," *NYT*, June 20, 1941.

[46] Flynn, *The Draft*, 22–23.

the kind of work that the CME had conducted in the previous fifteen years "hopelessly out of date."[47]

"Youth" in Transition

The establishment of the Selective Service System affected the lives of young Americans in many ways. For example, the American Youth Congress (AYC) and other left-wing political organizations by young people that had flourished in the 1930s had already lost their vitality by the end of the decade, as their members fiercely disagreed over their stance on the crumbling international order, especially the Nazi–Soviet Pact of 1939; selective service furthered the growing ideological fracturing among them.[48] In Washington, D.C., the *Washington Post* reported how a meeting of Catholic college students in March 1941 ended up in an "unscheduled but heated debate" over selective service. A participant initiated the debate by claiming that youth were forced to face military training and war because of the enormous power that the federal government had assumed. Individual rights and liberties no longer held much meaning, he maintained. Another student attacked him, asserting that such an observation was un-American.[49] On October 16, 1941, a National Youth Day Rally was held in New York City by an interventionist group to commemorate the first anniversary of the Selective Service registration, while youth groups in Chicago led by a Youth Committee Against War protested such celebrations of youth conscription.[50]

Another significant change that affected young people was prompted by the expansion of the defense industries, which resulted in the rapid decline in youth unemployment. Columbia University announced in the spring of 1941 that over 90 percent of its graduating students had secured jobs and that the placement opportunities of that year "far

---

[47] John Nevin Sayre to Friends of the C. M. E., October 16, 1940, p. 1, "Military in General Corres. 1936–40" folder, Box 68, National Self Government Committee Records, New York Public Library, New York, NY.

[48] Robert Cohen, *When the Old Left Was Young: Student Radicals and America's First Mass Student Movement, 1929–1941* (New York: Oxford University Press, 1993), 279, 308–12; "The Youth Congress Loses a Pillar," *NYHT*, January 2, 1941.

[49] "Draft Debate Stirs Catholic Youth Parley," *WP*, March 3, 1941.

[50] "McNutt Asserts Youth Will Win War and Peace," *NYHT*, October 17, 1941; "'Welfare Fete' Ironic, Youth Groups Assert," *Chicago Daily Tribune*, October 16, 1941. Earlier in 1941, a proposal for a resolution to designate October 16 as National Youth Day was presented to Congress, though it was never adopted. Harold R. Moskovit to FDR, October 27, 1941, Folder: Youth Movements 1941, OF 58b (Youth) (Box 4), FDRL.

surpass any in the history of the appointments office at Columbia."[51] This vast decline in youth unemployment illustrates the sharp turn in young people's employment opportunities from the years of the Great Depression. As discussed in Chapter 3, the NYA and the CCC had already shifted their focus in the late 1930s from alleviating youth's financial difficulties to preparing young people for national defense work. The rising demand for young people, especially men by the defense industries as well as the military, further propelled New Deal's youth agencies to align themselves with war and defense efforts to justify their continuation. For example, the NYA opened a "health camp" in June 1941 to examine and treat young men rejected by the Selective Service Board for medical reasons.[52]

Arguably the most significant way that the country's shift from the Depression to military preparedness affected young people was the military's preference to draft young men. Although the Selective Training and Service Act of 1940 set the minimum draft age at twenty-one, it also set a mechanism to draft younger men within the draft age. On the one hand, as a "democratic" measure that represented the ideal of equal service, the Act was phrased in such a way as to avoid the appearance of allowing automatic group deferments, and its supporters emphasized that deferment would only be considered on an individual basis, such as in the cases of public officials, individuals engaged in activities critical to national defense or the public interest, ministers, men with dependents, and conscientious objectors. Students were allowed to complete the academic year if called in 1940 but were not to defer any later than July 1941.[53] This deferment policy, however, would result in the conscription of significantly more men under the age of twenty-five than older men, as these younger men were more likely to be single, have no dependents, and be unemployed or engaged in occupations that were not eligible for deferment. Moreover, unlike the debates over selective service during World War I, few legislators or other Americans insisted on raising the upper draft age limit and drafting older men before young

---

[51] "90% of '41 Class Placed in Jobs, Columbia Says," *NYHT*, June 8, 1941. See also Federal Security Agency, War Manpower Commission, *Final Report of the National Youth Administration, Fiscal Years 1936–1943* (Washington, DC: GPO, 1944), 20–21.

[52] "NYA Plans Health Camps for Youths," *WP*, January 14, 1941; "NYA Camp for Rejected Men to Open," *Atlanta Constitution*, June 1, 1941. See also "Defense Value of CCC Hailed on 8th Year," *WP*, March 31, 1941; Alfred Friendly, "Roosevelt Hints CCC Might Cure Draft Rejects," *WP*, October 4, 1941.

[53] Hershey, *Selective Service in Peacetime*, 169–71.

men. American society in 1940, in other words, was ready to tolerate the disproportionate draft of young men.[54]

Several changes to the selective service legislation made in 1941 further highlighted the step toward conscripting younger men. In August, Congress relieved men older than twenty-seven from induction. In Hershey's words, this arrangement reflected the public's recognition that "mechanized warfare was really a young man's war," and that it was therefore "inefficient to train the older men and then place them in the reserve."[55] Two days later, Congress passed the Service Extension Act of 1941, authorizing the U.S. President to extend the period of military service from twelve months to up to eighteen months, making draftees serve longer.[56] Of the 921,722 men who were inducted into the Army between November 1940 and November 1941, approximately 62 percent were men aged twenty-one through twenty-five.[57] The idea of equal service, which served as the foundation for the argument that selective service was democratic, meant that all men would serve in a capacity that would be best for their country, not that all men would have an equal probability of serving in the military. Even before the United States entered the war and conscripted minors, Americans had largely accepted the idea that young men would do the fighting.

The Japanese attack on Pearl Harbor invalidated the vague "neither peace nor war" premise on which the 1940 conscription Act was based. On December 13, 1941, Congress removed the territorial limits stipulated in the Act. Furthermore, inductees were now called for the "duration of the war and 6 months after its termination."[58] The entry into the war also forced American society to debate the lowering of the draft age.

The following week, Congress passed a bill that required all men of ages eighteen to sixty-four, inclusive, to register, although liability for military service was limited to men between ages twenty and forty-four, inclusive.[59] This new draft age resulted from a compromise between a House bill that kept the lower age limit at twenty-one and a Senate bill

---

[54] For a rare example in this period of a proposal to increase the draft age (in this case to include men up to age sixty), see Colonel William J. Donovan, "Should Men of 50 Fight Our Wars?" *This Week*, April 14, 1940, attached to Stuart A. Bishop to the Commandant, Ninth Naval District, April 15, 1940, "203 Age Groups, 1940" folder, Files from the Reference Library of the Research and Statistics Division, 1926–1969, Records of the Selective Service System, RG 147, NACP.

[55] Men between the ages of twenty-eight and thirty-six were still allowed to volunteer. Hershey, *Selective Service in Peacetime*, 47, 125–26.

[56] Ibid., 27, 47.   [57] Ibid., 17.

[58] Lewis B. Hershey, *Selective Service in Wartime: Second Report of the Director of Selective Service, 1941–42* (Washington, DC: GPO, 1943), 5.

[59] Ibid.

that made nineteen-year-olds liable for military service.[60] There were objections in the House to conscripting individuals under the age of twenty-one. Like their counterparts in World War I, some representatives opposed the plan based on the relationship between the legal majority and military service, emphasizing the fact that men under the age of twenty-one did not have the right to vote. Nevertheless, this line of argument was in the minority. A more frequent reason for objection was the supposed physical and mental immaturity of men below age twenty-one that mirrored the idea of immature "youth" forged in the 1930s, and that military service would interrupt their education and deplete colleges and universities.[61] The number of draft-age men enrolled in secondary schools and colleges did differ significantly between the two world wars. In 1916, the number of students in high school had been 1,700,000; in 1940, it was 7,100,000. Similarly, the number of college students had increased from 400,000 in 1916 to 1,400,000 in 1940.[62] The issue of lowering the draft age was, therefore, more intertwined with the educational sector than any other wartime in U.S. history.

Yet, major educational associations supported the draft of nineteen-year-olds. As noted in Chapter 3, they had been keen supporters of military preparedness (presumably as a defensive measure), supporting the transformation of the NYA and the CCC to defense training agencies, and the American Council on Education (ACE) and the National Education Association had jointly formed a National Committee on Education and Defense in August 1940 to strengthen education's contribution to national defense. The Committee was then serving as the Subcommittee on Education of the Joint Army–Navy Committee on Welfare and Recreation, and passed a resolution while the bill was being considered in Congress, endorsing the Senate bill to conscript nineteen-year-olds, "recognizing the gravity of the present

---

[60] Franklin D. Roosevelt supported the Senate bill that drafted nineteen-year-olds. Senator Robert Rice Reynolds (SC), speaking on S. 2126, December 17, 1941, 77th Cong., 1st sess., *Congressional Record* 87, pt. 9: 9905.

[61] Representatives John William McCormack (MA), Dewey Jackson Short (MO), Dow Waters Harter (OH), Charles Isiah Faddis (PA), George Anthony Dondero (MI), and Edouard Victor Michel Izac (CA), speaking on H.R. 6215, December 17, 1941, 77th Cong., 1st sess., *Congressional Record* 87, pt. 9: 9921, 9926, 9928, 9931, 9938. See also Senators Robert Alphonso Taft (OH) and Robert Marion La Follette Jr. (WI), speaking on S. 2126, December 18, 1941, 77th Cong., 1st sess., *Congressional Record* 87, pt. 9: 9972–73, 9977.

[62] Samuel A. Stouffer, et al., *The American Soldier: Adjustment during Army Life*, vol. 1 of the Studies in Social Psychology in World War II (New York: John Wiley and Sons, 1965 [1949]), 57.

situation and the necessity for mobilization of total manpower."[63] The educational elite's organizational support of the government in national emergencies could be traced to the period of World War I. They had developed a strong sense of commitment to national security since then, through such associations as the ACE, a product of World War I.

The lower draft age limit was eventually set at twenty in December 1941 as a compromise between the Senate and the House, but the urgent need for a larger armed force soon forced American society to confront the issue of further lowering the draft age. The debates about the appropriate age for conscription as well as how to prepare young men for military service raged across the country, and many of the arguments combined key strands of earlier debates that were discussed in prior chapters about the relationship between youth, education, and national security. In January 1942, for example, newspaper columnist Walter Lippmann articulated his thoughts on that relationship. The existing Selective Service System had been designed for a short emergency period rather than a long war, he pointed out, and therefore was only intended to raise an army out of men who were already adults. In other words, it was not meant to run preparatory training programs for young men below military age. Yet, he continued, since the war was expected to last a long time, there was an urgent need to train younger men so that they would be ready for high-skilled services that fighting a modern war required by the time they reached draft age.[64]

Lippmann's argument had been inspired by suggestions Harvard University president James B. Conant had recently made in a report on the role of higher education in wartime. The report pointed out that teens, in or just out of high school, were under "great but conflicting pressure" to make difficult decisions concerning which path to take after graduation. Without proper guidance and policy, it continued, a man might volunteer for a combat position when he would be better suited for other services, or a man with officer potential might decide to work in a factory rather than attend college because his parents couldn't afford it. In Lippmann's words, this could result in a haphazard and "unsatisfactory" allocation of young men to wartime roles that did not maximize their contribution to the war effort; one that was "inefficient, wasteful,

---

[63] Francis J. Brown to Capt. Francis V. Keesling Jr., letter reprinted at the request of Senator Robert Rice Reynolds (SC), speaking on S. 2126, December 17, 1941, 77th Cong., 1st sess., *Congressional Record* 87, pt. 9: 9906; Christopher P. Loss, *Between Citizens and the State: The Politics of American Higher Education in the 20th Century* (Princeton, NJ: Princeton University Press, 2012), 100. This committee will be further addressed in Chapter 5.

[64] Walter Lippmann, "Pres. Conant Right About Need to Plan College Program," *BDG*, January 24, 1942.

and unjust." Men over twenty years old were now spared from such a decision because once they were registered with the Selective Service System, not they but the government decided their wartime duties. Conant proposed that a selection of talented boys be made when graduating from high school, and those selected should be put under a special military organization, sent to college at the government's expense, and trained to become military or industrial specialists.[65]

It was precisely during the few years before the draft registration age that "the choices are made, the opportunities given or denied, which will determine whether the young man who registers is to become an officer, a specialist, or a deferred industrial worker," Lippmann argued. Without measures to provide "boys who have natural gifts of leadership and special abilities" with special training and select them without regard to whether their parents could afford to send them to college, he continued, a "talented" teen who could not afford college would wrongly decide to go into a factory or volunteer for combat. He argued that "if we are to have a democratic Army – one in which careers are really open to talent – we must take measures [...] to see to it that the corps of officers is not recruited chiefly from those whose parents could afford to send their sons to college." In a long war, Lippmann concluded, victory would depend much upon "how well we have managed to make the best possible use of all natural ability, regardless of the accidents of family income." As a practical matter, "this is one of the critical things we must mean when we say that we intend to fight this war as a democratic people."[66]

This argument illustrates the extent to which views about the role of youth in national security, which had evolved over the course of previous decades, merged with the idea of selective service as equal and democratic to establish a strong connection between access to education and military service. In other words, by this time, American adults had come to defend the selection of young men deemed "talented" solely from a military perspective as "democratic" and "American." The country's involvement in the two world wars, as well as the establishment of the SATC, ROTC, and other military–educational programs in educational institutions, had made American society to allow national security to define what "democratic" access to education meant. Hence, a young man's eligibility for Lippman's plan, which was considered "democratic" because it allegedly helped young men from families that could not otherwise afford a college education to receive one, was contingent on his usefulness to national security and his willingness to die for his country.

[65] Ibid.   [66] Ibid.

Lippmann's and Conant's comments also hint at how the transformation of young people who had been labeled as a "problem" in the 1930s into the nation's most valuable age group was rapidly being made. The military, schools, and industries were now all vying for the custody of youth, striving to attract as many as possible to their respective institutions. The induction of eighteen- and nineteen-year-olds into the military in 1942 would further transform the social perceptions of youth.

Plans to lower the draft age to eighteen were already being discussed long before this, even before the U.S. entered the war, but many Americans remained uncertain about it. In April 1941, FDR announced that a congressional committee would soon start hearings on proposals to change the draft age to eighteen through thirty, although he emphasized that such a step was not intended to be taken immediately.[67] A House Military Affairs Committee spokesman told the press in the same month, however, that the committee members were at the time "predominantly opposed" to such measures, adding that he believed that the average eighteen-year-old "has not reached the proper physical development to be able to make as desirable a soldier as he should."[68] Given that eighteen-year-olds had served as volunteers in previous wars as well as the ongoing war and had engaged in ROTC courses, it is striking how their physical immaturity was raised here as a reason for not conscripting them. The House spokesman's remarks demonstrate how controversial drafting minors remained, even though the draft Act amendment in 1918 had established a precedent that minors might be drafted in wartime if military necessity existed and the 1940 draft Act had set a mechanism to draft younger men in the draft age.

As the U.S. entry into the war in December 1941 necessitated the prompt and efficient mobilization of Americans for the military and the home front, War Department and Selective Service spokesmen pressed for an amendment to draft eighteen- and nineteen-year-olds. Hershey, who had succeeded Dykstra as director of the Selective Service System, argued that unless eighteen- and nineteen-year-olds were drafted, the supply of single men would be depleted in a few months, a situation that would require fathers and husbands to be conscripted.[69] This was a tough decision to make. The disruption of what was then known as the "family relationship" or the "American family" – an image of a

---

[67] "Selective Service Age Limits May Be Reduced to 18–30," *WP*, April 16, 1941; George Gallup, "51% Favor Lowering Draft Age to 18, Survey by Gallup Institute Indicates," *NYT*, May 11, 1941.
[68] "House Group Opposes Draft Age Lowering," *NYT*, April 17, 1941.
[69] "Married Men Face Draft in Few Months," *Los Angeles Times* (hereafter cited as *LAT*), August 22, 1942; "Pressure Seen for Drafting Youths 18–19," *WP*, August 23, 1942.

heterosexual couple cooperatively raising a few children, with the husband serving as the breadwinner – would elicit strong public opposition but so would draft of eighteen- and nineteen-year-olds. A Gallup poll of September 1942 indicated that the public was uncertain about who should be conscripted next. According to the poll, most favored drafting eighteen- and nineteen-year-olds over drafting married men *with* children, but sentiment was evenly divided when asked to choose between inducting eighteen- and nineteen-year-olds or inducting married men *without* children.[70]

On October 13, 1942, FDR finally announced that he believed it necessary to lower the draft age to eighteen.[71] On the following day, the bill to amend the draft Act to conscript men of ages eighteen and nineteen was introduced to Congress. Secretary of War Stimson opened the hearings before the House Committee on Military Affairs, stating that the War Department believed younger men were better soldiers and that lowering the draft age was not drastically new but was firmly in line with the U.S. military tradition: "I think I am stating the truth when I say that in every major war that the United States had had [sic] to carry through it has been largely carried through by men under 20, from 18 to 20." Because of the "terrific pace of modern war, which is more violent, more pressing, than ever before," he continued, there was an "imperative necessity" of creating as quickly as possible an army "more efficient, more determined, and more ardent […] than Europe and Asia can produce after 10 years of training and indoctrination." Juxtaposing youth in other countries and those in the United States, he argued that "[i]t is youth that is making the power of our enemies – youth, zealous for power and for the destruction of liberty. It is the strength of the armies that we have got to fight against. And, on the other side, it is American youth which is our strength and upon which the virility of our effort must depend."[72]

The debate over the amendment revolved around three interrelated questions: first, whether eighteen- and nineteen-year-olds were physically and mentally fit for military service; second, whether students should be given special consideration; and finally, whether inducting teens was less objectionable than conscripting fathers. As the war necessitated the passage of the Act, the debates were less about whether to pass it and more about how to make it look democratic and acceptable.

[70] George Gallup, "Low-Age Draft Favored before Taking Fathers," *LAT*, September 6, 1942.
[71] U.S. Congress, House, Committee on Military Affairs, *Lowering Draft Age to 18 Years: Hearings before the Committee on H.R. 7528 and H.R. 7694, A Bill to Amend the Selective Training and Service Act of 1940 by Providing for the Extension of Liability*, 77th Cong., 2nd sess. (Washington, DC: GPO, 1942), 1.
[72] Ibid., 3.

As in World War I, some people questioned the validity of drafting minors. A woman opposed to drafting teens named Mary E. Woolley (likely Mary Emma Woolley, a pacifist activist and a past president of Mount Holyoke College) wrote to FDR, arguing that "the wisdom of training for the army boys who are considered too immature to vote is open to question."[73] A mother of an "unmatured boy that wants to finish his education [first] if possible" asked FDR and Senators to give eighteen- and nineteen-year-olds voting rights before inducting them.[74]

However, the opinions linking the issue of the draft age to voting rights were overall very few. Instead, some people expressed reservations about the perceived immaturity of eighteen-year-olds. A House Committee on Military Affairs member argued that the bone structure of the eighteen- and nineteen-year-olds was still unstable and "what is true of the bone structure is also true of the brain structure, so far as maturity is concerned."[75] Military representatives argued otherwise, contending that eighteen- and nineteen-year-olds were physically superior to older men. They stressed that these young men were "perfectly indispensable" to building an army composed of highly trained, organized units required to win a modern war. In fact, the military representatives continued, eighteen- and nineteen-year-olds were "exceptional when compared with the older-age groups" for their adaptability to military training, responsiveness to leadership, good health and toughness, and their "desire for adventure."[76] Young men provided the principal element of elite troops in Germany and Russia, the military men insisted. The handling of modern weapons demanded, more than ever, "the stamina, flexibility, and courage so characteristic of youth."[77] Selective Service System director Hershey added: "when you have got to fly a plane, jump out of it, bounce around in a tank, and swim ashore, you don't want to be my age."[78] Hershey, born in 1893, had just turned forty-nine.[79] In short,

---

[73] Mary E. Woolley to FDR, September 25, 1942, Folder: "Selective Service Legislation, Oct. 1942", OF 1413 (Box 6), FDRL; Kristi Preiman, "Mary Emma Woolley (1934)," *Kappa Delta Pi*, https://web.archive.org/web/20050217130612/http://kdp.org/about/laureates/laureates/marywoolley.php (accessed December 23, 2023).

[74] A Mother to FDR, November 14, 1942, Folder: "Selective Service Legislation, Nov.–Dec. 1942", OF 1413 (Box 6), FDRL.

[75] House Committee on Military Affairs, *Lowering Draft Age to 18 Years*, 28.

[76] Ibid., 4–6; U.S. Congress, Senate, Committee on Military Affairs, *Lowering Draft Age to 18 Years: Hearings before the Committee on S. 2748, A Bill to Amend the Selective Training and Service Act of 1940 by Providing for the Extension of Liability*, 77th Cong., 2nd sess. (Washington, DC: GPO, 1942), 26.

[77] Senate Committee on Military Affairs, *Lowering Draft Age to 18 Years*, 23–27.

[78] Ibid., 40.

[79] George Q. Flynn, *Lewis B. Hershey, Mr. Selective Service* (Chapel Hill: University of North Carolina Press, 1985), 3.

to military leaders, eighteen- and nineteen-year-olds were physically mature enough to fight and yet mentally not too mature to be molded to military life.

The second issue concerned whether to allow students to finish the academic year before drafting them or serve while remaining in school, which was closely related to how to make the conscription of teens "democratic." Military leaders were against such a measure. Hershey insisted that group deferments defied the democratic principle of selective service and would work in favor of teens whose parents could afford to keep them in school.[80] A more democratic alternative to deferring students, supporters of the amendment argued, was to draft all eighteen- and nineteen-year-olds first, and then send those with special military talents to college at the expense of the government.[81]

Like Conant's and Lippmann's proposal examined earlier, this was supposedly a "democratic" measure for higher education that relieved individuals of educational expenses. President Edward C. Elliott of Purdue University, who was a member of the federal War Manpower Commission and was involved in developing the SATC program during World War I, argued that educational programs offered at colleges through the military would let "very superior young men" receive a college education irrespective of the financial conditions of their parents.[82] From a different perspective, Mayor Fiorello H. LaGuardia of New York City supported the idea of allowing students to remain in school while they serve. He proposed that high-school students who managed to matriculate in a college should be allowed to serve there as long as they kept up the required academic standing, and argued that such a plan was crucial to national interests, for, if "this war continues for 4 years, there will be a period in our country when only the physically unfit will have had a higher education."[83]

While military representatives were opposed to deferring students, they were not against deferring men with families, who tended to be older. Rather, they were ready to let go of older men if a sufficient number of servicepeople could be obtained from the younger population. Hershey was especially vocal on this issue, insisting that drafting fathers and husbands would disrupt American life and ruin the morale of the civilian population. The whole point of selective service, he believed, was to "hold our national life together." Or, in other words, to maintain the

---

[80] Senate Committee on Military Affairs, *Lowering Draft Age to 18 Years*, 36.
[81] House Committee on Military Affairs, *Lowering Draft Age to 18 Years*, 59–60.
[82] Ibid., 154–57.
[83] Senate Committee on Military Affairs, *Lowering Draft Age to 18 Years*, 74.

"family relationship."[84] Army Chief of Staff George Marshall added that eighteen- and nineteen-year-olds constituted "the sole remaining reservoir of individuals who have no dependents and who are, in general, either in school or employed on jobs which can either be dispensed with or performed by women."[85] The image of the "American family," undergirded by a widespread assumption about gender roles that assumed a breadwinner husband and a supporting wife, helped justify the draft of young single men as a democratic measure.

The passage of this amendment in November 1942 accelerated the disproportionate draft of young men that had begun in 1940. First, Hershey swiftly ordered that men of age forty-five and above should not be drafted. In December 1942, the Army declared that registrants thirty-eight years old and above were not acceptable for induction.[86] Until late 1943, men were selected for induction based on marital status and occupation, making young men who were single and without significant vocational experience useful on the home front the primary pool for the draft. Although the American public and politicians alike hesitated to support the draft of men with families, especially those with children, the exigencies of war led to policy changes in December 1943 and February 1944, ending dependency as a significant category of deferments. Still, men with families, who tended to be older than the younger men in the draft age that the military preferred, were prioritized in other deferment categories, such as occupational deferment. Additionally, starting in early 1944, a new selective service policy established that men between ages eighteen and twenty-five, both inclusive, were required to go through an additional round of approval procedure only required for this age group to be deferred.[87] By the time the war ended, nearly half of all U.S. servicemen were under the age of twenty-six.[88]

Selective service in World War II thus established the ages of eighteen to twenty-five as the primary group to be conscripted in wartime. Upon

---

[84] House Committee on Military Affairs, *Lowering Draft Age to 18 Years*, 79.
[85] Senate Committee on Military Affairs, *Lowering Draft Age to 18 Years*, 27.
[86] "President Signs 18–19 Draft Bill," *NYT*, November 14, 1942; Hershey, *Selective Service in Wartime*, 5, 12.
[87] Lewis B. Hershey, *Outline of Historical Background of Selective Service*, 1965 edition (Washington, DC: GPO, 1966), 11; Lewis B. Hershey, *Selective Service and Victory: The Fourth Report of the Director of Selective Service, 1944–1945, with a Supplement for 1946–1947* (Washington, DC: GPO, 1948), 49–50, 67–74, 115, 126–27, 141–42; Lewis B. Hershey, *Selective Service as the Tide of War Turns: The Third Report of the Director of Selective Service, 1943–1944* (Washington, DC: GPO, 1945), 131–32; Amy J. Rutenberg, *Rough Draft: Cold War Military Manpower Policy and the Origins of Vietnam-Era Draft Resistance* (Ithaca, NY: Cornell University Press, 2019), 32–36.
[88] Mapheus Smith, "Populational Characteristics of American Servicemen in World War II," *Scientific Monthly* 65, no. 3 (1947): 247.

signing the bill to lower the draft age to eighteen in November 1942, FDR announced, as if to reiterate Conant's and Lippmann's proposal, that a plan providing for the utilization of colleges and universities for the training of a limited number of men of the armed forces for highly specialized duties was underway. These men, he stated, would be selected "solely on the basis of their ability and without regard to whether or not they are now in college or whether they could otherwise afford to go to college." Furthermore, he promised that a study would be conducted to determine what steps could be taken to enable young soldiers to receive training and education after the war's end – a promise that would eventually materialize as the education provisions of the G.I. Bill of Rights of 1944, legislation that provided World War II veterans with a range of support to help them readjust to civilian life, such as loans for purchasing homes and business properties, unemployment allowances, employment services, and education.[89] As in World War I, therefore, adults framed the education of young men deemed useful militarily as a "democratic" educational opportunity. In a time in which educational credentials determined to a great degree one's economic success, however, this meant that the impact of military service on young men would long outlive the war. The consequences of these plans, which presented military service as a "democratic" educational opportunity, will be further discussed in Chapter 5.

While young men were destined for military service, women of all ages were expected to perform supporting roles. LaGuardia, testifying before the Senate Committee on Military Affairs, during the congressional debates over lowering the draft age, urged Congress to support the Army in allocating every woman, as well as every man, to a position they could serve best. He argued that the nation should "enlist 100,000 or 200,000 women to take charge of the kitchens, of the dining rooms, of the laundry, of the mending rooms, and of the permanent paper work." The mobilization of women for these tasks was needed, he continued, because at that moment, "every [male] soldier must learn how to peel potatoes and kitchen sanitation, and that is the most irksome and unpleasant duty that

---

[89] "President Signs 18–19 Draft Bill" ; "The President Begins to the Planning Looking toward the G.I. Bill of Rights. Statement on Signing the Bill Reducing the Draft Age. November 13, 1942," in *The Public Papers and Addresses of Franklin D. Roosevelt, 1942 Volume: Humanity on the Defensive*, compiled by Samuel I. Rosenman (New York: Russell and Russell, 1969 [1950]), 470. On the planning of this statement, see Robert P. Patterson to FDR, October 20, 1942, Folder: Selective Service Legislation Jan.–Oct. 1942, OF 1413 (Box 2), FDRL; Robert P. Patterson to FDR, with attachment, November 12, 1942, Folder: Armed Forces Comm. on Postwar Educational Opportunities for Service Personnel 1942–44, OF 5182, FDRL.

158   The Age of Youth

a soldier has to go through." LaGuardia assumed that such "irksome and unpleasant" tasks were something "women want to perform."[90]

Proposals to "conscript" women for national service on the home front or in the military, in fact, were occasionally made during the war. For example, Eleanor Roosevelt proposed the compulsory registration of women for war service on the home front, arguing that voluntary service was inefficient and wasteful.[91] These proposals never won broad support, however. Opposition was raised by women, too. In January 1943, for example, a group of women organized a National Committee to Oppose the Conscription of Women, arguing that the conscription of women for war work would be "detrimental to our national welfare."[92] The Selective Service System did not intend to conscript women either, for such a measure was thought to affect the morale of the home front.[93] The preservation of the "American family," which was one of the key grounds for the public's acceptance of the draft of young, single men, was ubiquitous throughout the war.

The pervasive image of the male soldier notwithstanding, a total of 350,000 women served voluntarily in the U.S. armed forces during World War II.[94] Indeed, women have "long been part of American military forces to a far greater extent than is usually appreciated," historian Linda K. Kerber points out.[95] The entry of women into the armed forces during World War II began when the U.S. Army established a women's corps in May 1942. Legally, the Women's Army Auxiliary Corps (WAAC) was not part of the Army but was rather intended to serve *with* it to release men in uniform from various types of non-combat work. A year after its establishment, the WAAC became the Women's Army Corps (WAC) and was given full military status. The Navy, the Coast Guard, and the Marines soon began to recruit women as well.[96]

---

[90] Senate Committee on Military Affairs, *Lowering Draft Age to 18 Years*, 73.
[91] "Register Women, First Lady Urges," *NYT*, February 16, 1942. See also "Asks Registration of Women 18 to 65," *NYT*, March 19, 1942; "Registration of Women Hits Snag in House," *WP*, April 1, 1942; "Roosevelt Sees No Present Need to Enroll Women for War Work," *NYHT*, May 2, 1942.
[92] "Statement on House Resolution 1742 (The National War Service Act) for the House Committee on Military Affairs by the National Committee to Oppose Conscription of Women," n.d., "WCOC-Governing Committee: Form Letters" folder, Box 1, Records of the Women's Committee to Oppose Conscription (DG 068), Swarthmore College Peace Collection, Swarthmore PA.
[93] Hershey, *Selective Service in Wartime*, 409.
[94] D'Ann Campbell, *Women at War with America: Private Lives in a Patriotic Era* (Cambridge, MA: Harvard University Press, 1984), 20.
[95] Linda K. Kerber, *No Constitutional Right to Be Ladies: Women and the Obligation of Citizenship* (New York: Hill and Wang, 1998), 261.
[96] Campbell, *Women at War with America*, 20. See also Leisa D. Meyer, *Creating GI Jane: Sexuality and Power in the Women's Army Corps during World War II* (New York: Columbia University Press, 1996).

The extent to which women's presence in the military changed the gendered understanding of the relationship between military service and citizenship was limited, however. As the American public was not yet prepared to embrace women in nontraditional gender roles, the military ensured that women's military service did not challenge prevailing norms. They endeavored to refute the public belief that the work would "masculinize" women and to portray women in the military as "feminine" and "domestically inclined."[97] As noted in Chapter 5, the postwar lives of women veterans were impacted by the persistence of the "American family" ideal, which centered on the male breadwinner and the women homemaker.

The debates over the draft of young men during World War II were based on the conscription policies that were developed during World War I, but they also incorporated ideas regarding youth, education, and national security that emerged in the years following World War I. This can be seen from how the lowering of the draft age proceeded during the war. The 1940 Selective Training and Service Act set the lower age limit at twenty-one, which coincided with the initial draft age during World War I and the age of legal maturity, although the military's preference for drafting young men was taken into account in the sense that it included measures to prioritize the draft of younger men than older men. Even though the U.S. entry into the war and the war's progress soon necessitated the conscription of minors, such a measure remained controversial, as evidenced by the heated debate in 1942 over lowering the draft age to eighteen years old. The supporters' justification for the measure to draft younger men drew on and reshaped the prevalent ideas about youth, maturity, and education in the 1930s. The young individuals' lack of advanced trade skills now suggested that they were immediately available for military duty, their unstable lifestyle and being unmarried meant that their induction would help maintain the "American family," and their mental malleability now indicated that they could adjust to military discipline. The draft was also presented as a "democratic" educational opportunity, as it was coupled with plans that ostensibly enabled "talented" men, regardless of financial means, to receive an education at government expense. This was also a logic that had been developed since World War I.

The strong connection between education and military service that was evident in the debates over lowering the draft age would soon be realized in the educational programs for soldiers and veterans, which will

---

[97] Elaine Tyler May, "Rosie the Riveter Gets Married," in *The War in American Culture: Society and Consciousness During World War II*, ed. Lewis A. Erenberg and Susan E. Hirsch (Chicago: University of Chicago Press, 1996), 135.

be discussed in the next chapter. U.S. Congress in World War I had also considered, toward the end of the war, rewarding soldiers with postwar educational benefits. Yet, only conscripted minors were to be eligible, from the assumption that military service was primarily an adult men's job. By contrast, in 1942, upon the passage of the selective service amendment lowering the draft age to eighteen, FDR stated in the aforementioned speech that "[t]his time we are planning in advance" for rewarding veterans with education after the war's end and did not specify what age range would be considered eligible; rather he said it would be made broadly available to young men.[98] This remark demonstrates how post–World War I developments in the relationship between youth, education, and national security defined "democratic" selective service in World War II – the blurring of the distinction between maturity and the legal majority (or between immaturity and minority) as a result of the spread of the "youth problem" as a problem of both teens and people in their twenties, the spread of the idea that education beyond grammar school was important for one's success in life, and the institutionalization of the idea that military training and service was a formative educational experience.

With the end of youth unemployment and the military draft of young men, "the youth problem," a phrase that had been so prevalent during the Depression, quickly fell into disuse. Symbolically, Congress decided that the roles of the CCC and the NYA had ended. Likewise, the AYCM failed to secure additional funds and disbanded in 1942.[99] As the next chapter reveals, educators no longer alluded to Nazi youth to call for greater attention to American youth, for the contrast between a devastated Germany and a prosperous United States had rendered the analogy meaningless. Adults throughout the war continued to problematize certain groups of young people, creating new labels such as "draft evaders" and "delinquents," but they were less likely to blame the problems on the characteristics of youth as a group. The people in the age group that had been deemed a serious problem in the 1930s were now considered patriotic men and women devoting their lives to the nation and making the world safe for democracy. The social consequences of this reconceptualization of "youth," as well as the new educational programs for soldiers and veterans, are what we will now turn to.

---

[98] "The President Begins to the Planning Looking toward the G.I. Bill of Rights," 470.
[99] Some members of the AYCM formed a Committee on Youth Problems to continue addressing youth-related issues for several years, but the new committee never reached the level of vibrancy and public attention that the AYCM had enjoyed. "Minutes of Committee on Youth Problems," September 9, 1942, Records of the American Council on Education, Box 193, "Committee on Youth Problems" folder, Hoover Institution Library & Archives, Stanford, CA.

5   Reimagining Youth during Wartime

In 1944, Charles H. Titus, a political scientist at the University of California, Los Angeles, who served in both world wars, wrote about how higher education institutions should accept veterans as students following the end of World War II: the "veterans went away from us as boys; they return to us as men."[1] He is not merely referring to the age of veterans, although many individuals did serve for multiple years and leave the military much older than when they entered. Rather, he builds on the image of boys maturing into men through military training and service, which had been proclaimed by various American adults in the preceding decades, including preparedness advocates in the 1910s, Reserve Officers' Training Corp (ROTC) supporters after World War I, and individuals concerned with the "youth problem" in the 1930s. World War II marked the peak of adults' grouping of young men as a distinct group, as they served disproportionately in the military, but it was also a moment that hinted at a shift toward a new conception of youth. As Titus stated, young men in the service were now seen as mature "men" rather than "boys."

In addition to the conscription of young men, the end of widespread youth unemployment and the rise of the United States as a world power contributed to the change in the perception of youth in American society during the war. The fate of the National Youth Administration (NYA) and the Civilian Conservation Corps (CCC) exemplifies how the circumstances affecting American youth were changing. The country's transition from the Great Depression to war in the late 1930s and early 1940s had severely harmed the legitimacy of these projects, exposing them to attacks from those who wished to see them terminated, such as Republicans who wished to undo the New Deal and educators who

---

[1] Charles H. Titus, "The University and the New Veteran," *Journal of Higher Education* 15, no. 2 (1944): 73; UCLA Library, Department of Special Collections, Manuscripts Division, "Finding Aid for the Charles Hickman Titus Papers, 1900–1965," *Online Archives of California*, https://oac.cdlib.org/findaid/ark:/13030/kt7z09p7mk/entire_text/ (accessed December 23, 2023).

saw these programs as a threat to the tradition of local control of education.[2] Franklin D. Roosevelt (FDR) and his supporters attempted to counter such criticisms by emphasizing the wartime utility of these agencies. One of them argued, for instance, that the CCC could serve as a "rehabilitation" program for the Selective Service System, transforming men deemed physically unsuitable for military service into combat-ready men by providing them with "proper diet, regular habits, and incidental corrective treatment."[3] The President believed that the NYA and the CCC had a "definite place in the all-out war effort," arguing that the NYA trained youth for the war industries, the CCC prepared Army reservations for maximum utilization, and some of the work done by youth in both agencies released soldiers for active duty. Moreover, he argued that since the majority of young people in the agencies were of pre-military age, the training they received was "preparing them for such service as they may be called upon to perform when they become of military age."[4]

Despite the support of these influential individuals, the future of the two agencies was bleak. By March 1942, enrolment in the CCC had decreased to 105,000 due to the end of massive youth unemployment and the urgent demand for a larger workforce on the home front and in the military. A few months later, the CCC was terminated. By then, work projects of the NYA that were considered non-essential to the war effort had been eliminated. The NYA was terminated in 1943 on the grounds that young people were no longer having trouble finding employment and that the NYA was duplicating the work of other federal agencies.[5]

The termination of the CCC and the NYA, as well as the 1942 decision to draft teens, signaled a major change in the cultural perception of youth

---

[2] "End of NYA, CCC as Units Urged," *New York Times* (hereafter cited as *NYT*), October 9, 1941; "Keep NYA and CCC, Roosevelt Urges," *NYT*, March 25, 1942; Calvin W. Gower, "The Civilian Conservation Corps and American Education: Threat to Local Control?" *History of Education Quarterly* 7, no. 1 (1967): 66–67; John A. Salmond, "Aubrey Williams: Atypical New Dealer?" in *The New Deal: The National Level*, ed. John Braeman, Robert H. Bremner, and David Brody (Columbus: Ohio State University Press, 1975), 229; Harry Zeitlin, "Federal Relations in American Education, 1933–1943, A Study of New Deal Efforts and Innovations" (PhD diss., Columbia University, 1958), 237–38, 304–305, 320–21; Charles H. Judd, "The Real Youth Problem," *School and Society* 55, no. 1411 (1942): 29–33.

[3] Rachel Louise Moran, *Governing Bodies: American Politics and the Shaping of the Modern Physique* (Philadelphia: University of Pennsylvania Press, 2018), 62.

[4] FDR to Paul V. McNutt, March 18, 1942, Folder: Official File (hereafter cited as OF) 268 CCC 1942–1945, OF 268 (Box 6), Franklin D. Roosevelt Library, Hyde Park, NY (hereafter cited as FDRL).

[5] Zeitlin, "Federal Relations in American Education," 118–19, 196, 323–24.

in American society. To some extent, the new perception resembled those of the years before the Great Depression. Once again, "youth" primarily indicated minors instead of the broader age range that the term had come to indicate during the Depression. Furthermore, the "youth problem" now implied teenage delinquency, and this was often associated with the prejudiced belief that nonwhite youth were destabilizing home front unity. On the other hand, one significant group of young people were now being treated as adults. When policymakers and educators contemplated plans to offer educational opportunities to young soldiers and veterans of World War II, they assumed they were addressing mature "young adults," not "boys" who needed to be educated because of their immaturity. The educators who had worked on the "youth problem" in the 1930s shifted their attention to other issues, such as juvenile delinquency, the education of soldiers and veterans, and finally, the postwar reconstruction of the world outside the United States. Yet, people in the age group that had been labeled "youth" were still affected by the military–educational programs that these adults developed, as well as the discourse that military training and service "democratized" access to education.

The Redefinition of Youth

Public attention to what American adults in the 1930s called the "youth problem" faded significantly after the United States entered World War II. The adults who had propagated the "youth problem" in the 1930s and created organizations and agencies to address the problem shifted their attention to other issues that seemed more pressing. The *Annals of the American Academy of Political and Social Science*, which had featured the "youth problem" in one of its issues in 1937 and declared that their interest in youth had superseded their interest in children (Chapter 3), returned to their study of children. The November 1944 issue of the journal was dedicated to "Adolescents in Wartime," discussing the education of "adolescents" defined as approximately fourteen to eighteen years old.[6]

The primary "youth problem" for the home front became the juvenile delinquency of boys and girls roughly fourteen to eighteen years old. In the federal government, it was the *Children's* Bureau of the U.S. Department of Labor that was put in charge of the problem. The bureau teamed up with the Office of Community War Services of the Federal

---

[6] Warren S. Thompson, "Adolescents According to the Census," *Annals of the American Academy of Political and Social Science* 236 (November 1944): 17.

Security Agency and other federal agencies supporting the home front, as well as private organizations addressing teens such as the Boy Scouts, the Girl Scouts, the Young Men's Christian Association, and the Young Women's Christian Association, to tackle the problem.[7] They explained to state and local agencies dealing with juvenile delinquency how the war had impacted the lives of the teens in question in many ways. They noted how, for example, engagements in wartime employment or military service had left parents with insufficient time for childcare, with a negative impact on children. They also noted how teens' entry into the labor market had brought them in closer contact with the negative influence of the adult world and how these situations had made the problem of misbehaving teens socially visible. According to the bureau, because of these new conditions surrounding young people, American adults were increasingly worried about teens that congregated on streets and crowded doorways of "inexpensive cafes and places of amusements" to seek relief from the "restlessness and tension of wartime," which gave rise to juvenile delinquency as an important social issue.[8]

While the "youth problem" of the 1930s had been seen primarily as impacting young men, adults now gave considerable attention to the behavior of girls. According to the Children's Bureau, as well as juvenile court reports that the bureau drew on, one of the factors that supposedly increased delinquency cases among girls was "the lure of the uniform," indicating that men in the military enticed girls into relationships considered improper. In other words, young men in the armed forces were given "the status of adults in responsibility and duties," which in turn led them to "exercise other rights of adulthood, of which one is freedom from supervision in their leisure-time associations." From the perspective of adults in charge of teens on the home front, then, young men in the armed forces were not youths in need of protection. Rather, they were now perceived also as "young adults" potentially threatening to girls on the home front.[9]

In other ways, adults detached service people from the once-popular conception of "youth," regardless of their physical age. In a 1943 issue of

---

[7] U.S. Department of Labor, Children's Bureau, "Conference with Youth-Serving Agencies," December 7–8, 1942, p. 19, "Youth" folder, Records Relating to Youth Problems, 1941–1945, Recreation Division, Records of the Office of Community War Services, Record Group (hereafter cited as RG) 215, U.S. National Archives at College Park, College Park, MD (hereafter cited as NACP).

[8] U.S. Department of Labor, Children's Bureau, "Barometers of Wartime Influences on the Behavior of Children and Youth," February 1, 1943, pp. 1–9 (the quotes are from p. 1), "Juvenile Delinquency, 1942–1943" folder, Records Relating to Juvenile Delinquency, 1942–1946, Recreation Division, RG 215, NACP.

[9] Ibid., 6, 8.

the *Annals of the American Academy of Political and Social Sciences* that featured economic issues concerning U.S. service people during and after the war, it was an expert on *adult* education that contributed an article on the education of veterans. Morse A. Cartwright was the director of the American Association for Adult Education, an educational consultant to the U.S. Office of War Information (a federal agency created in June 1942 to oversee war propaganda efforts), and the executive officer of the Institute of Adult Education at Teachers College, Columbia University.[10] Cartwright argued that an unprecedented number of men and women in uniform would be returning to civilian life after the armistice, requiring both public and private efforts to help them make postwar adjustments smoothly, and called for the development of plans to offer veterans training that led to employment. He noted that a high proportion of these veterans would be young, but his views of these young veterans were significantly different from the image of immature "youth" that had been prevalent in American society in the 1930s. "The whole range of individuals from 18 to 23 years of age will constitute a generation of *young adults* whose sole training in most cases will have been in the business of making war," he argued. For that reason, he continued, "[w]e must not make the mistake of considering this as a new 'youth' problem. These men, having faced the rigors of training and actual combat, will be 'adult' far beyond their years."[11] Cartwright thus clearly differentiated the problems of veterans from those of the "youth" in previous years.

When political and educational leaders discussed the "youth problem" in the 1930s, they primarily focused on young white people. As the problem subsided and their attention shifted to juvenile delinquency, however, some of them began to project their image of problematic youth onto nonwhite youth and stereotype them as crime-prone, violent, and threatening to social order, leading to what historian Luis Alvarez has termed the "racialization of juvenile delinquency" that spread following the U.S. entry into World War II.[12] This can be seen in the portrayal of a violent clash between white servicemen and young locals (mostly nonwhite men) in Los Angeles in June 1943, which became known as "Zoot Suit Riots" due to the attire of many of the latter group – symbolic long jackets and pegged trousers, sometimes accompanied by a pancake hat.

---

[10] Morse A. Cartwright, "Re-education of the Returned Soldier and Sailor," *Annals of the American Academy of Political and Social Science* 227 (May 1943): 121.
[11] Emphasis added. Ibid., 112.
[12] Luis Alvarez, *The Power of the Zoot: Youth Culture and Resistance during World War II* (Berkeley: University of California Press, 2008), 41, 43.

Young nonwhite zoot suiters – mostly Mexican American men, but also included Black and Asian American men – and other young locals were attacked by white servicemen on the streets early that month, sparking a series of clashes in the city and across the rest of the country. Racial tensions had been exacerbated by the entry of young men from diverse backgrounds into the military, leading some white servicemen to lash out at zoot suiters.[13]

Mainstream newspaper accounts of the clash reveal a racialized perspective on youth. The people on both sides were likely in the same age range – the mid-teens through mid-twenties. Nonetheless, newspapers clearly distinguished how they portrayed service people and zoot suiters. For example, they frequently highlighted the age – or the youth – of the zoot suiters but rarely specified the age of the servicemen involved. The *Los Angeles Times* reported how five young zoot-suiters – aged sixteen, seventeen, eighteen, twenty-two, and twenty-three – were treated at a hospital for injuries sustained during the confrontation with servicemen but mentioned the age of only one serviceman, age twenty-one, in the same article.[14] Other newspapers also attempted to identify the age of the zoot suiters. An article stated that the zoot suiters were typically between the ages of sixteen and twenty-five, while another said they were between sixteen and twenty years old.[15] They referred to zoot suiters as "youthful gangs," "teen-age hoodlums," "juveniles," and "youths," while neutrally describing their opponents as "servicemen," "sailors," and "soldiers."[16] A *Chicago Daily Tribune* editorial described the conflict as "a series of nasty little race riots between Americans in uniform and embittered Mexican bravos and toughs," capturing the zoot suiters with negative language while remaining neutral toward service people.[17] The prejudiced perspective of adults is also illustrated by the very fact that the conflicts were dubbed the "zoot suit" riots, despite the fact that servicemen initiated the attacks.

Adults named a variety of causes for the purported trouble caused by zoot suiters. Some observers, such as First Lady Eleanor Roosevelt, argued that the persistent racism they encountered in American society

---

[13] Ibid., 43, 155–57.
[14] "Riot Alarm Sent Out in Zoot War," *Los Angeles Times* (hereafter cited as *LAT*), June 8, 1943.
[15] "Los Angeles Barred to Sailors by Navy to Stem Zoot-Suit Riots," *NYT*, June 9, 1943; Lawrence E. Davies, "Seek Basic Causes of Zoot Suit Fray," *NYT*, June 11, 1943.
[16] "Issue Not Race Discrimination, Mayor Declares," *LAT*, June 10, 1943; "Zoot-Suit Fighting Spreads on Coast," *NYT*, June 10, 1943; Associated Press, "Army, Navy Promise to Halt Zoot Riots," *Washington Post* (hereafter cited as *WP*), June 12, 1943.
[17] "The Zoot Suit Riots," *Chicago Daily Tribune*, June 10, 1943.

was at the root of the problem, while authorities in Los Angeles denied the existence of racism in their city.[18] Regardless of their reasoning, adults, especially those who denied racism as a cause of the problem, tended to view zoot suiters as a problem of youth, which led to the development of solutions similar to those developed by adults in the 1930s to combat the "youth problem." For example, the *Los Angeles Times* stated that directing "the energies of groups of idle boys into constructive channels" would solve the problem, citing a local man who stopped boys from breaking windows by inviting them to dinner and raising funds for athletic equipment they could use.[19] A local police representative argued that young people over the age of seventeen who were not in the military should be compelled to work in farm or defense industries and that recreational facilities for them and stricter supervision of juvenile delinquents by police and probation departments should also be implemented.[20] A YWCA representative likewise advocated for farm work for teenage girls and boys, contending that such a program "might eliminate the zoot-suiters."[21]

The portrayal of servicemen as adults and zoot suiters as immature adolescents represents a significant shift in adults' perceptions of young people. Instead of categorizing all young people into a single group with shared characteristics, adults were increasingly inclined to classify them into distinct subgroups. In other words, they viewed service members as "young adults" (which meant that even if they caused problems, those problems were considered distinct from those that "youth" in the 1930s caused), and they saw the new youth problem as involving "juveniles" who were allegedly not contributing to the war effort due to their youth or other factors. Moreover, this new image of problematic youth frequently connoted nonwhite youth. The idea that nonwhite youth were prone to psychological problems and required adult supervision would also shape Americans' attitudes toward Japanese youth during the U.S. occupation of Japan (Chapter 6).

---

[18] "First Lady Traces Zoot Riots to Discrimination," *LAT*, June 17, 1943; S. Rottenberg, letter to the editor, *WP*, June 20, 1943; "Issue Not Race Discrimination, Mayor Declares"; "Who Is Really Stirring Up the Racial Prejudice?" editorial, *LAT*, June 15, 1943; "Mrs. Roosevelt Challenged on Zoot Statement," *LAT*, June 18, 1943; "Proberes Find Zoot War Is a Youth Problem," *Chicago Daily Tribune*, June 13, 1943.
[19] "Youth Gangs Leading Cause of Delinquencies," *LAT*, January 2, 1943.
[20] "Work on Farms Urged for Zoot Suit Youths," *LAT*, June 25, 1943.
[21] Genevieve Reynolds, "Light Farm Work Would Solve Zoot Suit Problem, Aid Food Supply, USO Official Says," *WP*, June 27, 1943.

The Recasting of Youth and the U.S. Rise to a Superpower

The reimagining of "youth" that took place during the war – from problematic "youth" as indicating an entire age group to the compartmentalization of the age group into such categories as young adults and immature juveniles – also had an international dimension. In other words, the ways that American adults understood their "youth problem" in relation to that of young people in other countries changed as the war proceeded. In the 1930s, the Great Depression and the psychological and political consequences it supposedly had for American youth had been considered comparable to the situations of foreign youth. This had terrified many adults, making the "youth problem" not only economic but educational and cultural as well, as discussed in Chapter 3. However, as this image of the "youth problem" faded from American public discourse, and as American society established its society and military as democratic and distinct from those of its enemies, the link between American youth and youth in other countries, particularly Nazi Germany, faded as well. This change in the perception of youth can be illuminated by comparing studies of the NYA and the CCC that were conducted in the 1930s and the 1940s.

Soon after its establishment in 1935, the NYA compiled a study of the unemployment, political activities, and education of young people in approximately sixty countries and regions across the world and steps that foreign governments had taken to solve their youth problems. The U.S. Department of State and the U.S. consuls around the world assisted the NYA in the project by collecting relevant data. The study was published in 1937 under the title, *Youth: A World Problem*. In this booklet, the author addressed how unemployed youth around the world were experiencing delinquency, demoralization, and despair, and explained how some governments had attempted to control youth lives by indoctrinating them, while other governments had taken more "constructive" measures to tackle the problem. In short, although the NYA recognized the differences in the responses of governments to the problems of youth, the assumption here had been that studying the situations of youth in other countries was useful for tackling the youth problem in the United States. The problem, indeed, was considered a "world problem," as the title suggests.[22]

The final report of the NYA published in 1944 indicates that their perceptions of American youth had changed, especially compared to

---

[22] W. Thacher Winslow, *Youth: A World Problem. A Study in World Perspective of Youth Conditions, Movements, and Programs* (Washington, DC: GPO, 1937), ix, xi.

youths of the wider world. It noted that the growing awareness among the country's leaders in the fields of education, industry, labor, and government of "what was happening in Europe, where Fascism had progressed alarmingly and youths' aggressive energies were being exploited by ruthless leaders determined to use the world-wide economic disturbances to their own ends" had led to the establishment of the CCC and the NYA. According to the report, frustrated and impoverished youth were "undesirable and dangerous" to democracy and "unmistakably social dynamite." The NYA, however, no longer alerted the American public to the mental instability of American youth. Instead, it boasted that the agency had helped "restore and buttress the faith of the youth in themselves and in their country," thereby implying that American youth had successfully taken the "right" path as opposed to those of other nations, thanks to the NYA.[23]

A similar change in the perception of American youth versus foreign youth can be found in the writings of Kenneth Holland, the associate director of the American Youth Commission (AYCM) who wrote extensively about the CCC. In 1937, Holland situated the CCC within the trans-Atlantic rise of youth labor camp programs run by both public and private organizations. He included in his analysis youth camps in Nazi Germany as well as those in countries such as Bulgaria, Switzerland, and the Scandinavian countries alongside the CCC. He argued that the concept of youth camps dated back to the early twentieth century when a group of professors at Heidelberg University proposed to the German government the establishment of an "'army of public peace' which would bring together for constructive work the different classes of German youth." Around the same time, Holland noted, the American philosopher William James published "The Moral Equivalent of War," in which James argued that the "conscription" of the entire young male population into an "army enlisted against Nature" would transform youth's negative energies into constructive ones.[24] The article demonstrates that Holland was keenly aware of the political intentions of the Nazi youth programs, but it emphasized the commonalities of "youth problems" around the world and situated the CCC within a global tide instead of highlighting the differences in the aims and intentions of the various projects in the United States and Europe. Holland thus maintained that "[h]ere in the

---

[23] Federal Security Agency, War Manpower Commission, *Final Report of the National Youth Administration, Fiscal Years 1936–1943* (Washington, DC: GPO, 1943), 77, 83, 233.
[24] Kenneth Holland, "The European Labor Service," *Annals of the American Academy of Political and Social Science* 194 (Nov. 1937): 152–53.

United States we are inclined to think that the work camp idea sprang full-grown from the minds of President Roosevelt and his 'brain trusters.' The fact is that European countries developed camps as early as 1920."[25]

By the time Holland and another contributor to the AYCM jointly published a study of the CCC in 1942, they had distanced the CCC not only from Nazi youth camps but also from other European programs for young people. The authors emphasized that the European programs "exerted no immediate influence" on the CCC and that it "is important to realize the essentially American character of the CCC even in its earliest stages." According to the authors, "camps and work in unsettled areas were an American inheritance three hundred years old. America had grown from cabins and sod huts pushing into forests or prairie, from surveying camps and railroad-building camps, from emigrants from the settled East living in wagons while they erected their new homes." Additionally, the authors situated the CCC within an American heritage of boys' camps, militia camps, and camps by private families and social groups. "Living in and working from temporary shelters and pioneer battling with the wilderness were both experiences in the American blood," they maintained.[26]

The change in how these educational leaders conceptualized the relationship between American and foreign youth reflected a broader shift in how the American public understood the role of the United States in world affairs. As the country emerged as the sole superpower during the war, an increasing number of Americans came to see that their situation was vastly different from that of the rest of the world. This contrast led them to believe in the moral superiority of the United States and the political system it represented, as well as the idea that the United States should be the agent of postwar reconstruction for the rest of the world.[27]

Among the educators who underwent this conceptual transition were those who had led the AYCM in the 1930s. Kenneth Holland, who had experience in international education before joining the AYCM and studying the CCC, was working for the U.S. Office of the Coordinator of Inter-American Affairs and the President's Advisory Committee on Education by 1944, considering the prospects of international educational cooperation within the Americas. After the war, he would become

---

[25] Ibid., 152.
[26] Kenneth Holland and Frank Ernest Hill, *Youth in the CCC* (Washington, DC: American Council on Education, 1942), 21–24.
[27] Daniel T. Rodgers, *Atlantic Crossings: Social Politics in a Progressive Age* (Cambridge, MA: Harvard University Press, 1998), ch. 11; Stephen Wertheim, *Tomorrow the World: The Birth of U.S. Global Supremacy* (Cambridge, MA: Belknap Press of Harvard University Press, 2020).

a long-time head of the Institute of International Education, a non-profit organization in New York City that has continued until today to administer many student-exchange programs, such as the Fulbright Program, on behalf of the U.S. government.[28] George Zook of the American Council on Education (ACE) also moved away from his work on the "youth problem" that had preoccupied ACE and other federal agencies in the 1930s, and, like Holland, became deeply involved in the international reconstruction effort, becoming a member of the U.S. delegation to the international conference that established the United Nations Educational, Scientific and Cultural Organization (UNESCO). After the war, he would chair the United States Education Mission to Germany.[29] For the remainder of the war, when these educational leaders addressed issues in American education, they did so most prominently through educational policies for soldiers and veterans. Although soldiers and veterans were no longer considered immature youth, however, the educational policies for these people that these educators helped develop continued to shape their educational experiences in various ways.

Education for Soldiers

In November 1942, when FDR signed the selective service amendment lowering the draft age to eighteen, he made two promises to the American public: first, the government would offer soldiers considered as talented the opportunity for training at higher education institutions, and second, the government would provide all young soldiers with educational opportunities after the war's end. The "youth problem" faded from public consciousness shortly thereafter, but the educational programs for soldiers and veterans that resulted from these promises continued to shape the lives of young Americans.

The President's promise of educational opportunities for veterans materialized as the Servicemen's Readjustment Act of 1944, commonly known as the G.I. Bill of Rights. This law would be remembered as the prime symbol of the "democratic" mobilization of civilians in the United States during World War II that uplifted many veterans from

---

[28] Kenneth Holland, "Inter-American Educational Relations," *Annals of the American Academy of Political and Social Science* 235 (September 1944): 76; David Jacobs, *Inventory of the Kenneth Holland Papers* (Stanford, CA: Hoover Institution Archives, 2008), 2.
[29] "George Zook Dies," obituary, *NYT*, August 19, 1951.

working-class families to middle-class status and created what would later be called the "Greatest Generation."[30]

The FDR administration began contemplating the treatment of veterans early in the war from the understanding that the lack of such preparation for the readjustment of World War I veterans back into civilian society had caused serious political and social ramifications. Indeed, World War I veterans had suffered from the economic recession after World War I and the Great Depression, which turned them into a powerful lobby that urged the federal government into the early payment of their bonus, a movement that in turn triggered the political satire of the Princetonian Veterans of Future Wars (Chapter 3). There was also a strong push from the veteran lobby for the establishment of federal support for veterans of World War II.[31] The bitter memories and experiences of the treatment of the veterans, as well as the powerful lobbying by veteran groups, had made the federal government aware of the need to better support veterans after demobilization.

In July 1942, FDR created a committee within the National Resources Planning Board (NRPB), a federal agency established in 1939 to oversee federal planning in national resources, public works, and the nation's economy, for a preliminary investigation on federal support for veterans. Although this committee was not intended exclusively to plan educational programs, it developed a two-tiered educational plan for veterans: a one-year educational support for all veterans and an additional three-year competitive scholarship for a select number of promising veterans whose education had been interrupted by the war or who had shown "particular aptitude and ability" in fields where "satisfactory and useful employment" could be expected. The work of this committee was succeeded by a second committee – called the Armed-Forces Committee on Post-War Educational Opportunities for Service Personnel – which FDR appointed shortly after making the above-mentioned promise to the American public upon signing the bill lowering the draft age to eighteen. This second committee focused solely on developing plans for the education of veterans.[32]

Leading educators had a considerable presence in the two committees. The first committee was chaired by Floyd W. Reeves, an AYCM member and a professor of administration in the Departments of

---

[30] Tom Brokaw, *The Greatest Generation* (New York: Random House, 1998).
[31] Keith W. Olson, *The G.I. Bill, the Veterans, and the Colleges* (Lexington: University of Kentucky Press, 1974), 3–4; Kathleen J. Frydl, *The GI Bill* (New York: Cambridge University Press, 2009), 2.
[32] Olson, *The G.I. Bill*, 8–11.

Education and Political Science at the University of Chicago. Francis Brown, a professor of sociology at New York University and another member of the AYCM, was a committee member.³³ The second committee, whose members included representatives from the government as well as higher education institutions, was headed by Frederick H. Osborn, a demographer who had built his career working on educational services for military personnel. He had chaired the President's Advisory Committee on Selective Service in 1940 and the Joint Army and Navy Committee on Welfare and Recreation in 1941 and directed the War Department's military morale branch.³⁴

The Osborn committee's plan, which was submitted to the President, largely followed the plan developed by the Reeves committee. The chief difference between the two plans was that while the Reeves committee recommended that veterans should have served at least three months to be eligible for the educational benefits, the Osborn committee suggested that the requirement be six months.³⁵ The President transmitted the Osborn report to Congress on October 27, 1943, proclaiming that the educational plan for veterans aimed to "enable those young people, whose education had been interrupted, to resume their schooling, and to provide an opportunity for the education and technical training of other young men and women of ability, after their discharge from the armed services."³⁶ He also expected that the announcement of the education plan would bolster soldiers' morale: "Nothing will be more conducive to the maintenance of high morale in our troops than the knowledge that steps are being taken now to give them education and technical training when the fighting is over."³⁷

In this announcement, FDR made a few assumptions about World War II service people and their expectations for education. First, he assumes here that many soldiers had been students before joining the military. Second, he believes that soldiers who had not been in school

---

³³ Ibid., 6.
³⁴ "Preliminary Report to the President of the United States from the Armed Forces Committee on Post War Educational Opportunities for Service Personnel," July 30, 1943, p. 1, "Armed Forces Comm. on Postwar Educational Opportunities for Service Personnel, 1942–44" folder, OF 5182, FDRL; Lewis B. Hershey, *Selective Service in Peacetime: First Report of the Director of Selective Service, 1940–41* (Washington, DC: GPO, 1942), 11–12; Christopher P. Loss, *Between Citizens and the State: The Politics of American Higher Education in the 20th Century* (Princeton, NJ: Princeton University Press, 2012), 94.
³⁵ Olson, *The G.I. Bill*, 11.
³⁶ "Message to the Congress on Education of War Veterans, October 27, 1943," in *The Public Papers and Addresses of Franklin D. Roosevelt, 1943 Volume: The Tide Turns*, compiled by Samuel I. Rosenman (New York: Russell and Russell, 1969 [1950]), 449.
³⁷ Ibid., 450.

upon entering the military would nevertheless wish to pursue an education or vocational training upon demobilization. Finally, this was the second speech by FDR, following the address he delivered to the American public in November 1942, where he declared that the federal government owed education to veterans – many of whom were young – who served in the war. This contrasts sharply with the World War I period, when a similar proposal for the education of veterans was rejected by U.S. Congress (Chapter 1). These assumptions, pronounced by FDR, suggest the evolution of the relationship between young people's access to education, work, and the government. In other words, schooling beyond grammar school had come to be perceived as a standard path toward a better job and life, and Americans had experienced the federal government's involvement in education through such programs as ROTC, the CCC, and the NYA.

The administration's bill for education for veterans, based on the Osborn committee's report, was met with another bill prepared by the American Legion. The final product – the educational provisions of the G.I. Bill of Rights of 1944 – was a product of a compromise between the two bills. There was little controversy among legislators over the overall objective of providing veterans with educational benefits. The debate instead centered on the specifics, such as the different qualifications that the two bills proposed. The administration's bill required six months of service to qualify for the educational benefits, while the Legion bill only required a ninety-day service. The former allowed all eligible veterans to enjoy one year of educational support and offered an additional three years of support to a select number of veterans, while the Legion bill restricted eligibility to veterans whose education had been interrupted by the war but promised them four years of schooling.[38]

One of the major issues was whether the benefits should be limited to those who could prove that their education had been interrupted or delayed, or whether all veterans who met the other requirements the bill set should be eligible for these benefits regardless of their prior educational records.[39] As scholars have demonstrated, the differences between the bills reflected ongoing debates over the proper scale and scope of the federal government, which had been sparked by the expansion of federal authority and jurisdiction under FDR's New Deal. For example, the

---

[38] Olson, *The G.I. Bill*, 15–17.
[39] Library of Congress, Legislative Reference Service, *Provision of Federal Benefits for Veterans: An Historical Analysis of Major Veterans' Legislation, 1862–1954*, House Committee Print No. 171, 84th Cong., 1st sess. (Washington, DC: GPO, 1955), 201–202.

conservative Legion appears to have been less interested in seeing this measure as an expansion of social welfare than in preventing veterans, who had learned "the art of destruction of both property and life," from aimlessly roaming the streets. A Legion representative maintained that the purpose of the educational benefits was to sympathetically help attune the veterans to the "peaceful pursuit of life" and give them "every opportunity to become disciplined forces for progress."[40] Some legislators argued that the danger of offering education to all veterans – including those who had been out of school for many years before induction – would be that too many veterans would take advantage of the benefits, especially if a period of massive unemployment followed the armistice. A Republican legislator warned that such a program would then lead to another federal program for war workers on the home front, and eventually to "a general education bill to give a free education to every citizen, man or woman, who made any contribution to this war, and that would include every American citizen practically from 18 to 88."[41]

The debates over the bill also replicated the discourses about youth, access to education, and national security that had been developed over the preceding decades. Some legislators, for example, argued that limiting the eligibility to veterans who had been fortunate enough to receive education before the war would work to the disadvantage of veterans from less-privileged backgrounds. One of them maintained that the soldiers were already experiencing the consequences of educational inequality in the foxholes, as men with more education were more likely to receive better assignments and treatment in the services.[42]

The final bill stipulated federal funding for one year of schooling for veterans who had served at least ninety days, including tuition, fees, and allowance. Those who had entered the military at the age of twenty-five or younger, as well as those who had entered at an older age but could demonstrate that their education had been interrupted due to their entry into the services, were eligible for additional support for schooling for up to a period equal to their length of service, with the total entitlement not to exceed four years. However, the demobilization process moved faster than predicted, leaving many veterans unemployed. As a result of legislators' concern about the negative impact that these veterans might have on economic and social stability, as well as complaints from veterans and others that the educational benefits were not as accessible as they should

---

[40] Frydl, *The GI Bill*, 111.
[41] Quoted in Library of Congress, Legislative Reference Service, *Provision of Federal Benefits for Veterans*, 207.
[42] Ibid.

be, an amendment was passed in December 1945 that expanded the law by eliminating the requirements that had been imposed on men who entered the military after age twenty-five.[43]

Yet, the fact that there was initially a cutoff age of twenty-five for the requirement of proof to receive extra educational assistance highlights the political impact of the developments concerning the ideas about youth, military service, and education that occurred between the two world wars. The proposed educational support for veterans during World War I (although it was never implemented) had only allowed those who had entered the military as minors to apply, demonstrating the link between reaching legal adulthood and military service. In contrast, the age of twenty-five as the cutoff for receiving the full amount of federal financial aid for education in World War II reflects both the growing consensus that young people of this age should be prepared for jobs in schools and colleges as well as how the age range of eighteen to twenty-five had come to be established as the main group for soldiering.

The G.I. Bill had a tremendous impact on young people's lives as well as the country's educational landscape in the years after World War II. Before the enactment of the law, some educators had worried about the negative impact that the influx of veterans, whom they perceived to be socioeconomically distinct from regular college students, might have on higher education institutions, or assumed that only a small number of them would enroll in college. For example, in December 1944, Robert M. Hutchins, the president of the University of Chicago, had written that veterans would turn college campuses into "hobo jungles."[44] On the contrary, veterans behaved maturely and often surpassed regular students in academic excellence, signaling to the American public that they were no longer "youth" but mature adults.[45] Moreover, a total of 7.8 million people, which amounted to 51 percent of all veterans of World War II, took advantage of the educational benefits. This meant that the benefits were eventually used by a greater number of veterans than the planners had originally expected.[46] Contrary to the public perception

---

[43] Ibid., 208–209; President's Commission on Veterans' Pensions, *The Historical Development of Veterans' Benefits in the United States: A Report on Veterans' Benefits in the United States*, Staff Report no. 1, House Committee Print No. 244, 84th Cong., 2nd sess. (Washington, DC: GPO, 1956), 156; Olson, *The G.I. Bill*, 17; Suzanne Mettler, *Soldiers to Citizens: The G.I. Bill and the Making of the Greatest Generation* (New York: Oxford University Press, 2005), 61.

[44] Olson, *The G.I. Bill*, 27–28; Joseph F. Kett, *The Pursuit of Knowledge under Difficulties: From Self-Improvement to Adult Education in America, 1750–1990* (Stanford, CA: Stanford University Press, 1994), 417; Loss, *Between Citizens and the State*, 114–15.

[45] Kett, *Pursuit of Knowledge under Difficulties*, 417–18.   [46] Mettler, *Soldiers to Citizens*, 7.

that most veterans used the G.I. Bill to go to college, 5.6 million used them for vocational training or education below the college level, while 2.2 million attended colleges and universities. Still, in the peak year of 1947 alone, veterans made up nearly half of all higher education enrollments.[47] On the eve of World War II, approximately 160,000 Americans graduated from college each year; by the end of the 1940s, about 500,000 did so. By 1952, a majority of the nation's veterans between twenty-five and forty-four years old had graduated from high school (58 percent of the veterans between twenty-five and thirty-four years old, and 51 percent of those between thirty-five and forty-four years old). By contrast, among nonveterans in these age groups, only 38 percent were high-school graduates.[48]

The G.I. Bill, on paper, guaranteed educational opportunities to all soldiers, regardless of race, gender, or socioeconomic background. But as historians have shown, it did not benefit all veterans equally, and the bill's stratification of veterans mirrored the stratification of young people in earlier military–educational programs. Black soldiers, for example, had expressed great interest in pursuing education by taking advantage of the G.I. Bill and their interest was even greater than that of their white peers, according to an Army study conducted in 1944. This study indicated that 29 percent of white enlisted men and 43 percent of Black enlisted men indicated an interest in pursuing further training or education after the war after the G.I. Bill was announced, while only 7 percent of enlisted men had done so before the announcement.[49] However, racial discrimination was firmly imprinted at every stage concerning the G.I. Bill, from policymaking to implementation. Segregationist legislators from the South, occupying important Congressional positions and collaborating with segregationist associations for veterans, succeeded in writing into the bill the principle of local administration of the G.I. Bill benefits, which led to the denial or severe limitation on Black veterans' access to the benefits at the local level.[50] Additionally, the military disproportionally – and often in a discriminatory manner – gave them dishonorable discharges, disqualifying them for the benefits. Between August and

---

[47] Frydl, *The GI Bill*, 35; Mettler, *Soldiers to Citizens*, 42; Kett, *Pursuit of Knowledge under Difficulties*, 417.

[48] Ira Katznelson, *When Affirmative Action Was White: An Untold History of Racial Inequality in Twentieth-Century America* (New York: W. W. Norton, 2005), 116; John Modell, *Into One's Own: From Youth to Adulthood in the United States, 1920–1975* (Berkeley: University of California Press, 1989), 204.

[49] Sarah Turner and John Bound, "Closing the Gap or Widening the Divide: The Effects of the G.I. Bill and World War II on the Educational Outcomes of Black Americans," *Journal of Economic History* 63, no.1 (2003): 151.

[50] Katznelson, *When Affirmative Action Was White*, 122–24.

November 1946, for example, 39 percent of Black men were dishonorably discharged from the service while only 21 percent of white men were discharged as such.[51]

For Black men who made it through these discriminatory barriers, the higher education opportunities they were offered were qualitatively and quantitatively limited, both in the North and the South. Institutions outside the South, for example, had long restricted the admission of Black students, and historically Black colleges and universities (HBCUs) in the South, at which 95 percent of Black veterans would use the G.I. Bill's educational benefits, were disproportionally few. In 1947, while Black people made up 25 percent of the population of the South, colleges for white people outnumbered those for Black people by more than five to one. Moreover, HBCUs lacked the funds, facilities, staff, and space to accept all veteran applicants. A survey of these institutions indicates that they had to turn down 55 percent of veteran applicants due to the lack of space. Black veterans who attempted to take advantage of the G.I. Bill's sub-college-level opportunities, such as vocational, technical, and apprenticeship training, likewise faced barriers because of white Southerners' opposition to training them and the lack of quality schools open to them. A study conducted then of Black veterans concluded that it was "as though the GI Bill had been earmarked 'For White Veterans Only.'" In short, historian Ira Katznelson argues, the G.I. Bill widened, rather than closed, the educational gap between Black and white people.[52]

The G.I. Bill had discriminatory effects on other individuals as well. Women made up approximately 2 percent of all U.S. veterans of World War II, but they were less likely than male veterans to claim their benefits as a result of pervasive gender stereotypes that were engrained in both the law and public perceptions of female veterans. For instance, they had to demonstrate their financial independence from a male breadwinner in order to qualify for the same amount of G.I. Bill stipends as male veterans while they pursued an education. As historian Lizabeth Cohen has demonstrated, the bill reduced the likelihood for women of this generation, veterans and nonveterans alike, to receive a college education due to legal discrimination that discouraged female veterans from pursuing an education and because educational institutions reduced the number of women they admitted to make room for male veterans. Due

---

[51] Lizabeth Cohen, *A Consumers' Republic: The Politics of Mass Consumption in Postwar America* (New York: Vintage Books, 2003), 167.
[52] Katznelson, *When Affirmative Action Was White*, 129–40. The quote is from p. 115. See also Turner and Bound, "Closing the Gap or Widening the Divide," 149n7, 153.

to the gendered image of the veteran as masculine, they frequently discovered that while their male peers were praised and admired by the civilian population and benefited from being a veteran, their veteran status had negative consequences for their postwar lives, such as discrimination by potential employers. In fact, as historian Margot Canaday notes, the military restricted the number of women in their institution to 2 percent of the total force until 1967. This meant that most resources for this program were intended for use by men – and heterosexual men, as veterans identified as homosexual were denied G.I. Bill benefits. As Canaday demonstrates, the G.I. Bill "institutionalized heterosexuality" within federal welfare policy, bolstering the prevailing cultural norm of the American family consisting of a male breadwinner and a woman homemaker while relegating to second-class status individuals who did not conform to this model.[53]

Although the G.I. Bill offered an educational opportunity to many veterans who would not have otherwise had it, then, it also highlighted the limits of the attempts to broaden access to education through military service, or of seeing war as a "plastic juncture" for such change. During the debates over the Selective Training and Service Act of 1940, the AYCM had advocated for greater federal support for young people in return for the service young men would offer (Chapter 4). Yet, their idea of using military service as leverage for reform did not translate into what they had expected.

The consequences of the second promise FDR made to soldiers and other citizens in November 1942 – that the government would allow talented soldiers to pursue a college education at the expense of the government – were likewise ambivalent, not just for civilian adults who expected the war to be a "plastic juncture" but for the military, too. The primary plan that materialized for these soldiers – the Army Specialized Training Program (ASTP) – drew on older plans dating back to the late 1930s, when higher education leaders had expressed support for military preparedness efforts and began planning for the education's commitment to military policy in case the United States entered World War II.

In November 1939, the ACE appointed Francis J. Brown, who was New York University professor, AYCM member, and future member of the Reeves committee on veterans' educational benefits discussed above, as a mediator between the federal government and the educational associations addressing the role of higher education in national defense.

---

[53] Mettler, *Soldiers to Citizens*, 11, 144; Cohen, *Consumers' Republic*, 138–40, 143; Margot Canaday, *The Straight State: Sexuality and Citizenship in Twentieth-Century America* (Princeton, NJ: Princeton University Press, 2009), ch. 5 (see especially pp. 171–72).

Then, in August 1940, the ACE and the National Education Association (NEA) held a joint conference to discuss the role of education in national defense with fifty-five educational organizations around the country. As a result of this conference, the National Committee on Education and Defense was formed, with George F. Zook, ACE president, and Willard E. Givens, executive secretary of the NEA, serving as co-chairmen. The committee was later made the Subcommittee on Education of the Joint Army–Navy Committee on Welfare and Recreation, which played a central role in developing educational programs for the military.[54] The ACE held several other major educational conferences before the Japanese attack on Pearl Harbor, inviting government officials and military officers, as well as educational representatives, to discuss the needs of educational institutions in the national emergency and implement educational programs for national defense.[55] Individual educational institutions also mobilized their resources for national defense, as mentioned in Chapter 3. In the first few months of 1941, more than 200 institutions of higher education established national defense committees.[56]

These educators became actively involved in national defense issues even before the United States' entry into World War II in part because of their frustration and critical view of what happened after World War I. By the time the country began to shift its attention from the Great Depression to military preparedness in the late 1930s, they had come to believe that the makeshift mobilization the United States experienced in World War I had produced chaotic consequences for higher education. Their memories of the Student Army Training Corps (SATC) had become particularly bitter. Higher education leaders now considered the establishment of the SATC as having come too late in the war, and Army officials assigned to SATC units as having been too dictatorial. Moreover, they now believed that the SATC had been terminated too abruptly and too soon after the armistice because of insufficient

---

[54] V. R. Cardozier, *Colleges and Universities in World War II* (Westport, CT: Praeger, 1993), 4–5.

[55] Ibid.; American Council on Education (hereafter cited as ACE), *Organizing Higher Education for National Defense: The Report of a Conference Called by the National Committee on Education and Defense Held in Washington, D.C., February 6, 1941* (Washington, DC: American Council of Education, 1941); ACE, *Higher Education Cooperates in National Defense: The Report of the Conference of Government Representatives and College and University Administrators, Held in Washington D.C., July 30–31, 1941* (Washington, DC: American Council on Education, 1941); Charles Dorn, *American Education, Democracy, and the Second World War* (New York: Palgrave Macmillan, 2007), 29–30.

[56] ACE, *Organizing Higher Education for National Defense*, 34.

planning, leaving many higher education institutions in a financial plight. The educational leaders' calls for early planning and engagement in the World War II period, therefore, built on memories of World War I that had become increasingly gloomy.[57]

Thanks to these early efforts, these educational leaders were confident by the time the United States entered World War II that they were better positioned than in World War I. Samuel P. Capen, who had served as the first ACE director between 1919 and 1922, declared in early 1942:

> We have now ... the American Council on Education, which represents us all; and we have a fortified Office of Education which is something more than a reporting agency, as it was in 1917, and which has direct and clear channels to the other operating agencies of the government. We have a roster of scientific personnel already more complete than anything we ever had during the whole course of the last war. [...] And we have also a Selective Service System which is a year and a quarter old [...] and which recognizes the necessity of providing through deferments for the complete preparation of skilled specialists.[58]

The federal government's planning for the use of higher education for military purposes during the war followed that of the educators. In August 1942, the War Manpower Commission (WMC), a federal agency in charge of manpower planning, appointed a committee to study the use of higher education for military policy. The committee was chaired by Edward C. Elliott, the president of Purdue University and a WMC member, and included another educator, but it was otherwise dominated by military officials. A report the committee produced demonstrated the tough stance of military officials toward higher education, stating that all "able-bodied male students are destined for the armed forces."[59]

From the fear that higher education institutions would be controlled by the military, the ACE established a committee on their own to mediate a wartime relationship of higher education to the federal government that met their needs. Chaired by Cornell University President Edmund E. Day, this committee proposed to FDR the establishment of a college training corps to be set up on campuses throughout the country to train

---

[57] Cardozier, *Colleges and Universities in World War II*, 4, 9.
[58] Quoted in Gene M. Lyons and John W. Masland, *Education and Military Leadership: A Study of the R.O.T.C.* (Princeton, NJ: Princeton University Press, 1959), 56.
[59] Cardozier, *Colleges and Universities in World War II*, 7; Lewis B. Hershey, *Selective Service in Wartime: Second Report of the Director of Selective Service, 1941–42* (Washington, DC: GPO, 1943), 120.

technical experts useful for the military.[60] On October 15, 1942, FDR wrote to the Secretaries of War and Navy asking them to study the use of higher education for the war effort, in light of the decline in college enrollment. On December 12, 1942, the Army and Navy jointly announced the establishment of college corps programs along the lines suggested by the educators.[61]

The ASTP, launched in March 1943, along with its equivalents run by the Navy and the Army Air Forces, symbolized higher education's contribution to the training of military personnel during World War II. The ASTP's goal was to provide soldiers with specialized technical training prescribed by the Army at authorized colleges and universities in fields of study where Army training facilities were insufficient. Graduates of the program would be assigned to the Officer Candidate School, Army Service Schools, or other military service as determined by the Army.[62] It intended to address the needs of both the military and higher education. On the one hand, the Army could no longer anticipate a steady stream of college-educated draftees who were knowledgeable in subjects like medicine, engineering, foreign languages, mathematics, and psychology and who were qualified to serve as officers as a result of the draft age being lowered to eighteen. On the other hand, the lowering of the minimum draft age signaled a severe loss of student population for higher education institutions.[63]

A few supplementary programs were created as well to recruit preinduction teens to the ASTP and to develop a direct flow of young men into the ASTP before they entered active duty. One was a pre-induction testing program for men between the ages of seventeen and twenty-two who were not yet in the armed forces to identify potential candidates for the ASTP. Another was the Army Specialized Training Reserve Program, which provided scholarships to seventeen-year-old high-school graduates who passed the aforementioned pre-induction test and sent them to colleges and universities for instruction in ASTP courses. The scholarship paid for tuition, housing, food, and medical care, and participants were to be called to active duty at the end of the term in which

---

[60] Cardozier, *Colleges and Universities in World War II*, 7; Louis E. Keefer, *Scholars in Foxholes: The Story of the Army Specialized Training Program in World War II* (Reston, VA: COTU Publishing, 1988), 11.
[61] Cardozier, *Colleges and Universities in World War II*, 7–8.
[62] [War Department, Office of the Chief of Staff,] *Fifty Questions and Answers on Army Specialized Training Program* (Washington, DC: GPO, 1943), 5, 13.
[63] G. Marshall, "Memorandum for the Commanding Generals," April 1, 1943, reprinted in [War Department, Office of the Chief of Staff,] *Fifty Questions and Answers*, n.p.; Cardozier, *Colleges and Universities in World War II*, 7.

they turned eighteen. The program, according to the Army, provided "uninterrupted training for many of these young men who might otherwise lose valuable training time during a gap filled with uncertainty between high school and college," allowing them to "begin immediate preparation for the most advanced military duties they are able to perform."[64]

Higher education administrators were enthusiastic about the establishment of the ASTP. By the autumn of 1943, 196 colleges and universities, 76 medical schools, 39 dental schools, and 10 veterinary schools had contracted with the Army for the program. Enrollment reached its peak around that time, figuring at 145,000. More than 200,000 men had studied in the ASTP by the time the program was terminated in 1946.[65] With the establishment of ASTP, the production of reserve officers by ROTC was discontinued for the duration of the war, although the framework of the ROTC was maintained in colleges and universities for the resumption of the program after the war. Students in the advanced course of ROTC were sent to other officer training facilities of the Army or to ASTP to complete their training, while ROTC institutions were used as ASTP sites.[66]

---

[64] U.S. Army Service Forces, Army Specialized Training Division, *Essential Facts about the Army Specialized Training Program* (Washington, DC: GPO, 1943), 14, 16–17 (the quotes are from p. 14); J. A. Ulio, "Army Specialized Training Reserve Program," July 10, 1943, "ASTP World War II Preliminary Report Book 1" folder, Army Service Forces, Director of Military Training, Army Specialized Military Training, 1942–46, Historical File, Records of Headquarters Army Service Forces, RG 160, NACP; "Army Begins Training for Boy Reservists in Selected Colleges," *WP*, August 8, 1943. The development of this program was also motivated by the Army's need to compete with the Navy for young, skilled men, which recruited individuals as young as seventeen. John S. Diekhoff, "History of Army Specialized Training Reserve Program, from Its Beginning to 31 December 1944," May 15, 1945, p. 2, "History of Army Specialized Training Reserve Program" folder, Army Service Forces, Director of Military Training, Army Specialized Military Training, 1942–46, Historical File, Records of Headquarters Army Service Forces, RG 160, NACP.

[65] Cardozier, *Colleges and Universities in World War II*, 25.

[66] Millard W. Hansen, "A History of the Reserve Officers' Training Corps and the 55C (National Defense Act) Schools, 1939–1944," April 1, 1945, n.p. (pp. 5–22 of "Chapter I – Training Requirements," pp. 2–3 of "Chapter II – Organization of Training by Echelon of Command," p. 10 of "Chapter III – Training Program, Administration"), "History of the ROTC" folder, Army Service Forces, Director of Military Training, Army Specialized Military Training, 1942–46, Historical File, Records of Headquarters Army Service Forces, RG 160, NACP; I. H. Edwards, "Memorandum for the Commanding General, Services of Supply," December 17, 1942, p. 1, "ASTP World War II Preliminary Report Book 1" folder, Army Service Forces, Director of Military Training, Army Specialized Military Training, 1942–46, Historical File, Records of Headquarters Army Service Forces, RG 160, NACP. ROTC in institutions below the college level was maintained in World War II, although the War Department did not

As examined in Chapter 4, supporters of the draft law amendment lowering the draft age to eighteen praised plans that allowed young soldiers with military talents to study in colleges at the government's expense as democratic measures that offered young people, regardless of economic means, advanced training. To them, the ASTP represented a prime example of democratically mobilizing young Americans. The Army also utilized this rhetoric of the ASTP as a democratic educational opportunity, declaring that the selection of ASTP candidates were made on "a broad, democratic basis."[67] The War Department highlighted the ASTP's educational advantages for young soldiers in a 1943 leaflet intended to address common inquiries soldiers had about the program:

> The war may have interrupted your education. It may have stopped you short just when you were ready to go to college. If you can meet the qualifications, the Army Specialized Training offers you the chance to pick up where you left off. In some cases it will permit you to complete the job. In all cases it will provide courses of instruction which will raise your value to the Army to its maximum and *leave you better prepared for the years that will follow victory.*[68]

Interestingly, the War Department promotes here the ASTP not only as a program that would improve the soldiers' standing in the military, but also as one that would help them have a better life after the war. The pamphlet also explains how the ASTP was strictly a wartime program to serve military needs – and therefore that the Army prohibited soldiers from choosing the course to attend or participating in intercollegiate sports – but the overarching message is the ASTP's *educational* benefits, both long- and short-term. This implies that the military, like the civilians who argued that military service was an educational opportunity for young men, had internalized the discourse that associated military service with educational opportunity.[69]

Despite the claim that education during military service would help young men live better lives, it was evident to all involved that the ASTP was a program founded out of war necessity. As explained below, it was unavoidably far from a program designed to provide socioeconomically disadvantaged and minority students with a college education comparable to that provided to other civilian students, let alone the opportunity to pursue a subject of their choosing. Furthermore, even from a military

---

establish new units during the war. Hansen, "A History of the Reserve Officers' Training Corps," n.p. (p. 1 of "Chapter VI – The Junior Division ROTC.")

[67] U.S. Army Service Forces, Army Specialized Training Division, *Essential Facts about the Army Specialized Training Program*, i.

[68] Emphasis mine. [War Department, Office of the Chief of Staff,] *Fifty Questions and Answers*, 3.

[69] Ibid., 5, 7, 19.

standpoint, the program did not produce the desired goals. The disparity between the rhetoric of military service as an educational opportunity and how the ASTP operated demonstrates the limitations of the idea that a war could be transformed into a "plastic juncture" for broad social goals.

Unsurprisingly, wartime policy was meant to serve military needs, not educational ones with long-range objectives. Like the SATC during World War I, the ASTP was focused on fields of study that served military ends. The largest programs were in engineering, followed by foreign language and area studies, psychology, and professional education such as medicine, dentistry, and communications. Soldiers had no control over whether or not to enroll in the ASTP or what subject they would study there.[70]

Moreover, although FDR's announcement on educational programs for soldiers discussed above suggested that the ASTP would be open to a broad range of soldiers, the exigencies of war meant that the ASTP would only train those who were already equipped with expertise in relevant fields of training. The basic eligibility criterion was the soldiers' performance on the Army General Classification Test, a test administered by the Army to determine each soldier's basic literacy level, and there were additional criteria that limited the pool of candidates.[71] The basic engineering course, for example, was only open to high-school graduates under the age of twenty-two who had taken relevant courses in high school. Meanwhile, the advanced course in engineering was only open to men who had completed at least one year of college, including at least one year of education in mathematics and either physics or biology. Likewise, enrollees in the language and area studies programs were required to have previous college training in at least one foreign language out of the thirty-four languages specified by the ASTP.[72]

Additionally, the program was less accessible to older soldiers who had not received any college-level education: it accepted soldiers aged 22 and older only if they had completed at least one year of college (but no more than three years), had majored in mathematics, physics, chemistry, psychology, or engineering, or had knowledge of a foreign language. Furthermore, the duration of the ASTP for each participant

---

[70] Cardozier, *Colleges and Universities in World War II*, 24; [War Department, Office of the Chief of Staff,] *Fifty Questions and Answers*, 7–11.
[71] [War Department, Office of the Chief of Staff,] *Fifty Questions and Answers*, 6–7; U.S. Army Service Forces, Army Specialized Training Division, *Essential Facts about the Army Specialized Training Program*, 2. On the Army General Classification Test, see Loss, *Between Citizens and the State*, 102–103.
[72] Cardozier, *Colleges and Universities in World War II*, 27–28, 33.

could be as short as twelve weeks.[73] The extent to which ASTP offered a college education to young people who had previously found it beyond their reach, unsurprisingly, was strictly dependent on military ends.

Finally, the ASTP did not last long. By the time the first trainees completed their studies in the fall of 1943, the Selective Service System was experiencing a severe manpower shortage. The Army reported a shortage of 200,000 men at the end of that year, announcing that they would have to consider inducting fathers. In light of the pressing need for young soldiers, both military representatives and Congress urged that the ASTP students be transferred to military duty. In February 1944, the War Department announced that the ASTP enrollment would be reduced from 145,000 to 35,000 within a few months.[74]

Another significant limitation of the claim that ASTP democratized access to higher education was the program's restricted accessibility to young Black men. In December 1943, only 789 of the 105,000 ASTP students were Black soldiers.[75] As in past wars, Black soldiers in World War II were likely to be assigned to noncombat units, such as the Quartermaster and Engineering Corps, and relegated to unskilled, hard labor jobs, a situation they described as "nothing but slaves" and being "treated like wild animals."[76] Regardless of the level of schooling, aspirations, and competencies, therefore, they were likely to be assigned to low-level tasks with little chance for promotion or transfer to jobs that better met their talents, which narrowed their possibility of getting into ASTP.

For many young Black men, whose economic opportunities in civilian life were severely restricted, the military did serve as a "gateway to modern America," as historian Ira Katznelson put it. In other words, it offered them a place to live, meals, health care, and a steady source of income, along with a range of educational opportunities that they were

---

[73] [War Department, Office of the Chief of Staff,] *Fifty Questions and Answers*, 6, 12–13.
[74] The majority of the 35,000 men who remained in the ASTP were those enrolled in advanced engineering, dentistry, or medical courses. These courses terminated shortly after the war's end. Cardozier, *Colleges and Universities in World War II*, 37–39; "Army Slashed College Training, Shifts 110,000 Men to Line Duty," *NYT*, February 19, 1944.
[75] Katznelson, *When Affirmative Action Was White*, 110.
[76] As of April 1942, African Americans comprised 42 percent and 34 percent of the engineering and quartermaster units, respectively. Ulysses Lee, *The Employment of Negro Troops* (Washington, DC: GPO, 2001 [1963]), 128. The quotes are from Katznelson, *When Affirmative Action Was White*, 91. See also Samuel A. Stouffer, et al., *The American Soldier: Adjustment during Army Life*, vol. 1 of the Studies in Social Psychology in World War II (New York: John Wiley and Sons, 1965 [1949]), 495–97.

not able to receive at home, from basic literacy to vocational training.[77] Yet, the military, whose leaders persistently believed that Black people lacked the mental and moral qualities for advanced positions and needed white officers' supervision, failed to offer Black men who had entered the military with more advanced expertise to maximize their abilities. In March 1945, approximately 11 percent of white military personnel held an officer rank, whereas less than 1 percent of their Black counterparts held the same position. With white soldiers being provided with greater opportunities for education and vocational training that could serve them in their postwar civilian career advancement as well as for advancement within the military, the war, in the long run, widened the socioeconomic and educational gap between white and Black people.[78]

The unpredictability of the war's course, as well as preexisting socioeconomic and racial discrimination and inequalities, rendered the ASTP a frustrating program for many involved. Although some ASTP trainees subsequently recalled their ASTP experiences positively, the experiences of many other ASTP graduates were not pleasant. Many of them had hoped to attend the officer candidate school upon completion of the program, but few did so because the Army prioritized sending advanced ROTC graduates there. Because there was a scarcity of troops on the front lines, a large number of ASTP graduates were deployed to battlefields overseas as replacements, where they were given assignments that had little to do with their talents and areas of specialization. The haphazard deployment of ASTP soldiers even confirmed to the Army that the ASTP was a failure. In an Army general's words, the Army "lost valued leadership by forced assignment of these men to inferior positions."[79] The ASTP, therefore, helped prevent many higher education institutions from bankruptcy but left mixed results for the military as well as young servicepeople who participated in the program.

The creation of educational programs like the G.I. Bill and the ASTP highlights a broader transformation in American society regarding the understanding of youth, education, and national security. As military preparedness activities surged in the early 1940s and the "youth problem" of the 1930s faded from public consciousness, "youth" came to mean juveniles too young to fight or young nonwhite people supposedly problematic to the wartime social order. The educational opportunities

---

[77] Katznelson, *When Affirmative Action Was White*, 105–109 (the quote is from p. 106); Paula S. Fass, *Outside In: Minorities and the Transformation of American Education* (New York: Oxford University Press, 1989), 145–46.
[78] Katznelson, *When Affirmative Action Was White*, 109–112; Stouffer, et al., *The American Soldier*, 501.
[79] Cardozier, *Colleges and Universities in World War II*, 37–41 (the quote is from p. 41).

that adults created for soldiers and veterans demonstrate that adults considered servicepeople, including those in the age group previously considered immature youth in need of adult guidance, as "young adults."

These programs represented, in the eyes of higher education elites, the fruition of their decades-long work to improve relations with the federal government during times of national emergency. Many of them claimed that the military's educational initiatives geared at preparing young men for service, such as the ASTP, also served to increase access to higher education for individuals who previously thought it was out of their financial reach. The military had internalized this discourse as well. However, these programs reflected the stratification of young people based on national security needs that had developed in the years following World War I and which had incorporated both the stratified nature of military institutions and preexisting racism and socioeconomic inequality in civilian American society. Additionally, an educational opportunity offered through wartime military service necessarily worked within a hierarchical framework of military manpower allocation that stratified servicepeople into duties that met military demands. The ASTP, while touted as "democratic," was intended to train only people who had previously received education in fields considered beneficial for military purposes, making many others ineligible. Moreover, many young Black servicepeople were denied the opportunity to obtain ASTP training as well as G.I. Bill training. Finally, due to the nature of the war, many ASTP trainees were assigned to posts unrelated to their area of expertise, rendering the ASTP frustrating for the military as well.

The educational elite remained committed to preparing young men for military service throughout the war. Two weeks after the announcement of the drastic curtailment of ASTP, the War Department announced the broadening of the ASTP reserve program for seventeen-year-olds, with the strong push for this move from ACE educators, led by Harvard president James Conant. As if to reiterate the argument he had made during the nationwide debate over selective service about a college education program for soldiers as a democratic educational opportunity (Chapter 4), he argued that by "being sent as ASTP reserve students, they [the seventeen-year-olds] will have an opportunity for education which will benefit them in their subsequent Army careers and will serve as a basis for future education when the war is over."[80]

---

[80] Benjamin Fine, "Colleges Look to Army Training Program for 17-Year-Olds to Repeople Their Campuses," *NYT*, March 12, 1944. See also "Army to Expand College Program with Youths Below the Draft Age," *NYT*, March 4, 1944.

The higher education sector grew dramatically in the postwar years, thanks to the G.I. Bill. Some educators might have felt uneasy pursuing the merits of the institution while their students risked their lives for their country. A sign of such uneasiness can be examined in the writing of Dan W. Dodson, an education professor at New York University, who was thirty-six years old in 1943. He sent a letter that year to his NYU colleague Francis J. Brown, who was serving as an educational advisor to the Joint Army and Navy Committee on Welfare and Recreation, indicating that as a man of draft age, he felt "a little uncomfortable sitting around here" at the university, when "the need was as great elsewhere."[81] Few educational leaders that drove higher education's cooperation with the military during the war, however, expressed any sentiment that suggested they comprehended the horrors of the front lines or publicly and explicitly acknowledged that their efforts built on the suffering and death of many young men they helped send to war.

When the Princetonian Veterans of Future Wars gained national attention in 1936 for its scathing satire of World War I veterans (Chapter 3), the national commander of the Veterans of Foreign Wars – the organization representing real war veterans – had stated that the members of the Veterans of Future Wars would "never be veterans of a future war, for they are too yellow to go to war."[82] On the eve of the U.S. entry into World War II, however, the *Washington Post* reported that those "veterans" of the "future wars" were "becoming just that." They were either already serving in the military or were about to be called, and they received or would receive the standard monthly salary but not the bonuses they had demanded. Eventually, all Princetonian leaders of the Veterans of Future Wars served, except for one who was exempted due to physical disability. One of them never returned.[83]

---

[81] The letter indicates that he was not able to perform military service due to a physical condition. Dan D. Dodson to Francis J. Brown, June 2, 1943, "Dr. Brown Personal" folder, Joint Army and Navy Committee on Welfare and Recreation Subcommittee on Education Correspondence, 1941–1943, Records of the Joint Boards and Committees, RG 225, NACP.

[82] "Future Veterans' Change War Views," *NYT*, March 4, 1944.

[83] Edward T. Folliard, "'Veterans of Future Wars' Are Becoming Just That," *WP*, November 30, 1941; "Future Veterans' Change War Views"; Donald W. Whisenhunt, *Veterans of Future Wars: A Study in Student Activism* (Lanham, MD: Lexington, 2011), 35.

6 Youth in U.S.-Occupied Japan

By the time major hostilities ceased in the summer of 1945, the United States had become the world's military and economic superpower, surpassing other major powers whose strength had been drastically diminished by the war. Since the early years of the war, the country had been preparing for the postwar occupation of the Axis powers, and while the Army Student Training Program (ASTP) was largely terminated in the middle of the war, other military–educational programs continued to exist in higher education institutions and trained specialists for postwar occupation duty.[1] Indeed, the political and social reform of Japan and Germany, as well as the physical reconstruction of the two countries, marked another "plastic juncture" in which Americans with divergent views of social order had enormous expectations for change. In U.S. Secretary of State James Byrnes' words, the occupation of Japan was "the second phase of our war against Japan," which followed the "fighting phase" and centered on the "spiritual disarmament" of Japanese people.[2] Mobilizing Japanese "youth" was essential to this "second phase" of the war.

While Americans were gearing up for the occupation of Japan, young Japanese people were experiencing the end of the war in many ways. In the fall of 1945, twenty-two-year-old Yamada Taro returned to his home village in Hyogo prefecture in western Japan, after having been a Japanese Navy draftee for nearly two years. This must have been an unreal homecoming for him – the Navy had ordered him to go on a "suicide attack." Before his scheduled last day of life, however, Japan surrendered to the Allied powers. Yamada, who passed away in 2011, left no written reminiscences of his wartime experiences. However, his

---

[1] Benjamin Justice, "When the Army Got Progressive: The Civil Affairs Training School at Stanford University, 1943–1945," *History of Education Quarterly*, 51 no. 3 (2011): 330–61.
[2] "Statement by the Secretary of the State," *Department of State Bulletin* 13, no. 323 (1945): 300; Jennifer M. Miller, *Cold War Democracy: The United States and Japan* (Cambridge, MA: Harvard University Press, 2019), 26.

neighbors and family members recollect him as someone who was never enthusiastic about the war. During a farewell ceremony held in his village for young local men being inducted into the military, all inductees – except for him – customarily performed the "*banzai*" shouts to show they were happy to fight and die for the emperor. Yamada, instead, looked straight ahead, poker-faced, quietly asking his fellow villagers to take care of the family he would leave behind – his mother and seven siblings he had been supporting since losing his father during his last year of secondary school.³

While Yamada was adjusting back to civilian life, Kanai Satoshi, another young man in the same prefecture, was pondering over the future of *Seinendan*, the most popular youth organization in Japan of which he was part. *Seinendan* originated as a community-based youth organization for young men in their teens through mid-twenties with units in municipalities across the country, but by the end of the 1930s, it had been incorporated into militaristic Japan's war mobilization scheme. With the war's end, Kanai was developing a determination to reform and refresh the organization to meet the social needs of the new era.⁴ Finally, Saito Kayoko was a secondary school student in Tokyo with a distinguished background. Born to an upper-class Christian family, she was fluent in English. At a time when schooling beyond grammar school was unreachable for most children in Japan, she would soon attend an elite high school, dreaming of becoming a schoolteacher.⁵

There were no personal connections between these three young people, but they did have one thing in common: they were part of the age group that the U.S. occupation authorities in postwar Japan labeled as "youth"; that is, Japanese people in their teens through mid-twenties.

---

³ Interviews with Yamada Taro's wife and children by the author, Hyogo, Japan, January 1, 2018; interview with one of his children by the author, Hyogo, Japan, January 3, 2020; Yamada's resume in his family's possession. Out of respect for his and his family's privacy, his name has been changed. I thank Yamada's family for allowing me to access their private collection and publish the findings. Japanese names in this chapter are given in conventional Japanese order (surname-given name) except for Japanese author names that appear in the reverse order (given name-surname) in English-language publications. All translations of Japanese-language materials are mine.

⁴ Kanai Satoshi to Durgin Sensei, May 3, 1947, "Kinki" folder, Supreme Commander for the Allied Powers (hereafter cited as SCAP), Civil Education and Information Section (hereafter cited as CIE), Education Division, Physical Education and Youth Affairs Branch, Topical File, 1945–51, Records of Allied Operational and Occupation Headquarters, World War II, Record Group (hereafter cited as RG) 331, U.S. National Archives at College Park, College Park, MD (hereafter cited as NACP).

⁵ Saito Kayoko's curriculum vitae and autobiography enclosed in Kaneo Ohta to Mrs. Theodore Waller, November 6, 1951, CIE (D) 02329–02330, GHQ/SCAP Records (microfiche), Modern Japanese Political History Materials Room, National Diet Library, Tokyo, Japan (hereafter cited as CIE-NDL).

As previous chapters have shown, American society during the Great Depression conceptualized the term as signifying Americans in their mid-teens through mid-twenties, individuals mostly out of school but not yet considered as mentally mature as older people. This perception shaped the selective service policy for World War II, but as the United States rose to prominence as the world's superpower and young Americans bravely contributed to the war effort, American adults gradually became less inclined to see the problems of American youth as comparable to those of foreign youth. As a result, adults who had worked on the "youth problem" in the 1930s turned their attention to foreign youth, and young Japanese were the typical "youth" who fit into their image of young people in need of American tutelage. In fact, the Japanese government up to World War II had similarly labeled young people in roughly the same age range as *seinen* (youth), connotating that they were the youthful vanguards of the Japanese colonial empire. U.S.-occupied Japan, then, was a unique space in which the Japanese and U.S. conceptions of youth came into contact with each other.

As in the case of the United States examined in previous chapters, the rhetorical banner of "youth" in Japan up to World War II had a homogenizing effect, generalizing diverse people as a single, monolithic group of young men and women and flattening the diversity and inequality within the age group. Concurrently, the Japanese militarist government stratified young people based on their usefulness for national goals, which often reinforced existing hierarchies based on social class, gender, race, and ethnicity. The Americans who arrived in Japan after the end of the hostilities drew on both the U.S. and Japanese conceptions of youth to advance their national security objectives. That is, they rhetorically addressed young Japanese as a unitary group of people craving to be rescued from a militaristic dictatorship while stratifying them through policy in a manner similar to how the U.S. government and other American adults had stratified young Americans in the name of democracy, national security, and public good. The ways Americans in postwar Japan treated Japanese youth demonstrate how strong the link between youth, education, and national security remained. However, it also suggested that the period in which "total war" shaped cultural perceptions of the role of youth in national security was coming to an end, as the nascent Cold War was gradually reshaping the relationship.

Setting the Stage

In Japan, youth groups had existed locally for centuries before they were incorporated into the war mobilization scheme in World War II, providing moral support to their members, organizing local festivals, and helping fellow farmers during harvest seasons. Around the turn of the twentieth century, the word *seinen* gained prominence as a term to address young people from those aged approximately twelve (when people normally finished compulsory education) to those in their midtwenties (when they married). Like similar terms elsewhere in the world that addressed young people, *seinen* carried future-oriented connotations. Adults envisioned *seinen* as vanguards of Japan's imperial modernity – the youthful citizens that signified the country's farewell to its feudal past. The term also had gendered implications, primarily indicating young men, with young women often being referred to as *joshi* (girls, women) or *shōjo* (girls, young women) rather than *seinen*.[6]

By the early twentieth century, youth groups collectively called *Seinendan* quickly emerged as the predominant association for young men (*dan* means group), and national military and political leaders, sensing that *Seinendan* would be a useful medium through which they could reach young people across the country and the colonies, set out to include them under the umbrella of the Japanese state. The nationalization of *Seinendan* went hand-in-hand with similar moves aiming at placing other age groups under state management. People faced social pressure to join *Seinendan* and other age- and gender-segregated neighborhood associations, making local association membership a lifetime commitment. Men first entered a local boys' group as children, moved on to *Seinendan* once they left school, and joined other associations for older men once they reached their early or mid-twenties. Likewise, women joined girls' groups, female youth groups, and associations for older women. Groups for children and young people were led by older neighborhood adults, such as the groups' alumni and schoolteachers, teaching younger members of the community how local hierarchies worked.[7]

---

[6] Sayaka Chatani, *Nation-Empire: Ideology and Rural Youth Mobilization in Japan and Its Colonies* (Ithaca, NY: Cornell University Press, 2018), 13–14, 69; David R. Ambaras, *Bad Youth: Juvenile Delinquency and the Politics of Everyday Life in Modern Japan* (Berkeley: University of California Press, 2006), 3.

[7] Tani Teruhiro, *Seinen no seiki* (Tokyo: Dōseisha, 2002), 57–59; Katase Ichio, *Wakamono no sengoshi: Gunkoku shōnen kara rosujene made* (Tokyo: Minerva Shobō, 2015), iv–xiii, 61–62; Sheldon Garon, *Molding Japanese Minds: The State in Everyday Life* (Princeton, NJ: Princeton University Press, 1997), ch. 4; Takeyasu Hideko, "Josei no seiji sanka katsudō no tenkai to sono genkai: Sengoki no Tottori-ken chiiki fujinkai katudō o chūshin ni," *Gendai Shakai Kenkyūka Ronshū* 8 (2014): 40–41; "Outlines of Program and Policies for 1946," n.d., pp. 1, 3, "Materials Re Guidance" folder. SCAP, CIE, Education Division, Youth and Health Education Branch, Miscellaneous File, 1945–52, RG331, NACP.

This nationalization of youth groups, however, did not proceed as a simple top-down imposition of imperial goals on ordinary people; rather, it developed in a zigzag manner consisting of clashes and compromises between the state and its constituents over the aims, aspirations, and expectations of this nationalization. For example, a 1915 government decree that formalized a national network of *Seinendan* and set the upper age limit of *Seinendan* membership at twenty, which coincided with the minimum draft age, ignited public criticism that condemned it as a militaristic measure intending to make *Seinendan* a pre-draft training institution. Due partly to this opposition, the government revised the decree five years later to admit men of up to age twenty-five to *Seinendan*.[8] Additionally, some socially disadvantaged young men sought to appropriate the state's imperial goals for their ends. Young men in rural regions, for example, eagerly took up leadership positions in the government's *Seinendan* nationalization initiative as an upward mobility opportunity to overcome a public image of themselves as marginalized, backward-looking farmers as opposed to urban, educated youth who symbolized the country's modernization and material wealth. By so doing, they could claim that they, not their urban counterparts, were the vanguards of Japanese imperial modernism.[9]

By the late 1930s, however, with the state's grip over *Seinendan* and other communal groups tightening, young people were left with little leeway to appropriate the state's imperial goals for their ends. In January 1941, the government merged *Seinendan* with its younger boys' and girls' equivalents into *Dai Nihon Seishōnendan* (Greater Japan Youth and Children's Organization) to mobilize young people and children for war. In the spring of 1945, the government ordered the entire civilian population to prepare to take up arms against the anticipated Allied invasion of the Japanese home islands, thereby reorganizing *Dai Nihon Seishōnendan* into *Gakutotai* (Student Corps) for pupils and students and *Kokumingiyūtai* (Citizens' Volunteer Corps) for men between the ages of fifteen and sixty and women between the ages of seventeen and forty.[10] By the end of the war, therefore, *Seinendan* as a government's war mobilization apparatus had ceased to exist.

After the hostilities ceased in the summer of 1945, Japanese society was in unprecedented chaos. Nearly seven million people, including both

---

[8] Chatani, *Nation-Empire*, 33–35; Tani, *Seinen no seiki*, 58–59; Hirayama Kazuhiko, *Gappon seinen shūdansi kenkyū josetsu* (Tokyo: Shinsensha, 1988), Part 2: 21–30, 82.
[9] Chatani, *Nation-Empire*, ch. 2.
[10] Kitagawa Kenzō, *Sengo no shuppatsu: Bunka undō, Seinendan, sensō mibōjin* (Tokyo: Aoki Shoten, 2009), 68; Tani, *Seinen no seiki*, 14.

soldiers and civilians, were heading back to mainland Japan from overseas, and many others returned to their home communities, having been demobilized from wartime industrial work elsewhere in the country. Sixty percent of urban housing had been destroyed by aerial bombing, and with widespread hunger and poverty aggravating the situation, nine million people had been rendered homeless.[11] The unprecedented social confusion impacted young people in numerous ways. Young veterans, for instance, had extreme difficulty readjusting to civilian life. Finding work was one of their biggest challenges since civilians, who earlier hailed military men as national heroes, were now linking them with war crimes or erroneous stereotypes of unemployed men as thieves.[12] Veterans or otherwise, young people also found themselves in a state of despair or lethargy. Many of them developed a great distrust of older adults who had "indoctrinated" them into the imperial cause of war, and some blamed themselves for this manipulation.[13]

The occupation amplified the emotional restlessness among young Japanese. According to a U.S. officer in Japan, being occupied by young people from another country enjoying privileges out of their reach gave them a "deep feeling of inferiority."[14] Indeed, it was likely that the U.S. troops that young Japanese people encountered were of comparable age. For example, the median age of U.S. draftees in Japan in July 1946 was as young as twenty years and three months.[15] Yet, the contrast in living conditions between Japanese youth and U.S. troops was striking. Young Japanese people in the cities were being driven from their ancestral lands that had been bombed out during the war and which were requisitioned by the occupation forces. They saw neighborhood roads renamed "Texas Avenue," "Michigan Boulevard," and other American names unfamiliar to them. They witnessed the staggering gap between the makeshift shacks and shanties that many Japanese lived in and the luxurious mansions the U.S. officers occupied, and between homeless Japanese freezing to death

---

[11] Lori Watt, *When Empire Comes Home: Repatriation and Reintegration in Postwar Japan* (Cambridge, MA: Harvard University Press, 2009), 2; Michael Cullen Green, *Black Yanks in the Pacific: Race in the Making of American Military Empire after World War II* (Ithaca, NY: Cornell University Press, 2010), 32–33.

[12] Kitagawa, *Sengo no shuppatsu*, 73–77.

[13] "Seinen no shisō dōkō o kataru zadankai," *The Seinen* 31, no. 7 (1946): 12, filed in "Youth Movements" folder, SCAP, CIE, Education Section, Physical Education and Youth Affairs Branch Topical File, 1945–51, RG 331, NACP; Kitagawa, *Sengo no shuppatsu*, 78, 81.

[14] "Youth Affairs Program for Kinki Region," n.d., p. 3, CIE (A) 08828, CIE-NDL.

[15] Lindesay Parrott, "Curb on GI Crimes Ordered in Japan," *New York Times*, July 14, 1946; Susan L. Carruthers, *The Good Occupation: American Soldiers and the Hazards of Peace* (Cambridge, MA: Harvard University Press, 2016), 266.

and Americans enjoying Christmas shopping at Japanese department stores, now turned into post exchanges exclusively for the occupiers. Many also worked as servants for U.S. families or engaged in prostitution serving Americans to make ends meet, both of which involved intimate relationships that keenly taught them the economic richness of American life.[16] The physical visibility of young, khaki-clad Americans in everyday life thus vividly reminded Japanese youth of their subordinate status.

Amid this social confusion and distress, young people reunited, particularly in rural areas where *Seinendan* had flourished before the war. Although *Seinendan* as a state's war mobilization apparatus had been demolished during the war, *Seinendan* as communal groups had survived the war in many communities throughout Japan.[17] The return of young people from factories, overseas, and the military increased membership. In a village in central Japan, for example, half of the male members had served in the military. Theatrical performances that involved singing, acting, and dancing became a favorite activity of the new *Seinendan*. Although prewar youth organizations had been gender-segregated, and while some adults still frowned at the mingling of young men and women, postwar *Seinendan* activities increasingly became co-educational. Recreational activities run by youth organizations thus functioned to bring together young people with diverse wartime experiences and provided entertainment for rural communities that had limited access to movies and other sources of leisure.[18] Japanese newspapers published editorials arguing that *seinen* should lead the "New Japan," demonstrating the public's high hopes for youth as future leaders of the nation.[19]

The Japanese government also encouraged the reorganization of youth organizations, though with the conservative goal of preserving the national polity. On September 25, 1945, the Ministry of Education issued a statement to regional and prefectural governors, suggesting that youth organizations be reestablished locally. It stressed that the new organizations should demonstrate a departure from its wartime precedents – they should be "entirely free from officialism and militarism,"

---

[16] Murakami Shihori, *Kobe yamiichi kara no fukkō: Senryōka de semegiau toshi kūkan* (Tokyo: Keio University Press, 2018), 84–89, 100; Milton A. Smith, "Christmas Shopping in Japan Cheaper, Easier than in Big New York Stores," *Afro-American* (Baltimore), December 2, 1950; Jean Vanaervoort, "Middletown, Japan," *Far East Stars and Stripes Weekly Review*, October 5, 1947; Yoshimi Shunya, *Shinbei to hanbei: Sengo Nihon no seijiteki muishiki* (Tokyo: Iwanami Shoten, 2007), 107–109, 127–30.

[17] Chatani, *Nation-Empire*, 251; Kitagawa, *Sengo no shuppatsu*, 68–70.

[18] Kitagawa, *Sengo no shuppatsu*, 82, 90–95, 102–103, 119–21.

[19] "Seinen ni shokubō su," editorial, *Mainichi Shinbun*, October 4, 1945; "Nihon saiken to waga seinensō," editorial, *Asahi Shinbun*, February 7, 1946.

should avoid "regimentation," should be "managed through the spontaneous activities and mutual help of the youth," and should be "left to develop naturally."[20] At the same time, old assumptions about social order still loomed large. The statement suggested that the new youth organizations should be administered under a "Board of Advisors" composed of the heads of town and villages, schoolteachers, religious leaders, and other leading personalities in each municipality. Furthermore, the Ministry suggested that organizations for men and women should be formed separately, and while men and women from ages fourteen to twenty-five (from the time they normally finished eight years of elementary education through the time men reached voting age) were considered appropriate to join youth groups, women members were to be unmarried.[21]

Older ideas about social order lingered among young people as well in the early postwar years. For example, in a forum of young people that took place in central Japan in December 1945, participants discussed whether to abandon the emperor system, with many defending it.[22] A young individual published an opinion piece in a youth organization's periodical that was evocative of wartime language, arguing that "we need to defend the emperor system [...], the spiritual treasure of our country, to the death."[23] The idea of gender equality was not shared widely among all young people as well. A 1946 poll conducted in a village in central Japan indicated that 69 percent of young people there were happy that youth organizations no longer segregated their activities by gender. However, a young woman in the same village insisted that strong prejudice against women remained pervasive in her community. A young man in another village observed that, while the degree of gender inequality seemed to have lessened in public spaces, women in the household were still being abused "as if they were cattle or horses."[24] The fact that young people were openly discussing the emperor system or gender equality was a significant

---

[20] "Youth Organizations and Student Activities," December 23, 1946, p. 2, and Russel L. Durgin, "Japan's Youth Learning Democratic Principles," n.d., p. 1, both in "Materials Re Guidance" folder, SCAP, CIE, Education Division, Youth and Health Education Branch, Miscellaneous File, 1948–52, RG 331, NACP; Hyogo-ken Rengō Seinendan, *Hyogo-ken Seinendan-shi* (Kobe, Japan: Hyōgoken Rengō Seinendan, 1981), 51–54.

[21] "Youth Organizations and Student Activities," p. 2; Asahina Sakutarō, "Heiwa nippon kensetuno tameni," *Seinen* 30, no. 5 (1945): 2–7, CIE (A) 07287, CIE-NDL; Garon, *Molding Japanese Minds*, 159.

[22] Kitagawa, *Sengo no shuppatsu*, 108.   [23] Quoted in ibid., 109.
[24] Quoted in ibid., 113.

change from the war years, but these examples show that visions of the "New Japan" varied widely among young people in the immediate postwar period.

It was in such a milieu that the occupation authorities stepped into the lives of young people. Young Japanese people were naturally recipients of occupation policies directed broadly at the Japanese population, such as labor and agricultural reforms. But the authorities also created positions aimed specifically at supervising young people. The most noteworthy among them was the Youth Organizations and Student Activities (YOSA) Officer position created within the General Headquarters of the Supreme Commander for the Allied Powers (GHQ/SCAP)'s Civil Information and Education Section (CIE). This position was focused on supervising young people through extracurricular activities for students and communal activities for out-of-school youth. The CIE was in charge of disseminating democratic ideals and the American way of life to Japanese people through radio, books, movies, and other media, and addressing educational policies, broadly defined, such as the reconstruction of the Japanese schooling system, the separation of religion and the state, and the monitoring of the Japanese press.[25] As detailed below, the YOSA Officers and the programs for Japanese "youth" they led reflect how American ideas about "youth" were being projected onto young Japanese. The ways that the officers viewed "youth" as a distinct group and yet stratified them according to the degree of pro-Americanness also mirrored how American adults stratified young Americans based on their expected contribution to national security needs.

Three Americans assumed the title of the YOSA Officer during the occupation period. They were either experienced in youth work, familiar with Japanese culture, or both. Russell Luther Durgin, the inaugural YOSA Officer who held the position through June 1947, was a YMCA representative who had lived in Japan for three decades before the war. Donald M. Typer, his successor, also had YMCA experience, albeit in the United States, in addition to academic appointments at the University of Chicago and George Williams College. After Typer departed the office in May 1951, CIE director Donald R. Nugent doubled as the third and last YOSA Officer through the end of the occupation, and he had conducted graduate work in East Asian history

---

[25] Mire Koikari, *Pedagogy of Democracy: Feminism and the Cold War in the U.S. Occupation of Japan* (Philadelphia: Temple University Press, 2008), 79–80; "Organization Chart: Civil Information and Education Section," October 3, 1945, CIE (C) 00007, CIE-NDL; Takemae Eiji, *GHQ* (Tokyo: Iwanami Shoten, 1983), 115–28.

and education at Stanford University and had taught in Japan before the war.[26]

The YOSA Officers worked in liaison with other officers within the CIE such as adult education, vocational education, higher education, secondary education, and women's education officers, as well as officers in other relevant GHQ/SCAP sections. There were also U.S. officers across Japan who performed youth-related work under the leadership of the YOSA Officer in Tokyo. Collectively, these Americans, in Tokyo and around the country, engaged in wide-ranging projects, such as conducting surveys of youth organizations and students, issuing instructions for both Japanese and Americans on organizing and supervising youth organizations, hosting or attending conferences on youth organizations, and training Japanese youth leaders. Additionally, they supervised the Japanese Ministry of Education as well as Japanese government agencies in charge of youth affairs at the regional, prefectural, and municipal levels. Finally, they monitored and worked with existing youth organizations, such as the YMCA, the Young Women's Christian Association (YWCA), the Boy Scouts, the Girl Scouts, and *Seinendan*.[27] In this chapter, I refer to the three YOSA Officers and the Americans who worked on youth affairs under their leadership collectively as "YOSA officials."

These YOSA officials dealt with both children and young people but their role was geared toward the supervision of those aged roughly fifteen to twenty-five through youth groups, since as many as 80 percent of these people did not attend secondary school and, therefore, could not be supervised through formal education channels.[28] Witnessing the rapid reestablishment of youth organizations across the country, Durgin considered that while some organizations seemed to be endeavoring to become democratic, others appeared to follow "more or less along traditional lines even in the use of the old name, Sei Nen Dan."[29] That the mere use of "Sei Nen Dan" in organizations' names upset him indicates the great extent to which he saw *Seinendan* as an undesirable relic of the Japanese militarist empire and what Japanese wartime youth organizations stood for: centralization, militarism, enforced membership, and

---

[26] Nihon Seinendan Kyōgikai, *Nihon Seinendan kyōgikai nijūnenshi* (Tokyo: Nihon Seinendan Kyōgikai, 1971), 52, 59, 102, Supplement: 24–25, 29–30; Takemae, *GHQ*, 116.
[27] "Youth Organizations and Student Activities," pp. 5–9; "Outlines of Program and Policies for 1946," p. 2.
[28] "Outlines of Program and Policies for 1946," p. 2; "Youth Organizations and Student Activities," pp. 4–5.
[29] Russell L. Durgin, "Decentralization," June 20, 1946, p. 2, "Materials Re Guidance" folder, SCAP, CIE, Education Division, Radio Education Branch, Miscellaneous File, 1948–52, RG 331, NACP.

top-down administration. However, *Seinendan* was by far the largest organization for young people. Moreover, its pervasiveness in rural communities rendered it the most realistic channel through which to reach young people across the country. Instead of dissolving *Seinendan* altogether, therefore, the YOSA leadership chose to closely monitor the group and supervise young people through it.[30]

Supervising Japanese Youth

The YOSA officials pushed forward with youth-related work with unwavering confidence in the political and cultural superiority of the United States to Japan. They operated on a simplistic worldview that dichotomized Japanese history based on the moment that U.S. troops had landed on Japanese shores in the fall of 1945, frequently contrasting the "education in the past" with the "new education" introduced to Japan by the United States, with "the past" indicating a premodern, feudal time that had supposedly remained unchanged for centuries. Durgin, for example, proudly claimed that thanks to the occupation, "for the first time Japan's youth has had the opportunity of operating on its own."[31]

Armed with such a cultural assumption, naivety, and arrogance, YOSA officials launched policies for "youth," optimistic but confident in their ability to teach young Japanese democratic values and renew youth organizations in Japan. A 1947 report of local *Seinendan* activities written by Clifton J. Phillips, a CIE officer based in Hyogo prefecture, offers a glimpse of this. Surveying youth organizations in thirty-two communities across the prefecture, Phillips concluded that while certain features of the old pattern of youth organizations still existed, new organizations were "developing gradually towards democratic procedures and democratic ideology."[32] According to Phillips, with the

---

[30] Ibid.; "Outline of Program and Policies for 1946," pp. 1–2. For the number of members in various youth organizations in Japan, see "Youth Activities in Kinki Region, as of June 1, 1950," CIE (A) 09273–09274, CIE-NDL.

[31] Durgin, "Japanese Youth Learning Democratic Principles," p. 1. See also "Change of Education in Japan," n.d., CIE (A) 08828, CIE-NDL. In a similar manner, Americans in Germany emphasized the contrast between pre-occupation Germany and the country occupied by the United States, showcasing how the occupation brought freedom and happiness to German children and youth. Frederick Simpich, "Uncle Sam Bends a Twig in Germany," reprinted from the *National Geographic Magazine* (October 1948), filed in "German Youth Activities" folder, SCAP, CIE, Education Division, Physical Education and Youth Affairs Branch Topical File, 1945–51, RG331, NACP.

[32] Clifton J. Phillips, "Youth Groups in Hyogo Prefecture," May 22, 1947, pp. 3–4, "Kinki" folder, SCAP, CIE, Education Division, Physical Education and Youth Affairs Branch, Topical File, 1945–51, RG331, NACP.

federation of youth organizations above the county level unorganized and the intervention of village elders as well as local and prefectural governments dissipating, youth organizations operated autonomously and independently. He described a typical village as having multiple *Seinendan* units organized by smaller wards. Each unit had a young men's section and a young women's section, but both men and women considered themselves as part of a single youth group, and some of their activities were co-educational.[33]

Phillips noted a lag in the degree of democratic administration between youth groups in urban areas and their rural counterparts, with those in Kobe, the largest city in the prefecture, and its vicinities leading the way in progressive reform, while those in rural communities inclined toward maintaining older patterns of *Seinendan* organization. The latter, however, appeared to him as possessing "enough vitality to overcome this impediment." In other words, *Seinendan* might well, "through an alert, youthful leadership, become the medium for a bloodless revolution in the rural areas, where a virtual patriarchal system has long prevailed." Phillips was also excited to observe, during the election month of that year, youth groups holding educational meetings and roundtable discussions on the political responsibilities of young people.[34] Overall, then, he envisioned youth organizations, warmly supervised by Americans, as a major driving force of grassroots democracy in the "New Japan."

In fact, the prospects of focusing on *Seinendan* as an avenue through which to guide Japanese youth were not promising, and not all Japanese individuals saw the intervention of the occupiers in the lives of young people favorably. After Japanese people were freed from the government's war mobilization scheme in the summer of 1945, new organizations for young people, such as those organized around professions, political beliefs, or hobbies, rapidly emerged, offering young people a new sense of belonging as well as recreation opportunities. Accordingly, many local *Seinendan* groups increasingly became dormant after the initial postwar comeback mentioned earlier. Critics denounced *Seinendan* as government-made and coercive, and that its only active members were those in leading positions of the organization. As the CIE tightened its grip over *Seinendan* in the following years, it encouraged the reorganization of *Seinendan* along voluntary, decentralized, and

---

[33] Ibid., pp. 1–4; Clifton J. Phillips, "Report on Survey of Five Seinen-Dan in Hyogo Prefecture," January 22, 1947, pp. 1–2, "Kinki" folder, SCAP, CIE, Education Division, Physical Education and Youth Affairs Branch, Topical File, 1945–51, RG331, NACP.
[34] Phillips, "Youth Groups in Hyogo Prefecture," pp. 2, 4; Phillips, "Report on Survey of Five Seinen-Dan in Hyogo Prefecture," p. 2.

democratic lines, as well as its engagement in physical education, group work, and other supposedly healthy, unpolitical activities. Some Japanese people soon came to regard such an intervention in the same light as the top-down, coercive efforts of the prewar and wartime Japanese government.[35] The CIE's loud propagation of the terms "orientation," "discussion," "demonstration," "recreation," and "evaluation" as keys for successfully running democratic organizations made the Japanese ridicule *Seinendan* during the occupation period as U.S.-controlled "*shon-shon Seinendan*" ("shon" refers to the transliteration of "-sion" and "-tion" in English words).[36]

Despite these cloudy prospects, the occupiers remained optimistic about the democratic potentialities of youth organizations, and this optimism was reinforced by their encounters with young Japanese collaborators who paid them the utmost deference. The YOSA leadership had, in fact, concluded that the greatest problem with Japanese youth organizations was the shortage of competent youth leadership owing to young people's lack of experience in running organizations and doing so democratically. Because of the lack of proper leadership, Durgin noted in June 1946, "ideological extremes" were spotted in some localities. In some communities, according to him, communist youth were attempting to "infiltrate wherever possible into local youth organizations (rural, industrial, and student)," while in other communities, former military officers were beginning to be looked to for leadership.[37] The U.S. occupiers considered that the ideological threat from both the right and the left could only be removed by establishing an army of young Japanese leaders fully immersed in the essence of democracy and actively promoting it.

To YOSA officials, therefore, young Japanese people who seemed to willingly accept U.S. rule over them signaled an encouraging prospect for their endeavor. In February 1947, Durgin, accompanied by Phillips and another U.S. representative, visited Kande village in Hyogo prefecture,

---

[35] Kitagawa, *Sengo no shuppatsu*, 126–39; Horiuchi Yasumura, "Naniga kansei Seinendan ka," *Seinen Bunka Jihō* 1, no. 4 (1946): 10–12, CIE (A) 07215, CIE-NDL; Paul S. Anderson, "Information for Tokyo Youth Affairs Conference," January 4, 1950, pp. 1–2, CIE (A) 08839, CIE-NDL; Kobayashi Tetsuro, "Japanese Youth Specialist Report for January 1951," CIE (B) 08253, CIE-NDL.

[36] Hyogo-ken Rengō Seinendan, *Hyogo-ken Seinendan-shi*, 71–72.

[37] Durgin, "Decentralization," p. 1. See also "Outlines of Progress and Policies for 1946," p. 1. The Japanese Communist Party, reconstituted by the occupation authorities, was making a strong comeback after decades of suppression by the Japanese government, and its increasing militancy posed a threat to the occupation authorities even before the Cold War made the occupation policy more conservative and anti-communist in the late 1940s. John W. Dower, *Embracing Defeat: Japan in the Wake of World War II* (New York: W. W. Norton, 1999), ch. 8; Miller, *Cold War Democracy*, 44, 57–58.

Figure 6.1 The Youth Branch meeting with Kande village representatives.
Photo enclosed in Kanai Satoshi to Durgin, May 3, 1947, NAID: 425588. Courtesy of the U.S. National Archives.

where he convened with local government officials, youth leaders, and committee members of local organizations (Figure 6.1). The local youth leaders, who had attended CIE's youth leadership training conference in Tokyo the previous summer, respectfully welcomed Durgin and likened his visit to a long-awaited reunion with their beloved father.[38] They offered explanations of the status of young people in Japan that neatly overlapped with the Americans' understanding of it – how they had been indoctrinated in the sacredness and righteousness of their country up to the war years, how, after the war, crime, black markets, inflation, and moral deterioration became rampant in Japan, and how such a situation propelled them to establish new *Seinendan* units with the conviction that young people should work to build a "good, peaceful Japan."[39] The U.S. officers were then introduced to wide-ranging fields of activities that the

---

[38] "Kande-mura Youth Association Welcome Speech," n.d. p. 1, "Kinki" folder, SCAP, CIE, Education Division, Physical Education and Youth Affairs Branch, Topical File, 1945–51, RG331, NACP.
[39] Ibid.

new *Seinendan* units in the village were working on, such as social work, physical training, cultural activities, and educational programs.[40]

After their visit, the village's *Seinendan* leader wrote a thank-you note to Durgin, expressing his determination to make youth organizations the central driving force of the new democratic Japan and asking him for additional guidance. Kanai Satoshi, the youth leader mentioned at the beginning of this chapter, addressed Durgin in the letter as *sensei*, a Japanese word used to signify mentor or to show respect to people of high social standing. The village, he told Durgin, had been incorporated into the nearby city of Kobe after his visit to the village. In Kanai's view, *Seinendan* in Kobe had been dormant because of the physical damage caused by the wartime bombing and the lack of interest of municipal authorities in youth affairs. He had been encouraged by a former village mayor to take up a job at the municipal office to devote himself to the development of youth and children's associations in the city. He asked Durgin whether he would agree.[41]

While developing close ties with youth organization leaders to influence out-of-school youth, the occupiers also placed college students at the top of their hierarchy of young Japanese and welcomed the development of pro-U.S. student groups that they expected would turn the "New Japan" into a junior partner of the United States. Most of the young people with whom the CIE officers were to deal were out of school, but the officers thought that college students were important because they would go on to become leaders in various sectors of society. The occupiers, therefore, considered that dealing with student organization activities was among the most important of their tasks "from the standpoint of quality rather than quantity" as a "very large proportion of the future leaders in every walk of life will be found here."[42] As such, they paid close attention to the unwanted political activism of college students on the left and the right, even though such students were a small minority. At the same time, they warmly supervised pro-U.S. students who seemed ready to accept their ideal of social order.[43]

---

[40] "Kande-mura Seinendan jigyō to soshiki," n.d., pp. 1–2, and Russell L. Durgin to Mark T. Orr, "Report of Kwansai Trip," February 25, 1947, pp. 2–3, both in "Kinki" folder, SCAP, CIE, Education Division, Physical Education and Youth Affairs Branch, Topical File, 1945–51, RG331, NACP.

[41] Kanai to Durgin Sensei. [42] "Outline of Program and Policies for 1946," p. 4.

[43] Frank Kawamoto to Dr. Bells, "Report on the Second National Conference of the Federation of All Japan Student Self Governments (Zengakuren)," June 6, 1949, CIE (A) 07203, CIE-NDL; "A Poll of Student Opinion at Meiji University," August 19, 1948, CIE (C) 06534, CIE-NDL; "Research Report: Student Organizations in Japan," January 29, 1949, CIE (B) 04422, CIE-NDL; Paul S. Anderson, "Known Communist Youth Organizations and Publications," August 25, 1948, CIE (A) 08844, CIE-NDL.

An example of a pro-U.S. student activity that the CIE supported was the Japan–America Student Conference, an annual cultural exchange event between college students in the United States and Japan that had been inaugurated in 1934 at the initiative of an association for college students studying the English language in Tokyo but had been suspended since 1941. In 1947, when it reconvened in Tokyo for the first time since before the war, forty-eight Americans and seventy-six Japanese participated in the four-day conference, and the numbers grew in the subsequent years.[44]

Due to travel restrictions, the U.S. participants of the conferences held during the occupation were not college students from the United States but rather Americans already in Japan, such as members of the occupation forces, teachers, missionaries, and businesspeople. All Japanese participants, in contrast, were college students.[45] The relationship between the two groups was predictably far from equal. Americans acted as tutors, while the Japanese were considered pupils. The Americans highlighted the differences between Japanese society of "the past" and that of "the present" as did YOSA officials, while the young Japanese participants faithfully thanked the Americans for teaching them the essence of democracy. For instance, in one of the photos from the conference report of 1949 showing delegates discussing various social and cultural issues in both countries (mainly in Japan), an American woman is speaking with a confident facial expression while Japanese participants look at her. The caption for the photo reads: "Sorry, I can't agree! [sic] with you there!"[46] Here, the ability of a woman to freely voice her thoughts and disagree with others is shown as an example of gender equality, democracy, and free speech – all concepts that Americans in Japan propagated to Japanese people. Such examples abound in the reports of the conferences conducted during the occupation, indicating how the annual conferences were designed as settings where the tutor–pupil dynamic between Japanese youth and U.S. occupiers developed.

On student activism in postwar Japan, see Naoko Koda, *The United States and the Japanese Student Movement, 1948–1973: Managing a Free World* (Lanham, MD: Lexington, 2020).

[44] Japan Student Association, "The Tenth Japan–America Student Conference, 1949," n. d., n.p. ("Brief History") and p. 38, CIE (D) 02086, CIE-NDL.

[45] Japan Student Association, "The Eighth Japan–America Student Conference, 1947," n. d., p. vi, CIE (D) 02085, CIE-NDL; Japan Student Association, "The Tenth Japan–America Student Conference, 1949," pp. 4, 43–47.

[46] Japan Student Association, "The Tenth Japan–America Student Conference, 1949," p. 20. See also Japan Student Association, "The Eighth Japan–America Student Conference, 1947," pp. 12–14.

This tutor–pupil relationship, seen in both Kande village and the student conferences, indicates how U.S. and Japanese conceptions of social hierarchy and the place of young people therein overlapped, allowing the U.S. occupiers to build on the ideas and structures of youth management that had been crucial to imperial Japan. As the previous chapters have demonstrated, American adults had identified young people in their late teens to mid-twenties as an age group potentially problematic to American society and therefore in need of adult supervision. While that idea changed within American society during World War II, as the youth unemployment problem disappeared, young men entered the military, and the United States became the world's superpower, the U.S. occupiers nonetheless projected their conception of "youth" onto young Japanese people identified as *seinen*, addressing them as a single group with distinct needs and problems while stratifying them in accordance with the U.S. national security goal of transforming Japan into a junior partner of the United States. For their part, the Japanese were accustomed to situating themselves and others in an imperial hierarchy based on supposed levels of modernization and self-governance, looking down on other Asian people and justifying Japanese rule over them.[47] Moreover, Japanese society itself was highly hierarchical. As we have seen, prewar youth in Japan had been taught to live within a hierarchy from their early days; they had also learned to appropriate it to their advantage.

A few points, then, can be drawn from the pro-U.S. youth's positive attitudes toward U.S. representatives, as evidenced by their reference to Durgin as their "father" and *"sensei"* and their faithful acceptance of U.S. tutelage in democracy: some Japanese youth leaders may have sincerely appreciated the U.S. patronage and the new society the occupiers were helping to create, while others may have been playing the pupil role with the pragmatic expectation that the CIE's patronage would lead them to a better socioeconomic opportunity in the new hierarchy created by the occupation. The two positions may have coexisted in one individual. Regardless, the convergence of the U.S. and Japanese notions of "youth" during the occupation established these pro-U.S. youth leaders as the occupiers' trusted collaborators.[48]

---

[47] Tsuchiya Yuka, *Shinbei Nihon no kōchiku: Amerika no tainichi jōhō/kyōiku seisaku to Nihon senryō* (Tokyo: Akashi Shoten, 2009), 93–97.

[48] A number of scholars have explored how U.S. imperialism, undergirded by the centuries-old idea of Western racial superiority, shaped the colonial, hierarchical relationship between Americans and Japanese during the occupation, which, in turn, propelled the rise of Japan as the United States' junior partner and Japanese society's

The YOSA officials' selective, top-down approach to young Japanese meant that many young Japanese were left out of their orbit. Among them were young women in rural regions. Yamada Taro, who we met at the beginning of this chapter, married a woman from a nearby village a few years after demobilization. Yamada's wife, recalling her youth in her late eighties, vividly remembered how U.S. airmen piloting fighters during World War II had indiscriminately strafed and killed her fellow civilian villagers on their way back from bombing raids against industrial plants, but she did not remember seeing a single American after the war. Personal memory often reflects the individual's preferences on what they wish to remember. Her testimony, therefore, does not guarantee that she did not see any Americans during the occupation or that her life was not influenced by the occupation. It does, however, imply that the occupation authorities had a smaller long-term impact on her life than the wartime U.S. military, perhaps partly because she lived in a rural region with substantial distance from urban hubs of the occupation, but also because young people like her – young rural women, out of school, with no command of the English language, and in no significant leadership roles – were off the occupation authorities' radar.[49]

Indeed, gender equality remained of secondary importance to the three YOSA Officers. For example, Durgin assumed that young *men*

---

oblivion of its colonial past. See, for example, Koikari, *Pedagogy of Democracy*; Tsuchiya, *Shinbei Nihon no kōchiku*; Dower, *Embracing Defeat*; Yukiko Koshiro, *Trans-Pacific Racisms and the U.S. Occupation of Japan* (New York: Columbia University Press, 1999); Naoko Shibusawa, *America's Geisha Ally: Reimagining the Japanese Enemy* (Cambridge, MA: Harvard University Press: 2006). The extensive literature on U.S. attitudes toward ruling nonwhite others in the name of education and the relationships between U.S. rulers and indigenous collaborators includes David Wallace Adams, *Education for Extinction: American Indians and the Boarding School Experience, 1875–1928* (Lawrence: University of Kansas Press, 1995); Jonathan Zimmerman, *Innocents Abroad: American Teachers in the American Century* (Cambridge, MA: Harvard University Press, 2006); Sarah Steinbock-Pratt, *Educating the Empire: American Teachers and Contested Colonization in the Philippines* (Cambridge, UK: Cambridge University Press, 2019).

[49] Interview with Yamada Taro's wife by the author, January 1, 2018; interview with one of Yamada's children by the author, January 3, 2020. On how memory changes over time, see Carol Gluck, "The Past in the Present," in *Postwar Japan as History*, ed. Andrew Gordon (Berkeley: University of California Press, 1993), 64–95. According to a 1950 report by the U.S. Public Affairs Office in Germany, six out of ten Germans living in the U.S.-occupied zone had either seen U.S. troops only occasionally or never at all. This finding suggests that, like in Japan, the U.S. occupation of Germany did not have a uniform impact on local people. Reactions Analysis Branch, Information Services Division, Public Affairs Office, "The German Public Views [of] the Conduct of the U.S. Occupation Forces," Report no. 6, Series 2, February 6, 1950, p. 1, CIE (A) 09174, CIE-NDL.

should be holding leadership positions in youth organizations.[50] During his visit to Kande village, the local youth leaders, apparently all men, proudly explained to him about a newly created "livelihood and welfare" section in their *Seinendan* unit, run by women. According to them, this section offered young women skills and knowledge in such fields as clothing, nutrition, and sanitation. To the youth leaders, it signified a complete break for their organization from the past, when young men and women had belonged to separate youth organizations and when their activities had been gender-segregated. As they now welcomed women as *Seinendan* members, they told Durgin, they created this new section to help women acquire the skills and knowledge to "scientifically conduct housework" and to prepare to become housewives. Despite this limited, gendered role they assigned women members of their organization, Durgin's report of the visit shows no indication that he problematized it or advised the youth leaders to reconsider the role of women in their organization. Perhaps he didn't see it as a problem as it nicely overlapped with the gendered role that women in the United States were required to fulfill after World War II – women in the United States were also expected to live as good mothers and wives.[51] Likewise, at a CIE conference on youth affairs held in January 1950 and attended by Americans working on youth affairs throughout the country, some participants based at the regional level reported how young women were still unable to participate in *Seinendan* activities as equals to men. However, Typer, the second YOSA Officer, simply stated in his conference report that the problem "will be improved gradually as women find a new place in Japanese life," revealing his naïve assumption that gender inequality would naturally be solved once Japan became a democracy.[52]

The rise of the Cold War intensified the CIE's selective, top-down approach to young Japanese. In late 1948, the CIE assessed that the developments in youth organizations that year "presented a somewhat mixed picture." While its programs to educate youthful leadership had improved, "severe incursions were made into the ranks of youth by Communist agencies" allegedly because many young people were still under mental distress. With the conviction that the growing communist

---

[50] Durgin, "Decentralization," p. 1.
[51] "Kande-mura Seinendan jigyō to soshiki," p. 1; Durgin to Orr, "Report of Kwansai Trip," pp. 2–3. On gender and women in postwar United States, see Elaine Tyler May, *Homeward Bound: American Families in the Cold War Era* (New York: Basic Books, 1988); Lizabeth Cohen, *A Consumers' Republic: The Politics of Mass Consumption in Postwar America* (New York: Vintage Books, 2003).
[52] D. M. Typer to Chief, CIE, "Report of Conference with CAFF Youth Officers," January 23, 1950, p. 10, CIE (A) 07344, CIE-NDL.

influence would not be offset by the "relatively slower processes of cautious development of organizations based upon democratic techniques of operation alone," the CIE decided that it would actively guide the Japanese Ministry of Education and other relevant agencies in the "direction of stimulating youth activities that are based not only on sound democratic procedures and ideals, but which *vigorously and actively* oppose youth organizations committed to subversive doctrines."[53]

Accordingly, U.S. occupiers in the later years of the occupation reinforced the top-down supervision of youth organizations. In the fall of 1949, they created American Youth Affairs Officers positions in each of GHQ/SCAP's eight Civil Affairs regions to monitor regional, prefectural, and local Japanese officials in social education and youth affairs as well as youth organizations.[54] In the following year, Youth Specialist and Assistant Youth Specialist positions were established at the prefectural level to have Japanese people, normally older than the *seinen* age, be in charge of advising fellow Japanese on youth organization administration at the local level, while reporting to CIE Americans at the national and regional levels.[55] The U.S. occupiers thus strengthened the hierarchical structure of youth organization supervision, with the U.S. leadership in Tokyo at the top, under which American Youth Affairs Officers at the regional level operated, who, in turn, supervised Japanese Youth Specialists and Assistant Youth Specialists at the prefectural level. Local youth organization leaders and ordinary youth members were situated further toward the bottom of this structure. This top-down approach to young people mirrors the conservative vision of democracy held by U.S. Cold Warriors, which equated democracy with elite-led stability.[56]

Fully immersed in this mindset, the YOSA officials were oblivious to the massive hierarchy they had established. For instance, they naively anticipated that the work of Japanese Youth Specialists would eventually contribute to the formation of a "new *private* youth agency" led

---

[53] Italics added. "Education Division Plans for 1949," n.d., p. 39, "3" folder, SCAP, CIE, Education Division, Physical Education and Youth Affairs Branch, Topical File, 1945–51, RG331, NACP.

[54] Paul S. Anderson, "Youth Program in Kinki Region," November 7, 1949, p. 1, CIE (A) 08836, CIE-NDL; Youth Affairs Officers resumes, CIE (C) 03340–03341, CIE-NDL.

[55] "Plans for FY 1952: Youth Organizations, Student Activities, Health and Physical Education," n.d., p. 2, CIE (C) 03325–03328, CIE-NDL; "Job Description: Youth Specialist and Assistant Youth Specialist," n.d., pp. 1–2, CIE (C) 03325, CIE-NDL. There were several women among the Youth Specialists, but most were men. See Youth Specialists resumes, CIE (C) 03340–03341, CIE-NDL.

[56] Miller, *Cold War Democracy*, 2–3.

autonomously by young people and focused purely on recreational activities.[57] The wartime idea of "youth" that the occupation authorities used to understand and stratify young Japanese was thus incorporated into U.S. Cold War policy.

Japanese "Youth" as a Junior Partner of the United States

What the CIE achieved by the end of the occupation was the strengthening of the social hierarchy of young people that had existed before the occupation. Pro-U.S. youth in Japan, with whom the Americans had developed a solid tutor–pupil relationship and who were placed at the top of this hierarchy, helped justify U.S. hegemony in East Asia and Japan's role as its junior partner. An international forum for high-school students conducted in New York City in March 1952, ostensibly to demonstrate to the American public and the rest of the world U.S. benevolence and internationalism, illustrates how this operated on an international scene.

The forum was held by the *New York Herald Tribune* (*NYHT*) and featured delegates from eighteen Asian and Middle Eastern countries and regions. Arriving in the United States in December 1951, the international students had spent twelve weeks with U.S. families, attended high school, participated in community activities, and traveled to Washington, D.C., and Canada before attending the forum.[58] The forum, however, was overshadowed by Americans' preoccupation with the Cold War. New York Governor Thomas E. Dewey, addressing the forum, insisted that the forum was a chance to fix "the fearful falsehoods about America that are constantly spread by the Communist dictatorship," such as those that depicted the United States as "a war-monger and an imperialist." To Dewey, the international students were cultural ambassadors who would help notify the world of his country's "determination to keep the blessings of liberty, to defend them, to enjoy them and to pass them on to future generations in all their glory."[59]

Most of the international delegates, however, were not convinced by this Cold War worldview, insisting that Americans needed to face other pressing issues such as decolonization and racial prejudice without the Cold War lens. A student from Burma, for example, urged Dewey to

---

[57] Emphasis in original. "Job Description: Youth Specialist and Assistant Youth Specialist," pp. 1–2.

[58] "Asian and Middle East Students Will Attend High School Forum," *New York Herald Tribune* (hereafter cited as *NYHT*), November 30, 1951; "Forum Addresses and Students Discussions Broadcast at Home and Overseas," *NYHT*, March 24, 1952.

[59] "Dewey Calls Upon Youth to Help Meet Red Peril," *NYHT*, March 24, 1952.

explain how she should make sense of a statement he had made elsewhere, in which he argued that her country "threw off British rule too quickly." Yet, the governor reiterated the Cold War logic, explaining to her that he believed that her country had wrongly divorced from Britain before developing skills in self-government, which, according to his observation, had caused much social confusion and "the threat of Communist invasion."[60] A student from Indonesia was frustrated at how most Americans blindly believed the United States was the best country in the world, looking down on her country. A Singaporean student told the U.S. audience that "[i]f I said San Francisco was in Mexico, you would stare at me and wonder at my ignorance; but you try to look for Singapore on the map of China." Some delegates mentioned they would have appreciated a visit to the U.S. South to see what the racial situation was like there.[61]

The sole delegate that stood out in her overwhelmingly positive comments on her experience in the United States was Japanese. The delegate chosen by the Japanese Ministry of Education was Saito Kayoko, the eighteen-year-old student from Tokyo mentioned at the beginning of this chapter. She was born to a Christian family and was a student at an elite upper secondary school, as well as the daughter of a professor teaching economics at a university in Tokyo established in the late nineteenth century by Christian missionaries. Nugent, the CIE chief and last YOSA Officer, described her as "a very worthy and charming girl."[62]

She must have indeed appeared charming to Dewey and the forum organizers. While many other international students were critical of the U.S. stance on world affairs, Saito, at least in *NYHT*'s coverage of the forum, delightfully told the U.S. audience how thankful she was for the great opportunity she had been given and the friendliness of the Americans she had met during her stay in the United States. In addition, she sprinkled her remarks with references to world peace, stating that Japanese people had now "come to love, and wish, for peace" and held a "strong desire to co-operate with all the people of the world" to become "the good cosmopolitan, [and] the world citizen." She may have made these idealistic, future-oriented remarks to conceal her fear that she, as a Japanese representative, might be blamed for her country's

---

[60] Ibid.
[61] "Visiting Students Introduced, Tell of Homelands," *NYHT*, March 24, 1952.
[62] "Asian and Middle East Students Will Attend High School Forum"; "More of Understanding and Less of Prejudice Is Urged for 'The World We Want,'" *NYHT*, March 24, 1952; D. R. Nugent to Mrs. Theodore Waller (draft), n.d., CIE (D) 02329, CIE-NDL; Saito Kayoko's curriculum vitae and autobiography enclosed in Ohta to Mrs. Waller.

wartime aggression. However, her comments as published in the newspaper do not indicate that she was overwhelmed by such concern. According to the *NYHT*, she even rendered the atomic bomb unproblematic. She told the U.S. audience that before coming to New York, she had asked a Japanese boy who had survived the atomic bombing of Hiroshima what he would say to Americans about the bombing. According to Saito, the boy told her positively that "[w]e must be sure that such a thing does not happen again anywhere in the world" and suggested that people of the two countries "forget everything about the past and think about helping each other in the future."[63]

Saito's case alludes to the "marriage" between U.S. Cold Warriors and urban conservative elites in Japan that historians have pointed out – a coalition that fashioned postwar Japan into a socially conservative, pro-U.S. nation.[64] Additionally, archival sources indicate that a woman student was preferred as the Japanese delegate to the forum by either the Japanese Ministry of Education, the CIE, or the forum host, which hints at the gendered nature of postwar U.S.–Japan relations as Naoko Shibusawa has demonstrated.[65] Saito behaved ideally for the Cold Warriors – she seemed to have forgiven the United States for its atrocities, forgotten about the many atrocities her country had committed, and slipped securely under the U.S. arm. By the end of the occupation, therefore, Japanese youth had come to represent, for U.S. Cold Warriors, people successfully liberated from their militarist and feudal past thanks to U.S. generosity.

Left out from the Americans' self-satisfactory image of young Japanese, however, were thousands of young people in Japan that were placed toward the bottom of the social hierarchy. An American Youth Affairs Officer working at the regional level reported in 1951 that, in some remote rural areas, young people still faced group pressure to conform to the whims and orders of the town's bosses.[66] A publication in 1952 by a rural *Seinendan* unit described how rural women were still suffering from the community's ignorance of their right to education, political participation, and free speech.[67] While urban regions rapidly recovered economically,

---

[63] "More of Understanding"; "Visiting Students Introduced."
[64] Miller, *Cold War Democracy*, 12–14; Michael Schaller, *The American Occupation of Japan: The Origins of the Cold War in Asia* (New York: Oxford University Press, 1985), 48–51. For how this relationship played out in 1950s Japan, see Sayuri Shimizu, *Creating People of Plenty: The United States and Japan's Economic Alternatives, 1950–1960* (Kent, OH: Kent State University Press, 2001).
[65] D. R. Nugent to Mrs. Theodore Waller, draft (October 1951), CIE (D) 02330, CIE-NDL; Shibusawa, *America's Geisha Ally*.
[66] "Monthly Activities Report for May 1951," n.d., p. 9, CIE (A) 09252, CIE-NDL.
[67] Kitagawa, *Sengo no shuppatsu*, 117–18.

rural youth continued to face grave financial difficulties.[68] Local hierarchies, gender inequality, and the socioeconomic gap between urban and rural regions were all topics that the YOSA leadership failed to confront. Moreover, their policy decisions soon boomeranged. Although the YOSA officials intensely monitored the political activities of college students, or perhaps because the monitoring increased students' distrust of U.S. authorities, radical college students spearheaded social movements against the Peace Treaty of 1952, which tied Japan geopolitically to the United States, and against the maintenance of U.S. military bases on Japanese soil after the treaty restored Japan's independence. Students were also at the center of the Japanese protest movement against the U.S.–Japan security treaty renewal in 1960.[69]

While Saito was developing close ties with the U.S. occupiers, Yamada Taro found a career that he would pursue for his lifetime. After demobilization, he had begun as a clerk for the municipal employment bureau. By 1949, he was working for the prefectural Labor Standards Inspection Office, a newly established governmental agency whose mission was to check whether employees abided by labor laws and to ensure the safety of workers. That year, he passed the national examination to become a Labor Standards Inspector and devoted the rest of his life to the protection of the rights of workers and others in socially disadvantaged positions.[70] Meanwhile, Kanai Satoshi, the Kande village *Seinendan* leader who had addressed Durgin as a mentor, remained passionately committed to *Seinendan* activities in Hyogo prefecture, becoming the head of the prefectural association in 1952 and its adviser the following year.[71] Yamada, a politically liberal veteran; Kanai, the self-proclaimed mentee of the CIE; and Saito Kayoko, an elite, westernized high schooler living in the country's busy capital are just a few examples that demonstrate how the group that Americans labeled as "youth" was characterized by gender, age, geographical, educational, and socioeconomic diversity. "Youth" was both an illusion and an apparatus with which the U.S. authorities stratified young Japanese people. It allowed them to reinforce the top-down social hierarchy that had been created by militarist Japan, and make a small number of pro-U.S. Japanese youth slide into American arms while leaving many other young Japanese – including

---

[68] "Nōson no seinen ni," editorial, *Mainichi Shinbun*, October 4, 1950; "Nōson no seinen ni kibō to hōkō o," editorial, *Asahi Shinbun*, January 30, 1952; Katase, *Wakamono no sengoshi*, 33.
[69] Miller, *Cold War Democracy*, 151, 174, 203.
[70] Yamada's resumes in his family's possession; interview with one of Yamada's children by the author, January 3, 2020.
[71] Hyogo-ken Rengō Seinendan, *Hyogo-ken Seinendan-shi*, 118, 131.

those socially and economically disadvantaged – with little leverage with which to control their lives.

After the end of the occupation, *Seinendan* membership continued to decline, and the popularity of the term *seinen* declined as well. In the 1950s, Japanese sociologists began to explore the diversity within the group of young people labeled as *seinen*, segmenting them into such categories as "urban youth," "rural youth," and "delinquents."[72] The postwar recovery of the Japanese economy in the 1950s and the 1960s brought about a marked increase in high-school and college attendance and openings for blue-collar jobs, encouraging a large number of *Seinendan*-age youth to leave rural areas for school and jobs in the cities. As a result, with the increased mobility of young people and the diversification of their educational and career paths, public and educational institutions, as well as private businesses, increasingly took on the recreational and educational services for young people that village organizations such as *Seinendan* had offered previously.[73]

As *seinen* declined in popularity, however, another term that grouped together young people from diverse backgrounds – *wakamono* – gained public appeal. *Wakamono*, a term that is still in use and can be literally translated as "young people" (or "young person"), essentially refers to the same age group as *seinen* – teens to the twenties – but without the significant political undertones that *seinen* had carried.[74] This time, adults labeled young people as a distinct age group not because of war but because of Japan's entry into a period of long-term economic growth in the late 1950s and the various social changes that occurred as a result of the country's recovery from the war. Like their predecessors, adults in this period perceived youth as both full of promise and possibly destructive to society. While some viewed *wakamono* as lucrative customers for the expanding mass consumer market, others scowled at the rebelliousness of certain youths (like student activists) or the apparent lack of interest in society displayed by other youths, and still others viewed young people with mixed feelings as emblems of the growing homogeneity of modern society and culture.[75] Japanese adults' gravitation toward

---

[72] Furuichi Noritoshi, *Zetsubō no kuni no kōfuku na wakamonotachi* (Tokyo: Kōdansha, 2015), 52–53.
[73] Ibid., 52–54, 60–62; Tani, *Seinen no seiki*, 14, 198–201.
[74] *Kōjien*, 7th ed. (Tokyo, Iwanami shoten, 2018), s.v. "若者 [wakamono]."
[75] Tani, *Seinen no seiki*, 199; Furuichi, *Zetsubō no kuni*, 60–69. The Japanese government was an exception to the general trend of transitioning from *seinen* to *wakamono* when addressing young people. Until 2010, it published annual reports on children and youth that referred to youth as *seinen*. It began referring to them as *wakamono* in 2011. "Kodomo / wakamono hakusho ni tsuite," *Naikakufu*, www8.cao.go.jp/youth/suisin/hakusho.html (accessed December 30, 2021).

fantasizing about a mobilizable and manageable "youth," then, persisted with occasional ebbs and flows.

The policies for "youth" during the U.S. occupation of Japan symbolize the twilight of a period, spanning World War I to World War II, in which American and Japanese societies developed methods to mobilize and supervise their youth population for national security purposes. As the specter of total war receded, so too did the illusion of "youth" that had underpinned civilian mobilization efforts for the war in both societies.

Conclusion

In the first half of the twentieth century, different groups of American adults with varying agendas developed ideas linking youth, education, and national security. Universal military training (UMT) advocates in the early twentieth century claimed that young men should be "toughened" by military training, progressive educators believed that World War I would be a "plastic juncture" to advance social and educational reform, supporters of the Student Army Training Corps (SATC) during World War I and Army Specialized Training Program (ASTP) during World War II claimed that these were "democratic" programs that would benefit young men not only during the war but after it, and U.S. occupiers in Japan projected their view of youth and national security onto Japanese youth. Along the way, the cultural concept of "youth" was defined and redefined, as shown in how "youth" deemed problematic in the 1930s were recast as "young adults" in World War II. Young individuals handled these changes in a variety of ways, including young men who joined the SATC in search of a better life, students at land-grant institutions who protested Reserve Officers Training Corps (ROTC) requirements, and young Japanese who made use of the U.S. occupation to their advantage.

World War I marked the first moment in which American adults were confronted with the question of youth and their role in a national emergency. Legislators in 1917 decided that in principle, only men who had reached legal adulthood should be conscripted, and when the war necessitated the lowering of the draft age in 1918, they discussed ways to give draftees who were drafted under the age of twenty-one educational benefits that were not available to older draftees. The policies concerning youth and conscription that were implemented during this period and the debates surrounding them continued to influence the debates and policies concerning youth, national security, and education in the subsequent years. The argument put forth by UMT advocates – that military training would not only enhance the country's military preparedness but also "toughen" youth and turn them into mature men – continued to be made by advocates of other military training programs for young men, such as ROTC, military training in the Civilian Conservation Corps (CCC), and the ASTP. The discourse that military training and service was a "democratic" educational opportunity, as well as the idea that national security emergencies could be a "plastic juncture" to advance nonmilitary goals, also continued to shape debates and policies over youth, national security, and education in the years after World War I.

In the 1920s and the 1930s, the debates over compulsory ROTC training in higher education institutions revealed the developing connection between higher education institutions and the military, as well as how the relationship between youth, national security, and education established during World War I continued to affect young people's access to education. The debates also highlighted an evolving connection between social class, national security, and access to public higher education, as the majority of students impacted by the mandatory ROTC training attended public land-grant institutions. ROTC was situated at the intersection of education and national security, influencing the educational experiences of young people at a time when an increasing number of them aspired to an education beyond grammar school.

During the Great Depression, the "youth problem" that social commentators, educators, and government agencies highlighted as an economic, political, and ideological threat to American security spread the idea that "youth" now included men and women in their twenties and that they should be turned into responsible democratic citizens by the federal government's and adults' supervision. The government established programs to address the high rate of unemployment among this age group, but their conversion into military preparedness agencies in the late 1930s, as the nature of the national security emergency changed from the Depression to war, illustrates the haziness of the line between wartime and peacetime during this period. The public support for the introduction of military training to the CCC also highlights the enduring impact of the idea that military training was good for youth discipline and education on U.S. perceptions of youth.

These new conceptions concerning youth, education, and their role in national security influenced the debates over selective service during World War II. In the summer of 1940, American adults once again debated how to establish selective service as "democratic," and the passage of the Selective Training and Service Act of 1940 over a year before the United States entered the war reflected their belief that they were no longer living in peacetime. Yet, the lower limit of the draft age was set at twenty-one, illuminating how controversial the conscription of minors remained. When the draft age was lowered to eighteen in 1942, the supporters of the measure called for a "democratic" system of conscripting young men that linked military service with education. The ASTP was established due to such an idea of providing "talented" soldiers an opportunity to receive an education, but like the youth programs that came before it, it restricted access to the program for many young men, such as white men who had not been able to obtain an education that qualified them for the program and Black men of all social classes. The "democratic" educational opportunity motivated by national security concerns and requiring youth military service thus operated within established disparities and injustices both in the military and civilian society.

Another way in which the cultural concept of "youth" was linked to national security was how the situation surrounding young people during World War II – the conscription of young men, the end of youth unemployment, and the rise of the United States as the world's superpower – led to a major change in the image of problematic "youth" that was widespread in the 1930s. As the young people considered problems in the 1930s were recast as "young adults" contributing to the war effort, adults who had addressed the "youth problem" in the 1930s shifted their attention to other social issues, such as "juvenile delinquency" of younger boys and girls and nonwhite youth who were presumably more problematic. Yet, the policies for young people that they helped develop, such as the G.I. Bill of 1944, continued to affect the educational opportunities for young people and illuminated how they were built on longstanding inequality based on race, gender, and social class.

As the United States emerged from World War II as the world's superpower and widened its geographical scope of national security, American ideas about youth in national security came to affect young people elsewhere in the world. The U.S. occupiers in Japan thus merged their sense of youth and national security with the existing apparatus of *seinen* (youth) that the militarist government of Japan had used to mobilize young people for the war, identifying youth as a distinct group while stratifying young individuals by their value for U.S. national security.

By applying a "transwar" approach and examining American society from World War I to World War II from the perspective of youth, therefore, it becomes evident that war and military issues were intricately intertwined with political and cultural changes throughout periods of peace and war. The fact that it was an age of total warfare profoundly shaped the relationship between youth, education, and national security during this time. At the same time, this relationship also set the foundation for subsequent developments.

Consider, for example, how selective service during the Cold War both diverged from and expanded upon that which was implemented during

Conclusion

the two world wars. The Selective Training and Service Act of 1940 expired in March 1947, but with the relationship with the Soviet Union rapidly deteriorating, in June 1948, the Selective Service Act of 1948 became law, requiring men aged eighteen through twenty-five to register. Until the military reverted to an All-Volunteer Force (AVF) in 1973, selective service backed U.S. Cold War policy by conscripting men and encouraging many others to volunteer.[1]

In the two world wars, military service had been framed as an obligation of all men of military age. Therefore, although categories of deferment for men with dependents or in jobs deemed essential for the home front existed and functioned to draft young men disproportionately, the general rule was that deferments were granted only on an individual basis. As a result, young people were conscripted regardless of social class, and then stratified *within* the military. However, the Cold War led to a new military policy that centered on nuclear weapons, military alliances, and limited war mobilization of civilian society. The intense battle with the Soviet Union over military technology meant that scientific research was now seen to be a form of service on par with military service. In 1951, student deferment was established as a new deferment category in the Selective Service System, and opened a way for young men who could afford a college education to live out draft age without being drafted – they could be first deferred as a student, then land a job that was qualified for occupational deferment, and finally get married and have children to be deferred as fathers. By 1960, Selective Service System director Lewis Hershey had come to justify the extended deferments by arguing that they effectively guided the country's draft-age men toward activities that would best serve the interests of the country and elevating nonmilitary jobs deemed essential to the country's interests to the same level as military duty in terms of their contribution to the country.[2]

This new military strategy allowed for the explicitly unequal, selective procurement of military troops based on the open stratification of young men by educational attainment, social class, race, and ethnicity. For example, a disproportionate number of Black people joined the military in the years following World War II. Because of the structural discrimination against them in education and in the labor market, Black youth were

---

[1] Lewis B. Hershey, *Outline of Historical Background of Selective Service*, 1965 edition (Washington, DC: GPO, 1966), 12–17; George Q. Flynn, *The Draft, 1940–1973* (Lawrence: University Press of Kansas, 1993), 118.

[2] Amy J. Rutenberg, *Rough Draft: Cold War Military Manpower Policy and the Origins of Vietnam-Era Draft Resistance* (Ithaca, NY: Cornell University Press, 2019), 3, 70, 91–92; Amy J. Rutenberg, "Drafting for Domesticity: American Deferment Policy during the Cold War, 1948–1965," *Cold War History* 13, no. 1 (2013): 14–18.

less likely than white youth to be deferred on the basis that they were students or held key positions in the civilian industries. Additionally, they frequently faced discrimination from the local draft boards, which were predominately made up of white men. Because of the tremendous political, economic, and social discrimination they faced in civilian society, which increased their likelihood of being drafted, therefore, Black men chose to enlist in the military for a stable income, education, and job training.[3]

While the Cold War brought about these shifts in young people's roles in national security, Cold War military policy was also based on developments that took place during the total war period. Historians have noted that, when compared to the highly unequal distribution of service in the AVF with respect to race, class, and ethnicity, the U.S. armed forces during the Vietnam War (the last war in which the United States implemented the selective draft) were more representative of the country's demographics than is commonly recognized.[4] The key turning point in this interpretation of the history of military procurement in the United States is 1973, when the AVF was established. As I have shown, however, the groundwork for classifying youth in accordance with national security needs had already been laid in the years of the two world wars.

This book has also demonstrated the central role educational leaders played in developing the link between youth, national security, and education. Although some educators were against the development of such a link, such as those involved in the Committee on Militarism in Education, others were enthusiastic about the SATC's "democratic" potential, fiercely defended mandatory ROTC training from its critics in the 1920s and the 1930s, encouraged the conversion of the CCC and the National Youth Administration into military preparedness agencies in the late 1930s, helped strengthen the stratification of young people by their military value during World War II, and projected their conception of youth in national security onto young Japanese under U.S. occupation. Their motivations varied – some were motivated by patriotism, others by the desire to gain financial resources for their institutions, and still others by the belief that young people needed their direction – but they collectively helped fortify the ties between national security and

---

[3] Kimberley L. Phillips, *War! What Is It Good For?: Black Freedom Struggles and the U.S. Military from World War II to Iraq* (Chapel Hill: University of North Carolina Press, 2012), 13–14, 147–48, 151.

[4] Jennifer Mittelstadt, "Military Demographics," in *At War: The Military and American Culture in the Twentieth Century and Beyond*, ed. David Kieran and Edwin A. Martini (New Brunswick, NJ: Rutgers University Press, 2018), 93–94; Flynn, *The Draft*, 195. For an account that emphasizes the disproportionate service of men from working-class backgrounds during the Vietnam War, see Christian G. Appy, *Working-Class War: American Combat Soldiers and Vietnam* (Chapel Hill: University of North Carolina Press, 1993).

education, which had tremendous consequences for young people's educational paths.

Moreover, the firm relationship developed between the federal government and higher education authorities outlived the total war period, and after World War II, educators' involvement in national security policymaking became a matter of common knowledge. For example, they continued to intervene in selective service policymaking. When the selective draft was reestablished in 1948, they adamantly worked to secure student deferments, insisting that serving the country as students was as important as serving in the military, to make sure higher education would not lose human and financial resources.[5] At the same time, they also solidified higher education's role of training youth for military careers. *Education and National Security*, a pamphlet that the Educational Policies Commission (run by the National Education Association and the American Association of School Administrators) and the American Council on Education jointly published in 1951, declared that the armed services should be presented to students as an important career opportunity, for "[v]irtually all of the civilian occupations for which schools now prepare students are represented in the varied activities of the armed forces."[6] Meanwhile, starting with the Korean War, ROTC became a major institution for producing active-duty officers, not officers for the reserves, and ROTC provided 70 percent of Army lieutenants called to active duty during the said war.[7] Higher education institutions also continued to benefit financially from the G.I. Bill, which had originally applied only to veterans of World War II but was revised to extend educational benefits to veterans of later wars.[8]

A major change in the relationship between education and the military seemed to have arrived in the 1960s. Many institutions terminated the

---

[5] Christopher P. Loss, *Between Citizens and the State: The Politics of American Higher Education in the 20th Century* (Princeton, NJ: Princeton University Press, 2012), 119.
[6] Educational Policies Commission and American Council on Education, *Education and National Security* (Washington, DC: Educational Policies Commission and American Council on Education, 1951), 25.
[7] Michael S. Neiberg, *Making Citizen-Soldiers: ROTC and the Ideology of American Military Service* (Cambridge, MA: Harvard University Press, 2000), 37, 47; *The Oxford Companion to American Military History*, ed. John Whiteclay Chambers, s.v. "ROTC" (by John Whiteclay Chambers), www-oxfordreference-com.libproxy1.nus.edu.sg/view/10.1093/acref/9780195071986.001.0001/acref-9780195071986-e-0796 (accessed December 31, 2023).
[8] President's Commission on Veterans' Pensions, *The Historical Development of Veterans' Benefits in the United States: A Report on Veterans' Benefits in the United States*, Staff Report no. 1, House Committee Print no. 244, 84th Cong., 2nd sess. (Washington, DC: GPO, 1956), 158–59; Loss, *Between Citizens and the State*, 271n68; Keith W. Olson, *The G.I. Bill, the Veterans, and the Colleges* (Lexington: University of Kentucky Press, 1974), 104–108.

compulsory ROTC requirements in the late 1950s and early 1960s due to a growing consensus among the military and colleges that it was too costly, unpopular with students, and putting too much burden on students who were required to fulfill increasingly demanding curricular requirements to earn their college degrees.[9] This led to a steep drop in ROTC enrollments in these institutions, and in turn prompted various attempts to reform the program. For example, the ROTC Vitalization Act of 1964 instituted four-year scholarships to boost enrollment. This was a significant change from before, when only advanced-course students (in the third and fourth years) were offered stipends. The law also established a program consisting only of the two-year advanced-level training, supplemented by a six-week summer camp program, which indicated that the two-year basic course for first- and second-year students that many institutions had made compulsory for decades was, in fact, not militarily important. Despite these efforts, the rise of the anti-war movement in the late 1960s, followed by the introduction of the AVF in 1973, led to an enrolment drop in many institutions, such as the University of Illinois, which experienced an 82-percent decline from 1966 to 1974. In the following decades, the military and colleges attempted to fix this problem in various ways, such as by opening the program to people who had been barred or restricted from participating in the program, notably women and Black Americans, expanding the scholarship programs, revising the ROTC curriculum to raise the quality of courses and getting rid of simple drilling and other features in the curriculum that appeared too military to be in civilian educational institutions, and closing ROTC units in institutions where the enrolment was low.[10]

It may appear, then, that the relationship between youth, education, and national security was weakened in the late twentieth century. However, it proved to be extremely tenacious, and it continues to shape the lives of young people today. For one, even during the height of the antiwar movement on college campuses in the late 1960s, college authorities remained overwhelmingly in favor of keeping ROTC; ROTC is still an active part of many higher education institutions as well as secondary schools around the country today.[11] The fact that the age range required to register for selective service has remained eighteen through twenty-five until today is also one of the most obvious and persistent ways that the relationship between youth and national security that was developed in the years leading up to World War II has affected later years. Furthermore, although selective service registration was discontinued

---

[9] Neiberg, *Making Citizen-Soldiers*, 54–59; *The Oxford Companion to American Military History*, s.v. "ROTC."
[10] Neiberg, *Making Citizen-Soldiers*, 94, 98–99, 151–201.   [11] Ibid., 127–29.

in 1975, subsequent to the implementation of the AVF in 1973, in 1980, President Jimmy Carter requested that the registration be reinstated on the grounds that the Soviet invasion of Afghanistan posed a major threat to U.S. national security, which U.S. Congress immediately granted.[12] From 1982 to 2021, the registration was a prerequisite for men aged eighteen through twenty-five, both U.S. citizens and residents, to receive federal aid for higher education.[13] Except for those who had other financial means with which to pursue the education, then, young men's path to higher education hinged on their will to serve.

Throughout the first half of the twentieth century, military and national security issues were inextricably linked to political, social, and educational developments in American society, both during peacetime and wartime. Adults with various views of American society and young people's place in it embraced and institutionalized the notion that young people's service to the nation was a democratic, formative, and educational experience, and justified the stratification of young people according to their perceived importance to national security. The relationship between youth, education, and national security continues to influence young Americans and underpins the U.S. military empire today.

---

[12] Notably, this also marked the first time in U.S. history that a U.S. president requested the authority to register young women for military conscription, though only in noncombat positions; it was denied by Congress for a decades-old rationale of safeguarding the "family life." The Senate Committee on Armed Services, for example, argued that such a measure would result in an undesirable circumstance of a "young mother being drafted and a young father remaining home with the family." The "broader implications" of such a situation, the committee continued, should not be "ignored." James B. Jacobs and Dennis McNamara, "Selective Service without a Draft," *Armed Forces & Society* 10, no. 3 (1984): 361–62, 366–37; Jimmy Carter, "Selective Service Revitalization Statement on the Registration of Americans for the Draft," February 8, 1980, *The American Presidency Project*, www.presidency.ucsb.edu/node/249962 (accessed December 16, 2023); U.S. Congress, Senate, Committee on Armed Services, *Authorizing Appropriations for Fiscal Year 1981 for Military Procurement, Research and Development. Active Duty, Selected Reserve, and Civilian Personnel Strengths, Civil Defense, and for Other Purposes*, 96th Cong. 2nd sess., Report no. 96-826 (Washington, DC: GPO, 1980): 156–59; "Proclamation 4771: Registration under the Military Selective Service Act," July 2, 1980, *U.S. National Archives*, www.archives.gov/federal-register/codification/proclamations/04771.html (accessed December 16, 2023).

[13] Jacobs and McNamara, "Selective Service without a Draft," 373; Director of Selective Service System, U.S. Selective Service System, "Report on Review of Processes and Procedures Employed by Agencies for Appeals by Individuals Denied Federal Benefits for Failing to Register with Selective Service System, FT2022 NDAA, Section 529A," p. 4. www.sss.gov/wp-content/uploads/2022/08/FY2022-NDAA-SEC.-529a-7-28-2022.pdf (accessed October 1, 2022); Benjamin Collins and Cassandria Dortch, "The FAFSA Simplification Act," *Congressional Research Service Report R46909* (updated August 4, 2022), https://crsreports.congress.gov/product/pdf/R/R46909 (accessed October 2, 2022).

Index

ACE. *See* American Council on Education
ACLU. *See* American Civil Liberties Union
activism. *See* youth movements
Addams, Jane, 38, 81
adolescence, and youth, as distinct life stage, 8–9, 10
adult education, 165
Advisory Commission of the Council of National Defense, 47
African Americans. *See* Black Americans
"age of youth," 3
ALGCU. *See* Association of Land-Grant Colleges and Universities
All-Volunteer Force (AVF), in U.S., 6–7, 22, 219
American Association for Adult Education, 165
American Association of University Professors, 48
American Civil Liberties Union (ACLU), 120–21
American Council on Education (ACE), 48, 53, 108, 171, 221
   American Youth Commission and, 109
   military preparedness and, 127, 149–50
American Federation of Labor, 38, 118–19
American Legion, 82, 134, 174–79
American Peace Society, 122
American Youth Act, 105
American Youth Commission (AYCM)
   establishment of, 108–9
   military preparedness and, 126–27, 139–40
   Selective Training and Service Act of 1940 and, 179
   youth studies by, 169–71
American Youth Congress, 105, 146
Americanization, 33, 67
Annals of the American Academy of Political and Social Science, 107, 163, 164–65
armed forces, U.S. *See also* conscription; military training and service; Selective Service System
   All-Volunteer Force, 6–7, 22, 219

Black soldiers in
   discrimination under G.I. Bill of Rights, 177–78
   as officers, 186–87
   racial segregation in, 56–59
   racism against, 16
   during Civil War, 32
   "Dark Ages" for, 64
   education for, education levels by race and ethnicity, 56
   establishment of, 108–9
   G.I. Bill of Rights for, 59–60, 157, 171–72
   homosexuality and, 15–16, 179
   modernization of, 13–14
   racial segregation in, 56–59
   racism in, 16
   as volunteer force, 31
   women in, 158–59
      conscription of, 158
      Women's Army Corps, 158
   before World War I, 31
Army Specialized Training Program (ASTP), 179, 182–87, 216–17
   Army General Classification Test, 185
   Black soldiers in, 186
   cutback of, 186
   pre-induction teens and, 182–83, 188
Association of American Universities, 48
Association of Land-Grant Colleges and Universities (ALGCU), 82–83, 86–88
Association of State Universities, 48
Atlanta Constitution, 62, 125–26
AVF. *See* All-Volunteer Force
AYCM. *See* American Youth Commission

Baker, Newton D., 37, 38, 40, 47, 108–9
Baldwin, Roger, 120–21
Barnard, Eunice, 105, 107
Beale, Howard K., 142–43
Bentley, Jerome H., 98–99
biopolitics, theory of, 22

Index

Black Americans
  in armed forces
    discrimination under G.I. Bill of Rights, 177–78
    as officers, 186–87
    racial segregation in, 56–59
    racism in, 16
    in Army Specialized Training Program, 186
  education for, 56
    secondary school enrollment rates and, 80–81
  historically Black colleges and universities for
    Association of Land-Grant Colleges and Universities and, 82
    under Land Grant Act of 1862, 79–80
    military training at, 78–79
    under Second Morrill Act of 1890, 79–80
    Reserve Officers' Training Corps and, 78–79
  Southern Negro Youth Congress, 142
  in Student Army Training Corps, 56–59
Bourne, Randolph S., 13
Boy Scouts of America, 9, 163–64, 199
Brinkman, Paul, 61–62, 75
Brown, Francis, 172–73, 179–80, 189
Burke, Edward R., 136
Byrnes, James, 190

Capen, Samuel P., 181
Carter, Jimmy, 222–23
Cartwright, Morse A., 165
CCC. *See* Civilian Conservation Corps
CEST. *See* Committee on Education and Special Training
Chamberlain, George E., 37–38
child development, as academic subject, 9–10
Children's Bureau, 163–64
Christian Science Monitor, 115–16
Citizens' Military Training Camp (CMTC), 96, 119–20
City College of New York, 78
Civil Information and Education Section (CIE), 198–99
  Japan–America Student Conference, 205
  Youth Organizations and Student Activities (YOSA), 198–204, 207
  YOSA officers, 198
  YOSA officials, 199–200
Civil War, U.S.
  conscription policies during, 32
  military training during, 67

Civilian Conservation Corps (CCC), 96, 107–8, 111–23
  Army's involvement in, 119–20
  education in, 117–23
  eligibility criteria for, 112–13, 124
  enrollees in, 114
    public perception of, 113–15
    regional source of, 115
  enrollment in, 113
  establishment of, 111
  German youth programs compared to, 123–24, 169–70
  military preparedness through, 123–28
  military training in, 117–23
  positive public response to, 116–17
  in opinion polls, 121–22, 125–26
  purpose of, 115–16
  Roosevelt, F. D., support of, 96–97, 111, 123–25, 162
  termination of, 161–63
Clark, Grenville, 34, 35, 49, 135–36
CME. *See* Committee on Militarism in Education
CMTC. *See* Citizens' Military Training Camp
Coe, George A., 81
Cold War
  military service and, 219–20
  "transwar" approach in, 20–21, 218
  U.S. occupation of Japan and, 208–10
colleges and universities. *See* higher education
Committee on Education and Special Training (CEST), 48–50, 58. *See also* National Army Training Detachments; Student Army Training Corps
  Reserve Officers' Training Corps program and, 73
Committee on Militarism in Education (CME), 81–82, 88, 93, 142–46
Conant, James B., 150, 151, 152
conscription. *See also* Selective Service Act, U.S. (1917); Selective Service System; Selective Training and Service Act, U.S. (1940)
  during Civil War, 32
  post–World War I plans for, 134–35
  Joint Army and Navy Selective Service Committee, 134–35
Cornell University, 78, 92
Crowder, Enoch H., 38

Davis, Maxine, 102, 103
Day, Edmund E., 181–82

226   Index

deferments
  during Cold War, 219
  during World War II, 133, 147–48, 155, 156
Dewey, John, 12, 36–37, 81, 120–21, 142–43
  on "plastic juncture," 12–13
Dewey, Thomas E., 210
discrimination. *See* gender discrimination; racism
Dodds, Harold D., 139
the draft. *See* conscription
Durgin, Russell Luther, 198–99, 202–4, 207–8
Dykstra, Clarence A., 108–9, 145

educational associations, in U.S. *See also* American Council on Education; American Youth Commission; higher education; military training and service; Reserve Officers' Training Corps program; secondary education; Student Army Training Corps
  American Association for Adult Education, 165
  Association of Land-Grant Colleges and Universities (ALGCU), 82–83, 86–88
  Civilian Conservation Corps and, 117–23
  Emergency Council on Education, 48
  National Education Association, 48, 107–8, 149–50, 221
Einstein, Albert, 81–82
Eisenhower, Dwight, 131–32
Elliott, Edward C., 155, 181–82
Emergency Council on Education, 48
employment rates. *See* unemployment/employment rates

Fechner, Robert, 117–18
Filene, Edward A., 103–4
Fort Devens, 96, 128
Fosdick, Harry Emerson, 120–21
Foucault, Michel, 22
Freud, Sigmund, 81–82

gender discrimination
  G.I. Bill of Rights (1944) and, 179
  in Japan, 197–98, 207–8
G.I. Bill of Rights (Servicemen's Readjustment Act of 1944), U.S. (1944), 59–60, 157, 171–72, 174–79
  discrimination against Black veterans, 177–78
  discrimination against women, 178–79
  educational provisions of, 175
  homosexuality and, 179

Girl Scouts of America, 9, 163–64, 199
Givens, Willard E., 179–80
Great Britain, 35, 136
Great Depression. *See also* New Deal; "youth problem"
  educational elite during, 107–9
  as national security emergency, 4, 24
  U.S. military during, 64
  "youth problem" during, 98–107, 160, 217
    as "lost generation," 102–3
  youth unemployment during, 8, 100, 101–3
"Greatest Generation," 129, 171–72

Hall, G. Stanley, 10
Hamilton et al v. Regents of the University of California et al., 88–90
Happy Days (weekly newspaper), 117
HBCUs. *See* historically Black colleges and universities
Hershey, Lewis B., 145, 154–56, 219
high schools. *See* secondary education
higher education. *See also* Army Specialized Training Program; historically Black colleges and universities; Reserve Officers' Training Corps program; Student Army Training Corps; *specific institutions*
  increased enrollment rates for, 8
  Military Training Camp Association and, 139
  social value of, 4, 76
  before World War I, 76
historically Black colleges and universities (HBCUs)
  Association of Land-Grant Colleges and Universities, 82
  under Land Grant Act of 1862, 79–80
  military training at, 78–79
  under Second Morrill Act of 1890, 79–80
Hitler, Adolf, 103
Holland, Kenneth, 169–71
homosexuality, in U.S. armed forces, 15–16, 179
Hoover, J. Edgar, 117
Hopkins, Harry, 124–25
Howard University, 78–79
Howe, Louis, 110
Hutchins, Robert, 143, 176

Intercollegiate Student Council of the League for Industrial Democracy, 91
"interwar" period, in U.S., 17–23, 64
  conscription plans during, 134–35
  historical scholarship on, 18–19
Iwo Jima, symbolism of flag-raising on, 130–32

Index 227

James, William, 115, 169
JANSCC. *See* Joint Army and Navy Selective Service Committee
Japan, youth, in postwar era. *See also* Civil Information and Education Section; *seinen*; *Seinendan* groups
 Cold War and, 208–10
 gender equality in, 197–98, 207–8
 as junior partner of U.S., 210–15
 in Kande village, 202–4, 207–8
 mobilization of, 190
 pro-U.S. student activity among, 205
 seinen, definition of, 192–93
 "youth" in the U.S. and, 192
Japanese Communist Party, 202
Jefferson, Thomas, 69–70
Johnson, Louis, 123–24
Joint Army and Navy Selective Service Committee (JANSCC), 134–35
Junior Red Cross, 15
juvenile delinquency, "youth problem" and, 163
 racialization of, 165–67

Kanai, Satoshi, 191, 204, 213–14
Klein, Arthur J., 70–71

LaGuardia, Fiorello H., 155, 157–58
Land Grant Act (Morrill Act), U.S. (1862), 70, 71, 77, 79–80, 82–83
land-grant colleges and universities
 Association of Land-Grant Colleges and Universities, 82–83, 86–88
 HBCUs and, 78–81
 Reserve Officers' Training Corps program at, 79–88
Lippmann, Walter, 36–37, 150–51
Los Angeles Times, 125–26, 166
"lost generation," 102

MacArthur, Douglas, 64, 118, 131–32
Mann, Charles R., 49, 54–55
Mann, Thomas, 81–82
Marsh, Clarence S., 118
Marshall, George C., 64, 95, 156
masculinity, military service and, 14–16
Massachusetts Institute of Technology (MIT), 27, 70
Michie, Thomas J., 143
military preparedness, for youth
 American Council on Education and, 127
 American Youth Commission and, 126–27, 139–40

Committee on Militarism in Education, 142–44
New Deal and, 123–28
military training and service. *See also* Army Specialized Training Program; Reserve Officers' Training Corps program; Student Army Training Corps; universal military training
 access to education connected to, 16–17, 21–23
 access to public education and, 88–95
 gender and, 9–14, 15, 157–58
 masculinity and, 14–16
 patriotism and, 67–68
 Plattsburg movement and, 34, 63, 94
 in public schools and universities, 62
 before Reserve Officers' Training Corps program, 67–69
 student activism against, 75–79, 90–92
 university military training as influence on, 63, 65
Military Training Camp Association (MTCA), 34
 colleges and universities and, 139
 racism and, 34
 Selective Training and Service Act and, 135–36, 137
Militia Act of 1792, U.S., 31
Millard, Bailey, 125–26
MIT. *See* Massachusetts Institute of Technology
Mitchell, William D., 85–86
"The Moral Equivalent of War" (James), 115, 169
Morrill Act. *See* Land Grant Act
MTCA. *See* Military Training Camp Association
Muste, A. J., 142–43

National Army Training Detachments (NATD), 49–50, 55, 57
National Defense Act of 1916, U.S., 61, 72, 74–75
National Defense Act of 1920, U.S., 73, 75, 134–35
National Education Association (NEA), 48, 107–8, 149–50, 221
National Resources Planning Board (NRPB), 172
national security
 education access and, 16–17, 21–23, 220–21
 evolution of the concept in the U.S., 23
 youth and, 7–17, 21–23, 220–21

National Unemployment Census of 1937, 100
National Youth Administration (NYA), 98, 105, 107–8
  programs under, 110–11, 125
  termination of, 161–63
  youth studies by, 168–69
Nazi Germany, 4, 19–20, 103, 121, 128, 160, 168, 169–70
NEA. *See* National Education Association
New Deal, 85–86, 110–17. *See also* Civilian Conservation Corps; National Youth Administration; Roosevelt, Franklin D.
  National Resources Planning Board, 172
  preparedness and, 123–28
  warfare and, 99
  Works Progress Administration, 100–1
  World War I as influence on, 99–100
New Republic, 76–77, 120–21
New York Herald Tribune, 138–39, 141, 210
New York Times, 46–47, 83–84, 90, 105, 107, 116
Niebuhr, Reinhold, 120–21
Norris, George W., 81
NRPB. *See* National Resources Planning Board
Nugent, Donald R., 198–99, 211
NYA. *See* National Youth Administration

Osborn, Frederick H., 173
Outlook, 26–30

patriotism, through military training, 67–68
Perkins, Frances, 111–12
Perry, Ralph Barton, 35, 49
Phillips, Clifton J., 200–1
"plastic juncture," 12–13, 35, 99–100, 179, 190, 216
Plattsburg movement, 34, 63, 94
preparedness, 34–35, 84–85, 124–25
Progressive Era, definition of, 8–9
progressives, World War I and, 11–13, 36–37
public opinion polls, 121–22, 125–26, 136, 144–45, 153

racism. *See also* Black Americans; historically Black colleges and universities
  in Army Specialized Training Program, 186
  juvenile delinquency and, 165–67
  Military Training Camp Association and, 34
  in Reserve Officers' Training Corps, 81
  in Student Army Training Corps, 56–59
  in U.S. armed forces, 16, 56–59
  "Zoot Suit Riots" and, 165–67
Reed, David A., 119–20
Reeves, Floyd W., 108–9, 127, 172–73
Reserve Officers' Training Corps (ROTC), 5, 16–17, 216–17, 221–23
  Association of Land-Grant Colleges and Universities and, 82–83
  at colleges and universities, 4, 5, 16–17, 19–20, 66–67, 76–77
  Committee on Education and Special Training and, 73
  educational leaders' commitment to, 65–66
  federal government role in, 66
  Hamilton et al v. Regents of the University of California et al., 88–90
  at historically Black colleges and universities, 78–79
  at land-grant institutions, 79–88
  military training before, 67–69
  under National Defense Act of 1916, 61, 72, 74–75, 77
  under National Defense Act of 1920, 73, 75
  for Navy, 72
  origins of, 69–73
  participation demographics for, 66–67
  racism and, 81
  ROTC Vitalization Act of 1964 and, 222
  in secondary schools, 61–62, 66–67, 72, 75–76
  Student Army Training Corps replaced by, 73
  World War II and, 183
Reynolds, Robert Rice, 141–42
Richmond Academy, 61–63
Roosevelt, Eleanor, 106, 166–67
Roosevelt, Franklin D. *See also* New Deal
  Civilian Conservation Corps supported by, 96–97, 111, 123–25, 162
  on education for armed forces, 171–89
  national security and, 23
  on selective service, 123, 153, 156–57
Roosevelt, Theodore, 32–33
  Rough Riders and, 32–33, 131
Root, Elihu, 32–33
Rosenthal, Joe, 129–30
ROTC. *See* Reserve Officers' Training Corps
ROTC Vitalization Act of 1964, U.S., 222
Rough Riders, 32–33, 131
Russell, Bertrand, 81–82

Index

Saito, Kayoko, 191, 211–12, 213
SATC. *See* Student Army Training Corps
Sayre, John Nevin, 81
Schlesinger, Arthur M., Jr., 13
School Life, 71
Scott, Emmett J., 57
Second Morrill Act of 1890, U.S., 79–80
secondary education
   enrollment rates for, 80–81
   military training in, 61–62, 66–67, 72, 75–76
   social mobility and, 10–11
seinen (youth in Japan), 192–93. *See also* Japan
   conceptual evolution of, 192–93
   decline in popularity of, 214–15
   wakamono, 193, 214–15
Seinendan groups, in Japan, 191, 193–94, 199–200. *See also* Japan
   decline in popularity of, 214–15
   dormancy of, 201–2
   gender and, 197–98, 208
   Greater Japan Youth and Children's Organization, 194
   nationalization of, 194
Selective Service Act (1917), U.S., 31
   age parameters of, 41, 42–43, 46
      lowering of draft age, education and, 48
   opposition to, 38
   Student Army Training Corps under, 51–53
   Wilson and, 36–37
Selective Service Act (1948), U.S., 219
Selective Service System. *See also specific legislation*
   All-Volunteer Force and, 6–7, 22
   during Cold War, expansion of deferment categories, 219
   demographic representation through, 6, 11
   post-1973
      discontinuation of registration with, 222–23
      FAFSA Simplification Act (2021), 7
   registration requirements for, 7
Selective Training and Service Act (1940), U.S., 20, 34, 35, 82, 132, 135–46, 217–18
   age parameters in, 144, 147–48
      lowering of draft age, 41–46, 148–49
   American Youth Commission and, 139–40
   classifications of draftees under, 41–42
   deferments under, 133, 147–48, 156–57
   expiration of, 219
   Military Training Camps Association and, 135–36, 137
   opposition to, 140–42
      by Committee on Militarism in Education, 142–44
   universal military training and, 35, 135–36
   "youth" influenced by, 146–60
Service Extension Act of 1941, U.S., 148
Servicemen's Readjustment Act of 1944. *See* G.I. Bill of Rights
Sheppard, Morris, 138
Soule, George, 120–21
Southern Negro Youth Congress, 142
Stimson, Henry, 137, 138, 145–46
Studebaker, John, 108–9, 127
student activism. *See* youth movements
Student Army Training Corps (SATC)
   advertisement for, 28–29
   American Council on Education promotion of, 53
   application process for, 52
   Black Americans in, 56–59
   Committee on Education and Special Training, 48–50, 51, 58
   creation of, 46–60
   as democratic educational opportunity, 27–30, 56
   education administers' response to, 29, 53–54, 180–81
   educational legacy of, 60
   length of program, 52–53
   lowering of draft age and, 51–52
   National Army Training Detachments, 49–50, 55, 57
   in *Outlook*, 26–30
   racism in, 56–59
   under Selective Service Act, 51–53
   termination of, 54–55
   universal military training and, 46
   as "University of Uncle Sam," 27–29

Taft, Robert A., 141
Taft, William Howard, 35
Tagore, Rabindranath, 81–82
Thomas, Norman, 142–43
Thorndike, Edward L., 53–54
Time, 116
Titus, Charles H., 161
"transwar" approach, 20–21, 218
Typer, Donald, 198–99

UMT. *See* universal military training
unemployment/employment rates

230 Index

unemployment/employment rates (cont.)
  National Unemployment Census of 1937, 100
  for youth, 100, 101–3
United Nations Educational, Scientific and Cultural Organization (UNESCO), 171
universal military training (UMT), 14, 46, 216–17
  Military Training Camp Association and, 34
  military training of youth influenced by, 63, 65
  opposition to, 36–37
  Plattsburg movement, 34, 94
  Rough Riders and, 32–33
  Selective Training and Service Act and, 135–36
  Student Army Training Corps and, 46
  training of leadership for, 33–34
University of California, 88, 92–93
"University of Uncle Sam," 27–29. *See also* Student Army Training Corps
University of Wisconsin, 77, 92
U.S. Army. *See* armed forces
U.S. Department of Interior, 77, 113
U.S. Supreme Court, 88–90
U.S. War Department
  anti-ROTC groups and, 82
  Civilian Conservation Corps administration by, 113
  establishment of Student Army Training Corps by, 26
  Land Grant Act and, 72, 77
  Selective Training and Service Act, 137, 153

Veterans of Foreign Wars, 106, 189
Veterans of Future Wars (VFW), 105–7, 172, 189
Vietnam War, 220
Villard, Oswald G., 81, 120–21, 142–43
volunteerism, 31

WAC. *See* Women's Army Corps
Wadsworth, James, Jr., 82, 136
wakamono, 193, 214–15
Wallace, Henry A., 104
War Manpower Commission (WMC), 181–82
Washington Post, 115–16, 121, 146
Wells, H. G., 81–82
West Point, 69–70
Willkie, Wendell, 144

Wilson, Woodrow, 12
  declaration of war by, 37–41
  Selective Service Act and, 37–41, 46
WMC. *See* War Manpower Commission
women
  discrimination under G.I. Bill of Rights, 178–79
  as symbol to fight for in World War II, 15–16
  in U.S. armed forces, 158–59
  war mobilization of, 15–16, 158
Women's Army Corps (WAC), 158
Wood, Leonard, 32, 33–34
Woodring, Harry H., 123, 137
Woolley, Mary E., 154
Works Progress Administration (WPA), 100–1
World War I. *See also* Selective Service Act (1917); Student Army Training Corps
  antiwar movement after, 65–66
  Lusitania attack and, 35
  New Deal policies influenced by, 99–100
  "plastic juncture" and, 12–13, 35
  Wilson's declaration of war during, 37–41
World War II. *See also* Army Specialized Training Program; G.I. Bill of Rights; Selective Training and Service Act (1940); *specific topics*
  "Greatest Generation" and, 129, 171–72
  symbolism of flag-raising on Iwo Jima, 130–32
  "youth problem" during, 163–67
WPA. *See* Works Progress Administration

Yamada, Taro, 190–91, 207, 213–14
YMCA. *See* Young Men's Christian Association
YOSA. *See* Youth Organizations and Student Activities
Young Men's Christian Association (YMCA), 9, 98–99, 163–64, 199
Young, Owen D., 108–9, 127
Young Women's Christian Association (YWCA), 9, 163–64, 199
youth. *See also* Civilian Conservation Corps; Japan; National Youth Administration; *seinen*; "youth problem"; *specific topics*
  "age of youth," 3
  Civilian Conservation Corps' reconception of, 169–71
  as concept, 4–5
  adolescence and youth as distinct life stage, 8–9, 10

Index

child development as academic
  subject, 9–10
cultural construction of, 8–9, 216, 218
redefinitions of, 4–5, 7–17, 163–71
educational elite, the Great Depression
  and, 107–9
educational institutions created for,
  10–11
"democratization" of, 10–11
national security and, 7–17, 21–23,
  220–21
in Nazi Germany, 4, 19–20, 103, 121,
  128, 160, 168, 169–70
New Deal programs for, 110–17
unemployment rates for, 100, 101–3
youth in Japan. *See* Japan; *seinen*
youth movements
  against compulsory military training,
    77–79, 90–92
  American Youth Act, 105
  American Youth Congress, 105, 146
  Southern Negro Youth Congress, 142
  Veterans of Future Wars, 105–7, 172,
    189

Youth Organizations and Student Activities
  (YOSA), 198–204, 207
YOSA officers, 198
YOSA officials, 199–200
"youth problem"
  in *Annals of the American Academy of
    Political and Social Science*, 107, 163,
    164–65
  Children's Bureau, 163–64
  gender, 164
  during Great Depression, 100–7, 217
    definition of, 98–99, 109
    as "lost generation," 102–3
    unemployment rates and, 100, 101–3
  juvenile delinquency associated with, 163
  racialization of, 165–67
  Works Progress Administration and, 100–1
  during World War II, 160, 163–67
YWCA. *See* Young Women's Christian
  Association

Zook, George F., 108–9, 118, 171, 179–80
"Zoot Suit Riots," 165–67
  in popular media, 166

For EU product safety concerns, contact us at Calle de José Abascal, 56–1°,
28003 Madrid, Spain or eugpsr@cambridge.org.

www.ingramcontent.com/pod-product-compliance
Lightning Source LLC
Chambersburg PA
CBHW020047050925
32160CB00002B/15